The Dream of Stones and Winds
돌과 바람의 꿈

The Dream of Stones and Winds

JejuPEN Mook ② (30.12.2005)

Chief Editor Sung-Chan Oh
Compiler Prunsasangsa
Editors JejuPEN Publication Subcommittee

This collection copyright© 2005 by JejuPEN Mook

JejuPEN Mook ❷

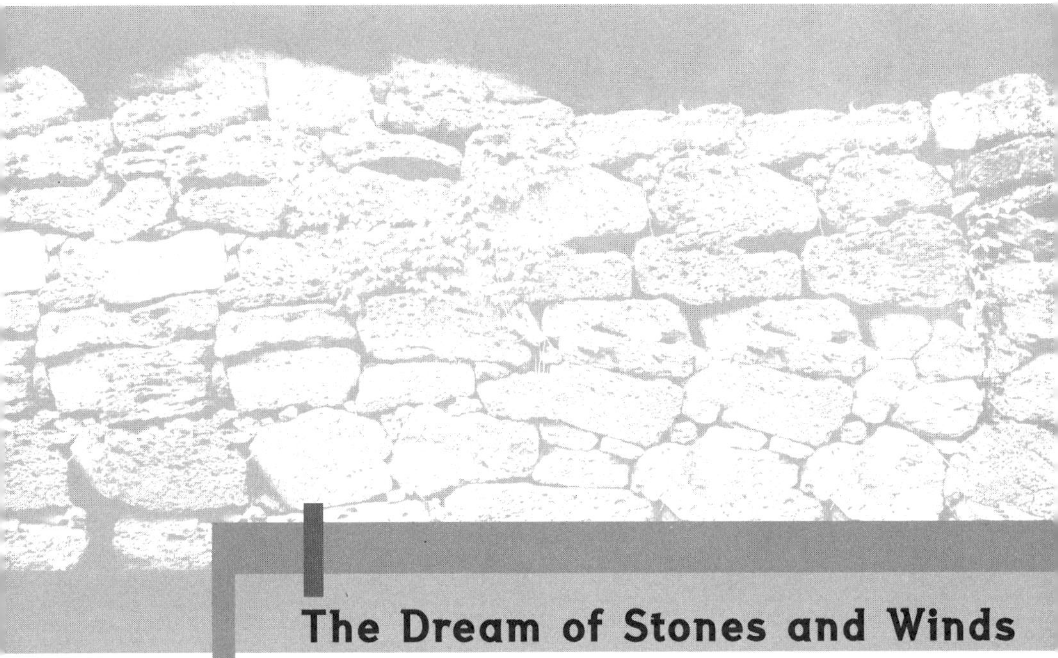

The Dream of Stones and Winds

Translated by Kyung-Ran Park

濟州

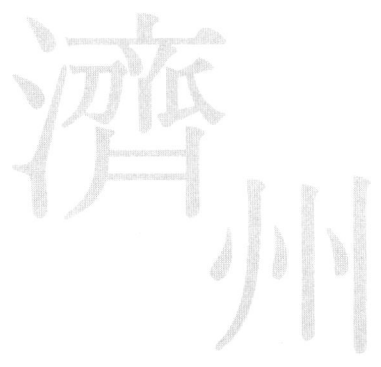

푸른사상

Preface

Well wishes for the publication of the second issue of JejuPEN Mook

Sung-Chan Oh
(President, JejuPEN International)

I am greatly delighted with the publication of the second issue of the Jeju PEN Mook English version following the first issue of *The Winds of Jeju Island* published around this time last year. I would like to express my gratitude to all the members for their passionate work whilst asking them for their continued enthusiasm.

Last year, we worked zealously on the publishing job and the result was successful. We sent the books to 140 representatives and board members of 50 PEN International member states as well as the members of PEN International Korea. After that, we received letters of encouragement from President IrYna Dybko Firipchak of the Writers in Exile PEN Centre American Branch and the representatives of London, San Francisco, and more. With one accord, they wrote that "we satisfied a literature need for a new area, Jeju Island", which phrase, cheered us all. They might have only been speaking out of courtesy, but such encouragement raised all our spirits while we were working on the second issue.

We call the second issue of JejuPEN Mook *The Dream of Stones and Winds*. It is well known by all, that Jeju Island is an island with an abundance of stone, wind and women. On the other hand, the good tradition of 'no need to have a locked gate as there are no thieves or beggars' has been our boast for generations. The stone and harsh winds might have been the first target to be overcome by our ancestors who lived on the island. Accordingly, I am not exaggerating to say that their history and their literary works reflect the ways in which they overcame the elements. Based on this assumption, we so named this issue.

Prof. Kyung-Ran Park, Ph.D. of the Graduate School of Interpretation, Cheju National University, is responsible for the translation and editing of all the poems, novels, plays, children's literature, and miscellaneous writings in this book, which were picked out by our very own PEN members. I appreciate her devotion and hard work whilst undertaking this project and fighting against the grueling summer heat.

As well, I would like to note that this project has been made possible because of the support given by the Jeju Provincial Government the same as they did last year. Finally, I promised myself as well as everybody else to continue the translation and distribution of our literary works despite the many unfavorable conditions we may confront.

Winter, 2005

▫ CONTENTS ▫

Preface Sung-Chan Oh 5

■ **Poetry**

Joong-Hae Yang 13
   The Most Beautiful Star Is··· 14   *At the Place of Exile* 16

Tong-Won Kang 18
   Jeju Island II 19   *Jejuu Island III* 21

Seung-Lip Kim 23
   Off-grade Product 24   *Leaf* 25

Yang-Soo Kim 26
   Zen Meditation 27   *Drinking A Cup of Coffee* 29

Yong-Kil Kim 31
   Downstream 32   *In The Autumn Forest* 34

Jong-Doo Kim 35
   University Tree 36   *Seogwipo Winter 1* 38

Gi-Cheol Na 39
   I in Seogwipo 40   *In Bijarim in Winter* 41

◻ CONTENTS ◻

Tae-Gil Moon   42

    Marado Lighthouse   43   *Ume Flower*   45

Seung-Haeng Shin   46

    April of Pascha   47   *Jeju in Praise*   50

Jeon-Hyung Yang   51

    Gueok-ri   52   *Jocheon-ri Wild Grass*   54

Young-Ho Oh   55

    Climbing Oreum on a Volcanic Island   56

    When I Go to Haengwon-ri   57

Bong-Taek Yoon   58

    The Place of No Longing   59   *Rain Water*   60

In-Soo Jeong   61

    Angling   62   *A Love Song*   64

Gi-Pal Han   66

    Island   67   *My Life In The Afternoon*   68

◻ CONTENTS ◻

■ Novel

Hyon-Sik Choi   71
The Faraway Mountain   72

Si-Hong Koh   97
Drifting Island, Ieodo   98

Sung-Chan Oh   120
My Hometown Where The Moon Rises   121

■ Children's Literature

Soon-Bok Kang   147
New Ramie Clothes in the Dresser   148

Jae-Hyong Park   156
Mr. Crow Oh   157

◻ CONTENTS ◻

■ Drama

Il-Hong Jang — 169
   The Choir Of Birds Which Makes Us Sleep   170

■ Essay

Tae-Gook Kang — 201
   It Takes Two To Hatch (Jultakdonggi) : The Moment of Enlightenment   202

Ga-Young Kim — 207
   My Heart Is A Flower   208

Myung-Chul Cho — 211
   The Travelers' Teahouse   212

Poetry

The Most Beautiful Star Is··· / At the Place of Exile
Jeju Island II / Jejuu Island III
Off-grade Product / Leaf
Zen Meditation / Drinking A Cup of Coffee
Downstream / In The Autumn Forest
University Tree / Seogwipo Winter 1
I in Seogwipo / In Bijarim in Winter
Marado Lighthouse / Ume Flower
April of Pascha / Jeju in Praise
Gueok-ri / Jocheon-ri Wild Grass
Climbing Oreum on a Volcanic Island / When I Go to Haengwon-ri
The Place of No Longing / Rain Water
Angling / A Love Song
Island / My Life In The Afternoon

Joong-Hae Yang

The Most Beautiful Star Is···
At the Place of Exile

Writer's Introduction

First recognized in *Sahsahnggye*. Former president of the Jeju Branch of the Korean Writers' Association and of the Jeju Branch of the Federation of Artistic and Cultural Organizations of Korea. Currently president of the Jeju Branch of the Federation of Korean Cultural Centers, board member of P.E.N. Korea.
Publications: *Waves, Songs of Halla, The Horizon*
Address: 108-306 Hyundai Apts, 943-3 Geonip-dong, Jeju, Jejudo, Republic of Korea
Phone: (064) 722-0523

The Most Beautiful Star Is…

Joong-Hae Yang

In the vast heaven
The most beautiful star is
The earth.

More beautiful than the sun rising in the east sky
In the morning
More beautiful that the moon going over a high mountain
In deep night
More beautiful than any stars flowing in the Milky Way
In the night sky
The most beautiful star is
The earth.

Though there're a myriad of stars in the sky
We're living only
Only this star.
There are mountains and oceans
In mountains and oceans it rains and blows
Grasses and trees bloom and bear fruit
Birds and animals

Even worms make love to each other

Among the myriad of stars
In this enormous space
How could there possibly be more beautiful
Stars than the earth?

People!
Let's love the star.
The star that loves us
And that we can love,
The most beautiful star among stars,
Let's love the earth

Like grass and trees
Birds and animals
Love the earth
Let us also love the most beautiful star
The earth.

At the Place of Exile

This is
The edge of the sky
Where you can't be driven further
Brutal place of exile.
A grudge from Hanyang
Flew to the end of an island
Crying out in the sound of waves.

Though waiting all day long
Waiting again and again
No soul to be seen,
The horizon of yearning
Only a boundless ocean
Only the sound of waves
The ocean cries out

People, forget not!
At the end of this island
There was a grudge that left the island
Exhausted by crying with the sea.

The story of this grudge

Still today

Weeping in the sound of the waves.

Tong-Won Kang

Jeju Island II
Jejuu Island III

Writer's Introduction

Graduated from the Department of English Language and Literature at Cheju National University. Honorary Ph.D in Literature. First recognized in *Poetry* in 1977. Former president of the Jeju Branch of the Federation of Artistic and Cultural Organizations and of the Jeju Branch of the Korean Writers' Association. Currently Cultural Committee Member of Korean Modern Poetry. Professor Emeritus at Cheju National University.
Publications: *The Fog Horn, Upstream and Downstream, Jeju Island Eulalia Flowers,* etc
Address: 255-18 Yongdam 1-dong, Jeju, Jejudo, Republic of Korea
Phone: (064) 753-1732

Jeju Island II

Tong-Won Kang

Jeju Island is a window
The window of the ground
The window of nature
Open always at any time
Towards the sky
Towards the light.
The world of light
Glittering through the window
Open all year round.
The light of origin
The light of life
That a god saw
At the dawn of creation
Is pouring down endlessly
By the grace of the heavens.
The window of Jeju Island
Never closed forever
The light of Jeju.
Birth and destruction
Death and resurrection

Repeat in a perpetual cycle
Along with the window of Jeju
Along with the light.

Jejuu Island III

In Jeju
When I have a bitter heart
Caused by people and between people
In the course of life
Even several times a day
Even though they are nearby
I miss the mountain and the ocean
In Jeju.
When I call them a mountain and an ocean in Jeju,
It will become just Halla Mountain
And Jeju Ocean.
In Jeju
On this earth anywhere
When I miss my hometown,
Its mountain and ocean
When I call them again
Ah! Mountain! Ocean!
That just becomes Jeju Island
Halla Mountain and Jeju Ocean.
Awake or close my eyes

A vivid appearance
Approaching as a clear deep blue light
Enough to make my eyes ache
Halla Mountain, Jeju Ocean!
And Beloved Jeju!

Seung-Lip Kim

Off-grade Product
Leaf

Writer's Introduction
Address: 402-11 2-Do 2-dong, Jeju, Jeju-do, Republic of Korea
Publications: Off-grade Product
Phone: (064) 753-3185, 019-9101-3185

Off-grade Product

Seung-Lip Kim

It was the time of giveaways for Hanil Soju.
A storekeeper often drank 25% Hanil Soju.
Outside the window
Stacked twinkling snow intoxicated by 25%.
The man made a slight cough to our country.
The round tag on the soju bottle, which he emptied, was awkwardly left
Like his sunken face.
Afterwards, he became a degraded product.
And he could have a grander cough towards our country.
In winter of that time he stopped drinking
His dear 25% Hanil Soju
The roof of the store quietly fell in
Degraded snow
Unceasingly piles on empty soju bottles

Leaf

1

Ugly mountain

Clean eyes of my love

Falling last in deep autumn

A leaf like an idiot

Flows

2

A corner of our country

In dreary heart secretly

Sitting, sighing

The sound of love prevailing

And deepens without notice

Yang-Soo Kim

Zen Meditation
Drinking A Cup of Coffee

Writer's Introduction

Debut in *Simsangji* in May 1990 with the Prize for New Writers. Four volumes of poetry include *Even The Wind Longs for Rest*. One of the prose publications is *The Memory Is As Sweet As Chocolate*. Member of Jeju PEN, Korea Poets' Society and the Sansang Poets' Society.

Zen Meditation

Yang-Soo Kim

Life
Though being a speck of a snowflake in a pot under fire
I am alive
Though being a moment in a blink of an eye
Bustling over the surface of water
With only a flash of energy
It's hot
Stiffen my tongue
Ice my heart
As if I am leaving far away and cannot return
After folding my childhood
Darkness is inscribed in history
Brightness is being left as a myth
My heart is in pain
Originally
What makes the world shake is said
Between people and people
What makes the void sealed is wind
What flitting of space and time
A piece of flower dropping her life

Since all that I can hold is not mine
It's lighter than breath

I can't meet enlightenment until I deny myself and
Give up today
Get rid of names and faces;
The burden of having relationships

I sometimes face you
With only practice to erase myself
Higher than a guardian hill
Like a butterfly flying lightly over a high rugged mountain

Finally
Reaching the blue ocean
The entire self is freed

Drinking A Cup of Coffee

I empty a bag of instant coffee
And pour the water
In a paper cup.

A sweet aroma like a unlighted window
Is as cozy as your heart.

A sip
Warms up longing
Another sip
Appeases pity
Again with a sip
I know you and I melt together.
Not to hurry
Or not too slow and quiet
What a delight
To keep warmth in hand long and deep
Swallowing the coffee like bodily fluid!
However,
When the empty cup

Becomes an abandoned heart
Lonely and desolate
When its sorrows grow bigger
Like an empty sky,
I am left in tears, thinking that
My infected love for caffeine
May also be abandoned.

Yong-Kil Kim

Downstream
In The Autumn Forest

Writer's Introduction

Jeju-do Cultural Award (Division: Art) and Seogwipo Civil Culture Award. Former president of the Seogwipo Branch of the Korean Writers' Association
Publications: *Duet of Sea and Island*
Address: 206 Jungbang Villa, 118 Seogwi-dong, Seogwipo, Jejudo, Republic of Korea
Phone: (064) 762-4943, 011-694-9229

Downstream

Yong-Kil Kim

In the jet-black darkness
The grass drops on her head
Heard the cry of a river
Passed over by the wind

Now the grass knows
It has come
Where the stream of a river ends

Lying down on the hill of the downstream
Memorizing the names of the shooting stars
The names to be erased
In the time of thinking

Traveling through thousands of miles
Becoming the flow of history that had been precipitated
The currents rise and fall as if groaning

When it penetrates the deep darkness
Reaching the ocean

The river will know
It is the beginning of lonely wandering
Without a line drawn.

In The Autumn Forest

Don't be so proud
You had a season of fresh green
Your arid lips
Like a raw structure

Before saying, "Ah! It's autumn."
Don't leave the forests
The mountain shadow in empty season
The darkness saturating to the ankle

Deserted forest
Dropping its body like a reed
Though my body is laid down
What would you do to me?

Jong-Doo Kim

University Tree
Seogwipo Winter 1

Writer's Introduction
First recognized in Sonyeon. Former president of Jeonnam Province Children's Literature Association and Jeju Province Children's Literature Association. Currently president of the of the Korean Writers' Association, Jeju Branch.
Korean Children's Literature Award, Socheong Literature Award.
Publications: *What Is Life? Garden with the Sun*, etc.
Address: 2423-15 Bonggae-dong, Jeju, Jejudo, Republic of Korea
Phone: (064) 721-1658, 019-721-1658

University Tree

Jong-Doo Kim

At a certain time
We used to call a tangerine tree
A university tree

With several tangerine trees
In a vegetable garden
We supported children to go to university
We treasured the trees as they are university trees

At a time we valued even boiled rice with barley
In autumn when tangerines were ripening into an orange color
In the households which grew tangerine trees,
The mothers and fathers were so complacent
They smiled, watching the golden fruit.

Selling tangerines for cash, they paid their debts for school expenses
Though preparing marriage expenses
For their sons and daughters
They were full of strength.

Recently

Wherever you go in Jeju

Tangerine trees are common

Though cut and rooted out

Once tangerine trees

Were called money trees which bore golden fruit

They were treated dearly as university trees

Seogwipo Winter 1

Snow that has fallen during the night
Immediately melts
In the rays of the sunlight at midday
In Seogwipo water winter.

The summit of Halla Mountain
Having settled down
With its white skin hat on
Only watches towards the evergreen port.

Powerless
Southward advancing snowy wind
Climbs down an ice wall
And dives into the ocean
In front of Seogwipo from where
Already picking up the Spring.

Gi-Cheol Na

I in Seogwipo
In Bijarim in Winter

Writer's Introduction
Born in Seoul in 1953, Graduated from the Department of Korean Language and Literature at Cheju National University. First recognized in *Poetry* in 1987. Member of Poems of Awakening.
Publications: *Longstanding Dreams of Islands, Namyang Inn, Crushing the Clouds*
Address: Gah-106, Cheonil Apts, 1699-4 ara 1-dong, Jeju, Jejudo, Republic of Korea
Phone: (064) 702-2726, 016-692-9652 / E-mail: nagc0914@hanmir.com

I in Seogwipo

Gi-Cheol Na

In Seogwipo there is a woman I call "Sundrops"
The deep blue waves of the ocean
Bring the flowers in full bloom
And get startled sometimes,
Scattering them in hundreds
Longing to be the shy 'Sundrops'

In Seogwipo there is a woman I call "Whistle Bird".
Even now my better-half is gone
I am not sad any more
Even now there is only a pair of chopsticks and a spoon
Set at my breakfast table
I am not lonely any more
I just try to become a 'Whistle Bird' for a short while.

In Seogwipo there is a woman I call *Sammaebong* Peak
One day I'll visit her,
Read the poems and see the pictures
Climbing up, down and around
The peak holds me firm from drifting away
Like the sound of a motor boat in front of Bird Island

In Bijarim in Winter

I gaze at an old nutmeg tree
With its head lifting
Towards the sky
A tightened bow string
Enduring the winds

I come to Bijarim and look at an old nutmeg tree
With its head lifting
I feel as if I could live
A hundred thousand years

Tae-Gil Moon

Marado Lighthouse
Ume Flower

Writer's Introduction
Former president of the Jeju Branch of the Korean Writers' Association,
Jeju Civil Award (Division: Art and Culture).
Publications: *Mara Island Lighthouse*, etc.
Address: 315-7 2-Do 2-dong, Jeju, Jejudo, Republic of Korea

Marado Lighthouse

Tae-Gil Moon

Whoever
Threw away
A stone of a peach?

Sprouted
In the space of a rock
Living with stars.

When she misses
Her old home
She just rolls her eyes.

With only a boat
Floating
The Island is not lonely

Towards the end of the curved
Sea horizon
Even when the sail of a scroll immerses

Towards the shore
To the shore
Again sets the fold of a mane.

She knows
People
Who she wants to lean on

The darling
Young lighthouse keeper
Marado lighthouse keeper

The North Star
With a frozen heart
Suffers the whole night

Ume Flower

In every valley of Halla Mountain
February blooms in lingering snow

Gentle, meek, countryman
Ah, is your face also blushing?

A budding willow
Closes its eyes again

Though living an entire lifetime
There is still an unaccomplished dream

The ghost wandering the nether world
Sprouted again from a stump

Incense burning
On the table of ancestral sacrifice
In the eldest grandson's house

Seung-Haeng Shin

April of Pascha
Jeju in Praise

Writer's Introduction

Pen name: Gusan. Poet and literary critic, member of the Korean Writers's Association, vice president of the Korea Literary Critics' Association, executive of Jeju P.E.N International.

Publication: *Encounter of Language and Literature*, *Identity of Poetry*, *Literature and Love*

Collections of Poems: *Island*, *Sea and Breath of Divers*, *Weather Strips*

April of Pascha

Seung-Haeng Shin

<1>

April

There was an exhausted voice

Enough to cause heartbreak

Breathless

On the fire polar

Fragile vengeful spirits are pierced

In the ocean a group of saw sharks

In the mountain red flags

April

Was fed up with Jeju Island

Your

Breath, wholly

Met empty morning

<2>

April

Tired, the day suffered from fatigue by a piercing wind

Oxen and horses flipped a whip

Excited traders

Though time passed

Unforgettable

Exhausted voice. That April

Was a brother during the day

Sitting in a dark-red wall

You

A mountain path of Golgotha

Again are having another long night

<3>

Jeju Island in April

Like a broken wreck

A baby, crying, is hung on the branches of a nettle tree

Scratched waves in the port

Also in the cave of Darangshi Oreum

In a thorn tree

How does April become

An unforgettable exhausted voice?

You
Become a squirrel tied to the electric chair

<4>
Now, April
You become the sacrificial ceremony dance to satisfy your grudge
From darkness to light
Oppression to freedom and liberation
This April became the life of Pascha
Connected from an ocean
Picking milk
Soothing sorrows…

The start
April of Jeju
Has become the voice of people

Jeju in Praise

Baekdu! Spread you chest!
Halla! Dance!
Here is the place love buds and the whole world live
The evergreen mountain
The invisible island, enchanting song
Jeju is a fantastic island and hometown of arts, planting tomorrow
Ah…
Waves!
Dance
Hoist a sail dancing together

Row your dream in an ocean hoisting a sail
Here is the place of youth crossing an ocean
Breathe
We cherish a sky, the future treasuring eternity
Jeju is the homeland of peace
Ah…
Waves!
Dance
Hoist a sail dancing together

Jeon-Hyung Yang

Gueok-ri
Jocheon-ri Wild Grass

Writer's Introduction
Member of the Hallasan Literature Society.
The Yeollin Literature Award and Korean Jayoo Poets Award.
Publications: *I Am a Rock, the Dandelion on a Street, Love Is Silent*, etc
Address: 38-1 Oilnam-Ro, Ora 1-dong, Jeju, Jejudo, Republic of Korea
Phone: (064) 725-3960, 010-6685-3960 E-mail: yih3960@hanmail.net

Gueok-ri

Jeon-Hyung Yang

How distant is it?
Gueok-ri, South Jeju Daejeong
Running for 50 years, at last
I had a glimpse of the dress of my little aunt
Wearing this world of woe and tumult in many layers.

The flames of April 3rd Uprising rose
Two people who had different thoughts
As far as millions of ri
Running to Gueok-ri
Risking their lives
The old school where they had debates is snow silent
A wailing cry of crows on the lookout hill is sad
Though the wind blowing in the Jibangteul Grandma shrine
Constantly performs an exorcism to ward off evil
I bury at least the grain of an old wound
A leap of fluttering resident birds
In the first place the dream of Gueok-ri was stars.

Gueok-ri!

Where could there be more of this dimming longing
Bowing down to a monument of a dutiful son
A traveler picks up broken pieces of pottery
Whoever walked longest reach Gueok-ri
Under the sky of Gueok-ri
Everybody becomes one of the stars in the sky.

Jocheon-ri Wild Grass

The wild grass carries autumn on her head in Jocheon-ri
All mothers from the nether land return
As if they open their hearts wide
Secretly burning incense in a refreshing sea wind
Draw down autumn fully in the village

Lifting the high sky higher
Under the low autumn sky displaying fireworks
A trimmed face of the flower
Is beautiful like the legend of the fire starter's daughter
Who wanted to shoot a fire

When several flowers begin to bloom on every roadside
People's hands are busy preparing for autumn
People's hearts palpitate with hope
For by chance somebody never heard of could come back
Climbing up Hurray Hill, trying to wave towards the faraway ocean

The throb of Jocheon-ri is waiting for autumn
The wild grasses carry autumn on her head in Jocheon-ri

Young-Ho Oh

Climbing Oreum on a Volcanic Island
When I Go to Haengwon-ri

Writer's Introduction
Former president of the Jeju Shijo Society. Currently vice president of the Jeju Branch of P.E.N. Korea and board member of the Korean Shijo Poets' Association. Korean Shijo Critics' Award.
Publications: *An Insignificant Reason*, *Climbing Oreum on a Volcanic Island*
Address: 324-10 2-Do 2-dong, Jeju, Jejudo, Republic of Korea
Phone: (064) 757-1361, 011-9660-6250 E-mail: jeju500@hanmail.net

Climbing Oreum on a Volcanic Island

Young-Ho Oh

At Mount Halla's hem
The sinner climbs again
Stepping on her thin back where her tendons jut over
Letting my steps lead
And confessing

Just watching a violet dancing
Having bloomed, knocking off a half-a-million year old thought
April wind flitting through a hole of a volcano rock

Now exhausted and bruised, even my own words I blame
Like a mother's bosom, so beautiful
Today, dreaming of new birth
Flowers bloom
Flowers fall

When I Go to Haengwon-ri

Windmills in Haengwon-ri are awake for 365 days.

Even with a light breeze, in a Dutch way

They flutter and collect energy

And brighten as far as a strange road.

In an ocean farm where desire and sadness are unburdened,

Fat flatfish are sleeping with their eyes open

Having a nightmare of being sold soon.

On a house-sized rock, half-submerged in the seawater

Women divers are dragging a net filled with fresh tot seaweeds

Whose hair is being washed in the waves.

The sharp sounds of women divers' breath penetrate into the ocean water

A hundred thousand times

Building a pillar for an old woman diver's house

The ocean bears another island on her bosom.

Bong-Taek Yoon

The Place of No Longing
Rain Water

Writer's Introduction

Born in Seogwipo.
New Writers' Award by Literary Trends with *Island Wind*, etc
Publications: *Farmers Also Yearn*, *Every Wild Flower Has a Name*
Address: 4316-5 Gahngjeong-dong, Seogwipo, Jejudo, Republic of Korea
Phone: (064) 739-2332, 011-9662-2340 E-mail: Seogwipo@hanmail.net

The Place of No Longing

Bong-Taek Yoon

If leaving quietly on a boat
At the time of daybreak
I might reach the island.
Though the seaway may be cut off
Longing keeps flowing.
Painful, raging waves of the far away island
Surge towards through welling lights.
Thou still stay there
Leaning on the poor port
Where longing still lingers
Becoming the shadow of a shipwrecked soul.
Embracing a longing which can't be shut
Though turning in my bed.
Thy sail will be set
Towards somewhere
When the west wind blows.

Rain Water

Soaking in, flowing

And staying in the mouth of a winter river

If I meet you, I'll drop an anchor

If you pass by,

I'll wait down the river.

Oh, rain water!

Twisting, turning and meandering.

Oh, poor rain water!

Flowing outside things

If I meet you again,

I will go over, gulping down my sobs

And say spiteful things.

I should take off my clothes

In poor rain water

And return···

In-Soo Jeong

Angling
A Love Song

Writer's Introduction
Bornn in Seogwipo.
New Writers' Award by Korean Literature in 1974, Jejudo Culture Award
Publications: *Samda Island*
Address: Gah-602, Samboo Jahngmi Aprs,1601-11 Samyang 1-dong,
Jeju, Jejudo, Republic of Korea
Phone: (064) 756-1846, 018-350-1846 E-mail: jung40@paran.com

Angling

In-Soo Jeong

Standing on the seashore I can see Udo[1])Island
Even though being alone I'm not lonely
Whether I cast a line or not
I'm glad not to be bored.

Udobong[2])lying face down in the ocean
In the bosom gently down the peak
The island village dimly falls asleep
Against the coral white beach[3])
The sea waves are dazzling to the eyes.

Measuring the sky with the tip of a fishing rod
As if giving the choking world a thrashing
I hit the sky, and
The curve flies with a whistle.

My life I have lived
Though passing time idly

---

1) Udo: An island 2.8km away from Jongdal-ri, Gujwa-eup, Jeju-do. So named as it looks like a cow lying on its stomach.
2) Udobong: The peak of Udo with a lighthouse.
3) A sand beach of rare corals, stretching along the south seashore of Udo.

I must draw a right parabola.

Out of the world like a twisted turban shell
Standing on the seashore where I can Udo
Let's cast a parabola to Udo.

A Love Song

In simmering broad daylight
Let's meet at Bejarim Forest*
Together between people longing for each other.
Don't take off your upper clothes
Ancient winds soaking out from the nutmeg tree
Will tickle your armpits.
Don't blow your nose.
The scent settles in every branch of the tree
Harboring and nurturing the wild orchids.

Let's meet at Manjang Cave**
All the year round
Together between lonely people.
Don't hug
On the way to the depth of ten thousand meters
You might have to carry the other on your back.
Don't scream
The sound of waking up lava sleeping thousands of years with a dragon's belch.

---
* The virgin forest of nutmeg trees in Pyeongdae-ri, Gujwa-eup, Jeju-do.
** So called as the length is *man jang* (ten thousand *jang*. 1 *jang* is 3m.)

In the middle of the night in summer

Let's meet on Rabbit Island***

Together between people who are going to soon break up.

Don't fret.

As long as you're in the flower garden of crinum

Under moonlight

The flower leaves will take care of you

Petting your faded love.

Don't clap your hands.

Blessing songs from waves splashing.

*** A small island off the shore of Hado-ri, Gujwa-eup, Jeju-do, the colony of crinum.

Gi-Pal Han

Island
My Life In The Afternoon

Writer's Introduction
First recognized in *Shimsahng* in 1975. Former president of the Jeju Branch and the Seogwipo Branch of the Korean Writers' Association
Jeju Culture Award, Seogwipo Civil Award, Jeju Literature Award
Publications: *Between Words and Silence*, etc
Address: 681 Bomok-dong, Seogwipo, Jejudo, Republic of Korea
Phone: (064) 732-4138, 011-694-4138

Island

Gi-Pal Han

Writing a poem
When the sound of water goes down
To the west where the moon's declining,
Absent-mindedly
I also sometimes
Want to get out into the world
Like that

The sound of surging waves
Clean echo of the wind
Sound like the cries of the island
I unload my whole junk thought
Tossing and turning
Sleepless night
If I become an island
By getting a light

My Life In The Afternoon

Washing my feet

Looking at a corn

On my little toe

Drinking a sip of water

Throwing instantly what's left

My life in the afternoon

What is life?

Over my magnifying glasses

The mirror of the sky shivering lightly

Like birds appearing

And disappearing in a flash

My daily life Losing something

Numerous stars pouring down every night

I don't know their names.

Novel

The Faraway Mountain
Drifting Island, Ieodo
My Hometown Where The Moon Rises

Hyon-Sik Choi

The Faraway Mountain

Writer's Introduction

Born in Hongwon, Hahmkyungnahm-Do in 1924. Awarded in the Spring Literature Contest of Josun Daily Newspaper in 1957 with *Deer*. Member of the Korean Writers' Association, Korean Novelists' Association, Korean Writers' Association, Jeju Branch.
Publications: *Red Dress*, *Black Cat Diary*, *Mountain at a Distance*, etc.
Phone: (064) 757-4525

The Faraway Mountain

It was snowy outside. I called Mr. T to suggest going stone searching.

"Where do you want to go?" he asked delightedly.

I replied, "I'd love to go close to the Sechongyo Bridge."

"Won't the road be blocked because of the snow last night?"

The morning news said a minibus will be running.

Even though the snow will be piling up all day?

Finally I answered, "If it's blocked we can come back."

We decided to meet at the inter-city bus terminal. The heavy snowfall during usu (one of the 24 seasonal divisions around February 18th) was the first in over two decades. However, snow piled up only around Halla Mountain but not near the coast. The temperature goes down 1℃ for every 100m. That means that if the temperature at the port is 0℃, it is -19℃ at the top of Halla Mountain due to its height of 1950 meters.

The bus was probably not crowded because it was Sunday. As the bus started to go down the snow-covered road, it seemed to be burdened. We were going up to around 500~700m and the temperature drop was reflected in the snowfall. The roads were cleared but the hail still fell continuously.

"It's more like snow fog than snowflakes," I said, drawing Mr. T's attention to the window.

"It's hard to see this sort of snow fog anywhere else besides Halla Mountain. The humidity of the fog can get climbers into trouble. You can't get it off once it sticks to your clothes."

"Incredible!" I exclaimed with admiration.

With twinkling eyes, he said jokingly, "What about the snow in your home province of Hamgyeong-do, uncle?"

"We have large flower-like snowflakes that come down all night⋯"

"Then, a lot of snow must be piled up."

"Yep. The snow falls, piles up, and melts then the cycle repeats over and over again until the middle of March."

"Large numbers of artists are believed to come down to Jeju from Seoul, but the snow-covered landscape of Jeju Island is notorious for the difficulties it poses to artists when they try to draw."

"How come? Snow-covered scenery must be the same everywhere."

"I also heard this from somebody, but it is said that the light of Halla Mountain is polarized, causing whole scenes to become white. Alternately, scenes become completely gray when back lights are shining, which greatly confuses artists."

"Completely gray?", I muttered to myself.

"Painters never know where to focus and mess up their canvasses with splotches of gray", T added.

"I see."

I lit a cigarette, feeling a bit confused. The windshield was continuously being cleaned by the wipers.

'The mess of gray' must be the right expression to describe Jeju in winter. That being said, my lost 'Faraway Mountain' was gray as well. I looked at T's face. He was looking out the window the whole time.

"That was the best landscape stone among the indigenous stones of Jeju Island. We'll never know who stole such a precious rock," he said while staring out the window.

"Your T-shaped 'Mokja' stone was also valuable."

We both liked them, didn't we?

"I decided to forget about it···"

'Faraway Mountain' was a beautiful dark-gray colored stone which was similar to Jeju's indigenous 'Mokdol' stone. The width was 30cm, which was perfect for viewing. Some might say it couldn't be 'the dark black stone' because it was not hard enough but it wasn't excessively soft like the flesh of pears. It was somewhere between a black stone and a pear with its quiet beauty. When it was placed on the cherry blossom-shaped saucer, the simplicity and tranquility became more distinctive.

'Faraway Mountain' was the most prized find I obtained soon after starting to learn about rock collecting. Six years ago I joined the 'Sangseok' Society and started spending Sundays searching for stones.

From time to time I went searching on my own, but most of the time, other members accompanied me. We scanned 'Waidocheon' Stream, 'Seongsanpo' Port, 'Biyangdo' Island and 'Gapado' Island.

It was a clear day in late autumn about a year after joining the club. I was passing through Halla Mountain alone on my way to Secheongyo Bridge. It was a long way away and I went for 30 more minutes from Seogwipo to the east by bus. I left home at 6 in the morning and was able to share a taxi, arriving in Seogwipo in an hour. I then transferred to a bus and arrived at S village a few minutes after 8 a.m.

The whole village was busy harvesting sweet potatoes. Maybe it was because of the tangerine trees and green camellia trees but the village seemed to be affluent at first glance. Right after getting off the bus, I suddenly stopped walking. From the end of the road which stretched to the east, a funeral hearse was coming. The bus slowly left and vanished into the distance and the funeral hearse, newly decorated with only white paper, continued to approach. "It must be a big family's funeral," I said casually, smiling at a guy standing next to me.
'Not really.'

The 67 or 68 year old man nodded and said, "It's the funeral of a woman diver." Since a 91-year-old veteran woman diver passed away, all the women divers were attending the funeral. As the funeral procession passed by, I heard the following chorus:

> "She lived in this world
> But she passed away somehow
> When will she come back?
> She can't come back once she is gone."

The funeral march and the line of the funeral procession was neat and orderly. I was standing with my hands clasped close to my chest and felt a lump in my throat. The stream of mourners passed through the village and headed into the corner leading to the footpath of the mountain.

The funeral marchers probably stopped because they encountered a steep hill.

"···I see, only women divers were casket-bearers and they went to bury her to complete the old woman's 91 years of ocean life," I thought to myself as I left that place. I headed over to the Secheongyo Bridge area which was located at the eastern part of the village.

It was quite a long way. One of Jeju's unique dry streams came into sight. I also could see the faraway horizon of the Yellow Sea. The ocean was particularly calm. I chose the muddy riverside under the bridge. Some meokdol stones were scattered around and they seemed to be pretty hard. Except for hermit crabs hiding from the sound of a person singing, and the sound of waves, it was tranquil.

"Rolling stones gather no moss." That's the basis of the beauty of stones. I continued moving slowly.

Three hours later, I stood up straight and looked around. I realized that I had been the only person out here for the whole day despite the beautiful weather. Oh, such solitude!

I glanced at the mountain where the funeral march had been. There was nothing else except for the dark blue sky and trees with dark red leaves. Chirp. Chirp. A sad sound, something like that of a bird, came from the ocean and drifted into my ear.

Shifting my gaze, I tried to determine where the sound was coming from. However, I could only see the quiet ocean and Bumseom or Tiger island on the horizon. How could it be so tranquil? Maybe it was because of the 90-year-old woman diver's funeral. I even forgot about myself amid the sounds of the ocean and started to search for stones again.

At about that time, I encountered 'the Faraway Mountain' and hurriedly left the area only carrying that rock. After a week, a cherry blossom-shaped saucer was placed under the stone I had named 'Faraway Mountain' and I started to talk to it. My 'Faraway Mountain'. It was a simple mountain-shaped stone with a main peak on the left and a generally-sloped shape. It had the shape of a nondescript mountain that can be seen anywhere in Korea.

However, one day when I came back home after drinking, I started to sing the following song in front of my stone:

> "I wandered today to the hill, Maggie,
> To watch the scene below,
> The creek and the creaking old mill, Maggie,
> Where we sat long, long ago.
> The green grass is gone from the hill, Maggie,
> Where once the daisies sprung. The creaking old mill now has been still, Maggie, since you and I were young."

How indiscreet for a guy in his fifties. I am embarrassed to say that I almost burst into tears. However, something came into my head and I was able to hum the whole tune to completion, after which I felt rather refreshed. I started to look at the mountain.

It was the hill at the back of the village forty years ago. Except for some pine trees at the southern end of the hill, it was almost bare, covered only with turf. Five or six-year old boys were flying paper airplanes. The winter of walleye fish and hairy crabs seemed to be continuing. I would feel like walking in the open air when I finally came out of hibernation. The boys soon got bored with throwing paper airplanes and changed the mood by playing war games. The boys grouped themselves together and started to play king of the hill to fight each other at the top of the hill. After several rounds they all got tired and lay on the ground. All of them tumbled to and fro on the grass and made wheezing sounds like, "Huff, huff" while catching their breath. Soon the sound of wind became clearer in my ears. They also noticed the smell of soil in the newly-growing grass. The boys looked around for something else to occupy their attention. The boys sat up.

"Wow, it's a flower!" Everybody gathered around the voice. "Yeah, it's really a flower!" They surrounded the violets in wonder. "Hey, there's one here, too- a yellow flower!" The voice came from the direction where a dandelion flower bud was. I stared at the flowers on the golden turf of the hill. Oddly, I cannot remember the faces and names of these boys. Even after concentrating for a while trying to remember the name of at least one, I failed. Nevertheless, my brain became refreshed with the images of little violets.

Since then, "The Faraway Mountain" has turned into the hill from my memory and led me to various thoughts- sardines littered on the white sand beach, dragon flies, sleighs, the suicide of an elderly person on the railroad tracks, royal azaleas, a snake, boys (was the boy's name Wondol?) and kite fighting in the autumn sky.

I was very much satisfied that memories of my hometown in each season came to mind thanks to 'the Faraway Mountain'. I also smiled from time to time with the thought that it must be a generous gift from the old woman diver whom I met at Sechongyo Bridge.

It was a day around Christmas Day. The members of Sangseok Society rock collecting club decided to have an exhibition. We rented the 'D' coffee shop and each member displayed their stones, up to three pieces. I only showed my 'Faraway Mountain'.

One night before the end of the exhibition, two stones were stolen. They were the T-shaped 'Mokjasoek' and my 'Faraway Mountain'. It was such a mysterious theft. We reported it to the police and the waitress of the cafe, but although some people were investigated, no clue was found. The thief must have been someone who knew rock collecting well. The thief must have waited until late at night (but still before the curfew), and hid it in his coat pocket. I was able to guess at least this much, but there was no progress in the investigation.

Maybe I would find a similar rock near Seochongyo Bridge. I could forget mine fairly easily, but T couldn't let go that easily. His T-shaped 'Mokjasoek' was so rare and famous that a Japanese tourist came to him and asked him to sell it for five hundred dollars.

One week after I lost 'the Faraway Mountain', I visited the Seochongyo Bridge despite my busy schedule. My hopes weren't realized and instead I had to settle for two Mokdol stones.

The second time was the same. I had the uneasy feeling that all the stones were laughing at me several weeks ago. How could I handle my treasure so carelessly? Why couldn't I appreciate the beauty of that single stone?

'We've reached the peak of 1100m.'

I was startled out of my reverie by the conductor's announcement. The snow fog seemed to have become lighter. Half of the route to Seogwipo is a downward slope descending the southern part of the mountain. The bus driver had to step on the brakes frequently.

"Was your T-shaped 'Mokjasoek' from Gapado Island?", I asked, breaking the silence.

"No, it was from Waedocheon Stream."

"Five hundred dollars is not a little sum of money for a rock, is it?"

'You're right, it's not, especially for me- but those who try to buy rocks aren't really professionals. Exchanges of stones can occur, but not with money.'

"Are you expecting to see it again?"

"Well, if it's my fate to see it again, I will. Karma is weird like that." He then proceeded to tell me the following story about destiny:

About 5 years ago, he had gone to Waedocheon Stream with P to search for stones. As everyone had different habits, each person chose stones differently, yet it was still rare for someone to pick one at first sight.

When they found nice stones, they remembered the location and thought over and over about whether or not to take the stones on their way home.

T was the person who found the T-shaped stone. Half of the stone was in the ground. The dark gray color was lively but it seemed a bit weak. They were about to go home when P held up the stone, looked it over and said to T, "If you like it, take it."

The stone didn't satisfy T, but he took it anyway and put it in his bag with another because he thought it would be rude to refuse P's offer.

After removing the dirt, he noticed that the stone was in the shape of the Letter "T". He stayed up all night touching and looking at the stone.

"So did you tell P about it?"

Of course not. He surely would've regretted it and I didn't want to argue with him.

When he saw it again later, he didn't realize what stone it was. I hid it in a cabinet and never showed it to him.

Hahaha. We laughed together. I don't expect to see it again. It was a punishment for my carelessness. T turned his sad eyes to the window.

A sign read '700m'. The bus was travelling fast through the snowy forest. The first thing we did upon arriving at S village was to drop by a coffee shop. A little street sign that read 'Wimi' was placed next to the post office. The inside of the cafe was all right. A pot or a flower vase was always on the counter, the tables were clean, and quiet music played in the background. They also had fairly good coffee.

Right after getting off the bus we headed for the coffee shop. Miss Kim welcomed us with a bright smile in the empty cafe. Narcissus flowers are already in bloom, I exclaimed, surprised at the flowers arranged with the pottery. We sat at a table close to the window and T ordered two cups of coffee.

I smelled the fragrance of the flower. It was so light that I was about to guess where it was coming from but lost it when the coffee was served.

"Why don't you have some coffee too, Miss Kim?" I asked her to join us.

"Sure, thanks, she said, leaving our table." Then she came back with one more cup of coffee for herself.

"You look prettier, Miss Kim," I insisted.

"Oh, stop it," she said, looking down at the floor, and added, "By the way, the lady is back."

"What do you mean by 'the lady'? The owner?"

"Yes."

"When?"

"The day before yesterday."

"Is she in?"

"She went to a hair salon."

"Are you talking about Ms. Cho?" T asked, breaking the silence.

Miss Kim clucked, "Come on, there aren't any other ladies here except for Ms. Cho!"

We could tell that she was joking by the way she talked.

"Did I make a mistake? Should we go?"

"Let Ms. Cho know that we will stop by again on our way back", I said.

Then we left the coffee shop. It wasn't snowing any more and the sun was brightening over the ocean.

"What just happened back there?" I thought while walking slowly.

Narcissus flowers in bloom out of season, the return of Ms. Cho-why did these meaningless events take the spring out of my step? I laughed at myself. However, the laughing depressed me and I started walking even slower.

I had thought that there wouldn't be a coffee shop there, but I unexpectedly found 'Wimi'. Perhaps due to my flustered state, Ms. Cho made a good first impression on me.

"My mother is from Wonju and my dad is from Shineiju." She was one of the displaced people. I asked her whether she was making ends meet 'in this poor village'.

"I'm managing somehow." She gave me a sad look.

On the third meeting, we drank soju with a conch shell dish.

I heard about Ms. Cho's past, about the 15 precious years until she opened a coffee shop. She married a man whom she met when she was 21. They met through an arranged date. Her father was satisfied with what the young man had and how he looked, but her mother opposed the marriage. Her mother complained that he didn't look like a man. Ms. Cho's parents argued about the prospective marriage for some time, but finally her father prevailed.

After three years of marriage, Ms. Cho divorced her husband after bearing one daughter. The guy had a morbid suspicion about her chastity. He could not sleep without a knife beside him. Her second marriage was not a legal one. She had to give up the relationship because the man went out every night.

That's when she started working at drinking houses. She didn't work in Seoul. She worked in cities like Busan, Masan, and Daegu in Gyeongsang-do province. She finally came to Jeju island three years ago. The coffee shop was her little but important property.

On the next occasion, I went to Sechongyo Bridge with T. The three of us, Ms. Kim, T, and I, headed for an oceanfront drinking house at sunset. The talk was mainly about rock collecting.

"I oppose placing stones indoors." Ms. Cho began.

T asked, "Oppose? how come?"

"Isn't it better for the stone to be left where it was born?"

"What about flowers placed in a room?" said T.

"You can grow flowers from seeds but that's not the case with stones. How can they be same?"

"I see. You are saying artificial things and natural things are different."

"I don't know about theory. I just feel that way."

"You must be right," I said.

"Whether it's a flower or a stone, it's all the same because they are leaving their place. Murder is murder. What's the difference?"

T retorted, "The flower will wither and die soon, so I think the flower is better off being picked and appreciated. In the case of stones, you don't even kill the stone by taking it, but instead make it stay at one place forever. Don't you think so?"

"A fool?" T said with wide eyes.

"Hahaha," I laughed out loud.

"Hey, T, think about it. Don't be too surprised. Even your T-shaped stone would've wanted to remain hidden in the ground. Because the beauty that the rock wanted to hide was made public, a theft ultimately resulted. Well, let's stop talking and have a drink," I said.

"I'm sorry, Mr. T," said Ms. Cho as she drooped her head.

"She's no ordinary woman- she's probably a veteran," I thought, while looking at alcohol-reddened eyes.

The window was open to the ocean. The sea breeze smelled of wild rose. We were all becoming mellow in that setting.

"Have you ever seen a butterfly in the middle of the ocean?" she asked earnestly.

"Butterfly?" T asked, intrigued.

"Hard to believe, isn't it? It was last summer. I was on my way back from Beomsom Island. Butterflies were flying in the middle of the water. The two little yellow butterflies had followed our motorboat. It was wonderful and fascinating. I watched the butterflies vanishing into the horizon.

Her eyes were sparkling. I've never seen a butterfly over the ocean but I now I know that butterflies not only fly over flower gardens but also over the ocean," I said, smiling.

"What's the poem?⋯ 'The ocean and the butterfly' if I recall correctly⋯"

"Hold on."

I thought for a while, rubbing my chin and said.

"I think the poem goes something like, 'Come back like a tired princess'- is that the right phrase? I can't remember."

"Like a tired princess?', she said to herself, then averted her eyes to the ocean. She made a rigid facial expression as if she was staring at something.

"I may have the collection of poems at home. I will write it down in a letter and send it to you" I said, breaking the silence.

"Really?" she said, smiling.

"I would never tell a lie to a lady," I said, smiling back.

After a few more rounds of drinking, T stood up first and suggested that we leave the place.

"I made some mistakes, but I've learned a lot. I really enjoyed this evening," she said politely. She was perfectly decent.

We went our separate ways at a bus stop.

The next day I found the collection of poems including 'The Sea and the Butterfly' and wrote down the whole poem on a piece of paper and put it in my pocket notebook. I promised to send the letter but I thought it would be better if I read it to her when we got together again.

We searched for stones at nearby places that summer but I didn't get a chance to go to the Seochongyo Bridge then or during the fall either. Around Christmas, I visited S village again.

The Wimi cafe was the first place I went. Miss Kim welcomed us with smile and said, "Ms. Cho met a man and⋯"

It turned out that the man was from the mainland and owned a tangerine orchard in Seogwipo City. Ms. Cho was busy taking care of the orchard and visited the cafe only twice.

"So you're handling this big place all by yourself?" I said after looking at the counter without flowers and dirty tables.

"Yes, she suggested hiring another girl but I opposed the idea."

"You speak standard Korean pretty well now," I said with a smile.

"It doesn't sound good at all, does it?"

"Yeah, not one bit. By the way, how do you deal with all the customers here? What do you do when you have to cook or when you have to go somewhere?"

"I know all the customers. When I am not here they play the record player and wait."

Miss Kim smiled again.

"I see."

I felt distracted.

"Do you want me to play a record?"

"Yes," I nodded.

She went back to the counter and the jukebox started up.

"Can you turn it down?"

"Sure."

She turned the volume down.

I pulled out my pocket book and took out the little paper on which the poem was written.

"Because nobody told it how deep the sea is/ the white butterfly is not scared of the sea at all/ It landed, thinking it was in a garden of green radish/ its little wings got wet/ and came back like a tired princess. It was sad because the sea is not a flower/ and a blue crescent moon is engraved on the butterfly's abdomen.

I tore the paper into little pieces, threw them into the ash tray, and left the cafe.

"Why are you so sluggish today?"

I walked more quickly in response to T's admonition.

T was waiting there. He asked, "Do you want to go the upper side of the bridge?"

Stones with special patterns like his T-shaped stone could be found in the riverbed on the upper part of the area and Meokdol stones like my 'Faraway Mountain' could be found in the lower part of the area which was close to the ocean. Neither of us could part from each other in order to achieve our individual purposes. That would be too selfish. That's why he was asking.

"It's up to you."

I wanted to insist going to the area which was better for me but I conceded out of guilt for my slow pace.

"Let's take a look at the upper part for about two hours."

T started to walk in front of me. We walked down the slope and entered the riverbed.

"T, why don't we do this today. All the stones found in the upper area are yours and all the stones from the lower part become mine."

"You mean cooperate? No problem. But we shouldn't be lazy."

"Definitely."

"Also, there's one thing that we have to make clear. If we fail to find anything precious today then I will not accompany you any more. I can't just follow you- I also need to go to Waedocheon stream."

"Then I will give up this place and go there with you."

"Really?"

"Yes."

"You're kidding. Then what about Ms. Cho?"

"What about her?"

"Don't deceive yourself. It's just between us," he said, grinning.

"I'm not deceiving myself."

"She is beautiful, friendly- almost perfect."

"Then why don't you try?"

"Well, I could but then you would never have the chance to see her."

"Hahaha."

We laughed together.

"Alright, let's get to work. Today could be the last day."

T looked at his watch, started to walk in front of me, and said, "Now it's one o'clock, so let's move to the other area at three."

We climbed far into the valley but could find nothing, so we had to move. I heard the sound of the ocean coming closer then I heard a lady's voice.

"Excuse me, sir!"

The valley rang with the sound of her voice.

I straightened up and directed my eyes to where the sound was coming. The voice was coming from the railing of the bridge. She was obviously calling to us while making little circles with her fingers.

"Yahooo"

I noticed that it was Ms. Cho and answered her back by waving my hands.

"Who is it?", asked T from behind my back.

"It looks like it's Ms. Cho."

"Then why don't you answer back?"

"Why, is it rude not to answer back?"

"Yeah, it sure is. You're cold-hearted."

"O.K., then why don't you run to her if you're so warm-hearted?" T joked.

"Let's quit what we're doing and go see her."

"I'll follow you soon. You should go ahead."

T agreed with me, but didn't want to quit yet. I cautiously walked quickly to her.

"I heard you stopped by my coffee shop," she said as we walked down the hill.

"Long time no see."

She was wearing a black sweater. I offered my hand, and thought that her face looked worn.

"I told Miss Kim that I would come by again on the way home. You didn't need to come all the way out here."

"I want to learn about rock collecting," she said, with a twinkle in her eye.

"What about your family?"

"I'm alone."

I almost blurted out, "Did you break up?" but I was able to control myself. I took a cigarette from my pocket.

"Didn't you say that it's undesirable to have stones in a room?"

"You haven't forgotten yet? I just said that because I was tipsy. I'm not going to obsess over anything. I'll just be searching for stones," she said firmly.

"Wow, it's been ages."

T approached.

"I guess you're not yet finished searching?" asked Ms. Cho.

"Yeah, not yet. We'll look around the area closer to the ocean then we'll go back."

Three of us came out onto the main road.

"On your way back, why don't you have dinner at my place. The mountain berry wine is ready."

She said she would be happy if we accepted her invitation to her humble house.

"I appreciate your offer, but I am worried that the mountainside might be covered with a lot of snow,' T said quickly, looking at me hesitantly.

"You can take the taxi late at night. In the worst-case scenario, you can take a bus early tomorrow morning and make it to work."
"Why not? She's doing us a favor. Let's promise to go home at seven."
"At seven o'clock? Are you sure?"
"You and I are both worried about getting home."
Ms. Cho, pleased, said, "Ok, then I will be waiting for you."
T said we would be there until five.

Ms. Cho was waiting for us in a jade green skirt and white top with light make-up.
"It's not a great place but," she said.
Her place was an approximately 16 square yard room behind her coffee shop. An old chest made of zelkova tree and a little table were the only pieces of furniture in this simple little room.

On the chest there were the narcissus flowers and a bookshelf. The flowers permeated the room with a refreshing fragrance. For dinner we had a 1.8-liter bottle of wine and side dishes including grilled dodok root (*Codonopsis Lanceolala*, a kind of tuberous mountain herb), roasted sea bream, as well as a conch dish.

Maybe because the wine was strong, I soon became tipsy after only drinking a couple of glasses.
"What's the worry? If we can't go tonight, we can still catch the bus early tomorrow morning," I said to T. He was worried that we might miss the last bus to Seogwipo at 8:30 pm.
"I know how you feel. But if you try to rush into something all at once, you

could get hurt. I think it'd be better to go home," he said bluntly.

"Oh, please. Maybe it didn't matter to you whether or not you found a stone at Seocheongyo bridge, but I was seriously hoping to at least find something similar to my 'Faraway Mountain'. But I failed again so what can I do? I should be able to drink at least."

I realized that I was getting drunk because it was hard for me to enunciate properly.

"You have to finish the bottle of wine you opened," Ms. Cho beamed, while looking down at the bottle.

"Alright, then. Let's drink to our heart's desire!"

T drank the glass of wine offered by Ms. Cho in one gulp.

"Now I'm seriously considering learning about rock collecting," Ms. Cho said after T offered her some wine.

"What about your family?" I asked.

"Do you know about Casino games?" she asked. She then kept silent for a while.

"I got into casino games recently- Blackjack, roulette, dice and Baccarat. I tried to stop him from playing, but it was impossible. Even after losing a 20,000 square yard orange orchard he's still crazy about gambling. He said that if I didn't like it, we should break up. What could I do? I decided to leave him. You said finding a stone is so hard, but so is finding the right person. If I marry again, I won't be a human being."

"The single life is not for everybody," I said.

"I know, so I tried to endure everything with my boyfriend. However now I'm fed up with it. It's filthy. It was best when I was alone. In this kind of season

I can befriend narcissus flowers and go rock collecting. I will live alone."
"Once, you said you would send me a letter about the Ocean and the Butterfly," she said, turning to me.
"I was carrying it in my notebook but one day I tore it up."
"Why?"
"Because the princess ran away."
"No way⋯"
"I will recite part of it to you."
"It landed down thinking it was in a garden of green radish/ it got its little wings wet / and came back like a tired princess."

"Cho Su-jin came back exhausted after landing in what she thought was a garden of green raddish. Hahaha. I am drunk."
She smiled.
I smiled and said, "You don't have little wings to get tired with."
"So, I am not going to land again?" she asked bluntly.
"We are talking too much about your sorrow."
The topic changed to Narcissus flowers.
"Wandang Kim Chonghee found the flower on Jeju for the first time. Until then, it was known as a Chinese flower, but when he was exiled to Jeju, people learned that the flower also grew in Korea, too. He wrote the essay praising the flower in the 'Collection of Wandang's works", I added, calming myself.
"The flower blooms from the end of January through February and March. During that season, all the flowers cover the mountains and fields like winter

snow. No matter where you go, if you just open your eyes, they will be filled with flowers."

"Where did he live when he was exiled?" asked Ms. Cho.

"You may know of Daejong village close to the base of Sanbangsan Mountain. He completed his works during his 9-year exile. He also found an orchid and pointed it out to the islanders."

"They didn't know that the orchid grew in the wild?"

"Probably not. Yeongyoung in China's Qing Dynasty was closer than Jeju Island. In January according to the Lunar calendar, young ladies enjoyed the fragrance of flowers from China."

"They enjoyed some kind of flower arrangement."

"Originally Korean flower arrangements centered on putting flowers in a vase. Just like the flowers in your room."

"Like the flowers in my room?"

She sounded surprised. Then she took a glimpse at her narcissus.

"Why don't we leave," T said, getting up.

"Please," I said, showing my opposition.

"The wine is almost finished too."

He pointed to the wine bottle with his eyes.

"What time is it?"

"It's eight ten. We can catch the last bus if we go outside now."

T hurried outside.

"What a pity," Ms. Cho said reluctantly. She stood up in the living room.

"Come visit us sometime in Jeju City. I will treat you to dinner," T said.

T and I left the room with empty backpacks. We came out to the main road through the coffee shop.

The waitress Miss Kim saw us and said, "Goodbye. I hope to see you again." Ms. Cho came with us to the bus stop to see us off. It was a clear, starry night. I could feel the cold night air on my neck. Maybe the roar of the waves sounded louder because of the wind from the south.

"So many stars," T muttered, slowing his pace.

"So many stones, too." I said.

"So many people, too," added Ms. Cho.

The bus arrived on time. About 6 people got off the bus but we were the only two to get on.

"Goodbye…"

I looked at Ms. Cho standing under the street light for a while through the window and said.

"You may not know the sadness of displaced people."

"Why not? I know it, too."

"If you know, you only know the concept. But you still do not know the real feeling of it."

"How big and deep is the real feeling?"

"It's so big and deep it makes you feel dizzy."

"Explain."

"Thirty years of absence from home. People say that nature even changes in the span of decades. Now it's been about three decades. I'm not exaggerating."

There is a hill at the back of my village where I used to play during my childhood. I wonder from time to time if I will be able to climb up the mountain and even if I will be able to die there."

"So you would exchange your life for a visit to your hometown?"

"Maybe it's my age. I came down here and now the way back is blocked. There's almost no way to go back to North Korea. At most, I might live two more decades. Thus sometimes I think that I could trade my life for just one visit back to my hometown. Ironically, however, I don't miss the people there. All I miss is the windflowers, the locust tree path, and other things belonging to nature."

"Are these thoughts clear in your memory?"

"They can't be. They're just vague. When I dream, though, it's all so clear. I play ball games in a wrong alley."

"In your dreams?" T asked.

"You aren't coming here anymore as you promised?"

"Of course I will. I'll return and find something. I am looking for the hill behind my hometown. I cannot stop it. I also have a female friend who wants to learn rock collecting."

I said, "Then I will surely accompany you."

To which I replied, "Thanks, but what about your T-shaped stone that you found in Waedocheon stream?"

"I've gotten a girl friend. Hahaha···"

Sure, I have to laugh. The North Korean dialect will disappear within 20 years in South Korea.

I thought about my Faraway mountain for a while and then mimicked him.

"I've gotten···"

The bus was running fast through the darkness.

Si-Hong Koh

Drifting Island, Ieodo

Writer's Introduction
Graduated in 1972 from the Department of Korean Language and Literature, cheju National University. New Writers' Award by *The Monthly Literature*. Member of the Korean Writers' Association, the Jejuhak Research Center. Commissioner of Jeju city Board of Education. Tamna Culture Award.
Publications: *A Handkerchief of the President*, *The City of Commandments*, etc.

Drifting Island, Ieodo

Chapter 1

Coming down from a hill in sight of the village, Eok-sun put down her straw basket on a rock and took off her headscarf. She dabbed off the sweat on her chest with the dirt-stained scarf. The strong smell of sticky sweat assailed her nostrils. Each time she gasped for air she tasted bitterness in her mouth. She felt trembling in her knees which were propping up the bag of millet ears. Breathing in long pants, she turned over her arms. Scratching among the millet for a newly-harvested sweet potato, she took one out of the bag and peeled it by scrubbing against the bag. She had left before breakfast.

A truck appeared from the corner of the road with clouds of dust swirling around. A cheerful song jingling from the speaker vanished into the dust right away.

"Good afternoon, dear culture and art-loving fellow citizens, this is Jeil road movie cinema, growing up and fed by your love. Tonight, the feature film, starring Gim Seung-ho and Hwang Jeong-sun, a real tear-jerker…"

A truck loaded down with eulalia grass passed by, drowning out her voice of the speaker.

After wiping the potato sap off her lips with the back of her hand, which was as rough as the edge of the straw mat, she crossed the road to enter the village. The cheerful songs coming out of the speaker made her feel bitter. Even a penny would be valuable to her. Every moment she took a step, faces of Eul-seon and Gil-su appeared on the jagged pieces of stone. Just thinking their asking for admission fees to watch a movie broke her heart. The mobile theater visited the village once every other month on the day of the 5-day local market and she had never given them the fee. She always lulled them by saying 'Next time' as if gently picking watermelon stems.

She unloaded her bag on the straw mat in the centre of the yard. She poured round bunches of millet ears out of the basket which made the sound of waves. She brushed the millet off the bag and the sea was still roaring. Diving seemed out of the question and the crashing sound of waves was a sign that the surf would strengthen. Eok-sun turned to face the soy-jar terrace and used a piece of stone as a stepping-stone, pulling her stumpy, log-like body onto the stonewall, overlooking the seaside. She stood on her tiptoes and thrust her head out in the direction of the port that stretched out to the sea. The waves had eased up a lot. Still, it seemed that the hot-dry wind had not gone completely. She regretted missing the appropriate tide time for diving. The fourth or fifth tide was just the right time for gathering seafood and since then the wind had blown continuously. The incessant wind had been worrying her.

The next day was the anniversary of her husband's death but she had nothing prepared. She would possibly have to remember it with just boiled water and burned rice. The anniversary of her father-in law's death was coming near within a month and she needed money to buy fertilizer as well as pay for tuition fees for her children. Even the old thatched roof needed to be changed.

Villagers thatched rooves for free but instead of wages, one should at least give a pack of cigarettes to them. The stone wall had fallen down during the last typhoon and remained untouched. The expenses were as numerous as holes in the stone wall. There wasn't even enough spare time to take a moment to think about how to spend the money in her pocket. The only way she could earn money was to dive. It was a matter of her life or death for her. The only place she could rely on was the land under the sea where she gathered marine products, staking her life on the gourd-shaped buoy. Every time winter was gone she wished that shiny silver sands covering the roof were broken pieces of pots or even sleeping pills to calm down the sea. She had no other wish but to dive, having the buoy as an islet. If only the sea were calm, she thought she could make a fortune. All the agar, brown seaweed, conches and abalones were treasures to her. When she kicked her ten toes in the air and dived into the ocean, she felt her windpipe swell painfully. The sea food was much more precious because it didn't require weeding and one didn't need to worry about fertilizing costs.

"Why are you standing with your lips pouting like that?"

Eok-sun was entering the earth-floored room and stepped down the terrace stone in wonder while approaching Eul-seon who was leaning against the stone wall near the yard.

"Did you go to school?"

Eok-sun remembered Eul-seon saying she would not go to school without the tuition money. Eul-seon was just fiddling silently with her rubber shoes using her toes.

"Did you argue with someone?"

Twitching her lips, Eul-seon shook her head.

"What then?"

"They turned me down because I didn't pay the money."

Eok-sun felt bitter against the teachers. It was not the first time yet she was filled with anger.

"Was Gil-su rejected too?"

"Yes," she said, "Gil-su went to the cinema with his friends."

"You should've told them about the strong wind. Why didn't you ask them to wait for a few days?"

"Such excuses don't work at all these days."

Eul-seon flung the book wrapper from her back into the room.

"That's good. From now on, quit school and learn to dive with me. You have done enough studying." The voice was quavering. She had even given birth to her daughter in the port on the way home from diving and wanted Eul-seon to at least finish middle school. Eok-sun felt her heart aching as much as back then.

She did not want her daughter to learn to dive. On her first visit to school to get her kids admitted, she saw a female teacher and noticed a female public servant sitting between men in the county office. She was so envious of them. Although there were some seventy households in Goet village, just ten families sent their daughters to elementary school. It was not just because of money.

Some had sons in high school and college but wanted daughters to be the source of family income. That was why villagers considered a family with many daughters as real rich folk. Having a daughter meant having a woman diver to make money as well as having a worker in the fields.

"I'd rather be a maid or nanny in the city or die than have to learn to dive. Eul-seon's furious voice surged down like a wave.

"What did you just say?"

"I said I'd quit school and make money."

Eok-sun felt her teeth clenched in anger. Setting up a millstone, she came out to the banister with a broom in her hand and pulled Eul-seon's hand; she was holding a pillar on her feet. She hit her daughter's back hard with the broom; people wouldn't use that on even a dog.

"Get out. Do you have any idea who has made my life this miserable?"

"Oww! I'm sorry for what I said. I take it back."

Squirming in her mother's grip, Eul-seon twisted her body towards the terrace stone of the house.

There was a sharp cracking sound; Rattle! Snap! The buoy fell on the stone entangled with the fishnet from the pillar. Eok-sun felt a crack in her heart then threw away the broom. She held the gourd which tumbled into the yard to her chest. It had a millet- grain sized crack around the stalk. Luckily, it didn't seem to be a problem for diving.

Chapter 2

Grinding grain in a stone mill, Eok-sun sang a mournful dirge mixed with sighs. Ieo, ieo Ieodo, was the road to Ieodo your last journey? Once you've gone, you never come back. Ieo, ieo, ieo hora. I finished patching up your socks and starching your clothes, waiting anxiously but you never returned. Ieo, ieo, Ieodo, on the millstone⋯

Worries smoldering in her heart accumulated into a little hill together with the buckwheat powder around the millstone. Thanks to the songs she sang while working, whether dashing through the fields or working in the sea, she could survive each day. The songs invigorated her soul.

"You must have gone to the field in the morning. I thought we'd go to the market together."

"I'd go if I had balls like a man but I can't go without them."

Eok-sun sang the millstone song again. Some ten gallons of barley or newly harvested millet would bring her something. They'd be sold at a giveaway price but in the end there'd be excited hip dancing and that was about it. Wearing her Sunday clothes, Bil-rae tucked up her skirt and took hold of the handgrip of the millstone. The shoulder of the arm grabbing the handle felt a lot less burdened.

"Let's go diving today. I'm in big trouble because I haven't prepared anything for Gil-su's father's memorial tomorrow."

"Don't even say the words you want to dive for the dead! The sea is still angry and Sun-deok's mom also promised to go to the market."

Eok-sun continued her sorrowful tune while the stone turned smoothly.

"The word 'diving' itself gives me creeps."

"You sound like a lucky woman."

After blowing her nose, Eok-sun wiped off her fingers in the crotch of her pants and then put buckwheat powder on the mat into a wooden basin.

"There is always another chance next year. Suppose you dive today in this weather and hold the service with seafood you pick. Will that bring your husband back from the dead?"

"Come to think of it, you're absolutely right."

What she said was true. She had performed the memorial rite for more than a decade since she was twenty-two years old and she had found the food set by the rule untouched by her husband, not even a spoonful of steamed rice. She hoped to set lots of food on the table as much as she could. Praying for his soul meant devoting herself to the sea. She believed it was for the King of the Sea. She felt like she was preparing a passage in the water which had been laid out by his boating songs. She was also creating one for herself.

That was why she prayed on her husband's memorial day without people watching. May God take me to Ieodo Island where there's lots of seaweed, abalone and conches while I cross from the East to the West···

His waterway was a path to Ieodo, the underwater treasure island.

"My back! Helping you grind buckwheat only hurts my back."

Letting go of her hold on the handgrip, Bil-rae patted her back with a grunt of pain.

"You crazy bitch! Didn't your man visit last night? Your back must hurt from making love, not because of me?"

Eok-sun slapped Bil-rae's buttock slightly with the broom used to sweep the powder out of the hole in the stone, giving her a sidelong glance.

"Speaking of which, nowadays I can't sleep at all when he's not around. It's a real problem."

"You should care for someone who represses the anxious heart with a sigh."
"OK, whatever. By the way, take me with you when you go to dive later."
"You must not have anything good enough for your hubby's meal that you changed your mind so quickly!"
"I will do it to help you out in preparing for the memorial service."
Sitting around the basin of buckwheat powder, Eok-sun touched Bil-rae's face.
"Thanks but you're pregnant…"

She couldn't say any more with her nose tingling. The sound of the angry sea blew in through holes in the stone walls. They had grown up together in the village living next door to each other but it was the first time that Eok-sun appreciated her friend's concern.

Chapter 3

The two women had grown up tagging along everywhere together. They started to practice swimming when they were about ten. In the summer time, they would do diving exercises near the port in shallow water wearing goggles. They spent all day together picking seaweed and agars.

They had owned all the tools they needed for diving since they were six or seven. They went out to the sea together with grownups to learn how to be divers. When they went into the sea, they wore a headscarf, a jacket, pants, diving goggles and carried a spear, a chisel to pick conches and abalones, a hoe to pick seaweed and a gourd to attach to a net to hold the sea crop. These were the only things they inherited from their parents. Eok-sun and Bil-rae were attached together like the gourd and net when making money in

Gampo, Guryongpo and Oeyeondo. They spent the night close by each other with the skin tanned by the sea wind and studied at the small night school in autumn and winter. They studied multiplication tables and how to spell their names. They also got married to the men living in the same neighborhood.

Somehow they were destined to be together. Both lost their husbands at the age of twenty, as if they had promised each other to become widows. Their husbands died in the same year. It happened to Bil-rae in summer, Eok-sun in autumn.

"I am the kind of a guy who would rather die in the sea like Gun-chil." Eok-sun's husband would resolutely say such things whenever he got drunk since the day Bil-rae's husband was found dead on the seashore in the neighborhood. Some people said sometimes idle talk foreshadowed actual events. One day, worried about not rolling up the fishnet he had cast in the sea, he disappeared into the dark with his fishing gear box after the storm cleared away. That night the wind was so powerful that it blew away all thatched roofs. Eok-sun stayed up all night by the seashore. Her husband and the boat with all the other fishermen never returned. The wail of widows could be heard everywhere in the port. His body was never recovered, not even a single strand of his hair. She had no choice but to give him up for dead.

Eok-sun was determined to devote herself to her dead husband and her kids. She had become a workaholic without knowing it. She worked as if possessed. She had been able to sleep well as long as her son Gil-su had showed sweet gestures.

The friendship between Eok-sun and Bil-rae became strained when Bil-rae became a mistress to Big Guy whose nickname came from his great height. She had paid no attention to the story that Bil-rae had decided to become the mistress or surrogate mother of Big Guy, the only son for four generations in his family. Even that night she could go to bed only after making sure again that the door was locked properly.

"You must think about your son Myeong-il and you mustn't do anything disgraceful. Don't ever consider giving birth to a son of a noble family to change your destiny."

"Living all alone for five years and just leaning on my son is so unfair and spiteful to me."

"Don't get yourself involved in the middle of a feud with the lawful wife. Carrying on your life with your son might be difficult for you right now but your later years will be peaceful. There is an old saying that even a stone Buddha would turn its back on a feud between a mistress and a lawful wife. You should keep that in mind."

"Maybe only God knows that. I just have no strength to stitch up my heart like a rip in a sock. You can't recover your youth once it's gone. Eok-sun, you might as well think it over seriously."

"You don't have to worry about me. Mind your own damn business."

Eok-sun lay down next to her kids and shut her mouth tight. She felt a kind of betrayal. It was shameful to have been a friend of such a whore all along.

It was the last time she saw Bil-rae. Anyway there weren't many chances to see her like there had been in the old days.

Bil-rae had done little manual labor since she had become a mistress. They ran into each other by chance in the street, but Eok-sun was the first to turn her eyes away. As if she had encountered a snake crossing the street, she spat and turned her back on Bil-rae.

However she couldn't refuse to sell the field adjoining her fence for building a house.
"Is he willing to build it for you without making sure whether it is a daughter or a son?" Eok-sun delivered the barb on purpose to Bil-rae who was big with child. Bil-rae snapped, "Are you going to sell the land or not?"
"Only if you will allow me to spend one night with your hubby."
They started laughing, the sound of which woke up kids and Eok-sun's face turned red as if caught in mischief.
"The construction will start next month, ok?" Bil-rae made her promise again and then left.
"I will sell it to you but you might be annoyed to live next to a widow asking for this and that."
"It's fine unless you lay your eyes on my husband,"
She said the words "my husband" loudly without hesitation which made Eok-sun envious.
"I will die as a mistress to the King of the Sea. All men in this world are not good enough."

And something strange happened. Eok-sun began having problems sleeping at night once Bil-rae moved in right next door. Her mind used to be like tightly and beautifully braided hair but became entangled little by little. She would stop working early, feeling weary at dusk. Like a mesh bag without a string, she often sat down carelessly anywhere and sighed. She just watched Bil-rae with a jealous look and felt hatred and betrayal for no reason.

She would patch up old clothes and holed socks with holes, while often staring at the lamp. After all, how one lived didn't matter because everyone died in the end. Bil-rae's seductive voice surged against Eok-sun's ears. Whenever that happened, she stung her thigh with a needle while doing patchwork. She wished there were no nighttime. At least during the daytime, she could work back and forth between the sea and fields all year around. She would forget to lock the door before going to bed and became short-tempered with the kids, which had never happened before. She had Big Guy do chores like fixing broken doors or piling stacks of grain stalks; indeed she became like Bil-rae. One day, she demolished a stone wall deliberately and had him rebuild it.

Chapter 4

The sky was still gloomy. Eok-sun had a large container on her back for the diving gear.
"You're gonna give us money for the movie today, aren't you?"
Gil-su asked while standing in the yard with a spoon in his hand. He had been having lunch in the kitchen.
"You were even kicked out of school because of money. Now you're talking about a movie?"
Eul-seon beat the back of Gil-su's head with the handle of her spoon.
"You are the one who told me to ask mom for money."

"Later, you're dead meat."

Glaring at him, Eul-seon hid in the kitchen.

"Go find someone who will buy your mom if you want to attend school and see movies…"

"Mom, you have said lying makes somebody a bad person and now you're breaking your word?"

"OK. Just keep the millet in the yard from being pecked by somebody's chickens."

"Awesome! You're the best, mom!"

Eok-sun headed for the sea with Gil-su's cheers echoing behind her. She decided to stay a few minutes longer under water. There were only a dozen of households that had radio sets in town so the mobile theater created a festive holiday mood. Children were as happy on that day as in the field in the autumn. Money didn't matter to them. Like a school of anchovies pursuing a brightly-lit boat, they rushed to the makeshift cinema nearby the bus station. Some kids with no money waited outside, hoping that the tent in front of them would be lifted automatically. They were just standing, wanting to see a the last scene of the movie

The same thing went for grownups. Joyful songs were heard only when the cinema visited the village and Eok-sun felt even more restless on those days. It had become worse since she had lost her husband. It was also partly because she tried to forget a guy working for the cinema who gave her first kiss before she got married and who never showed up again.

Even the last time she would not have rushed there if Gil-su hadn't been involved. That was the day after she had been told that Gil-su had to clean bathrooms at school everyday for a week as punishment.

By the time she had finished doing the dishes, Gil-su was still groaning; he kept on opening and closing the kitchen door, continuously asking for the admission fee.

"If you want to be a honey-bucket man, what's the use of movies?"

She wanted him to be dumbfounded.

"You said I should ask the teacher whenever I want to know something to get a good grade. That's why I did it."

"Yeah, but did I tell you to ask your teacher a question when she was in the bathroom?"

"I only did it because I missed the chance to ask questions in the first grade."

He explained what had happened. He did it because he wished to know what female teachers ate out of curiosity. It was the first time for him to see a teacher going to the restroom. While he was waiting for her to ask if she ate the same things as his mom did, unwillingly he looked through an opening left by a crack on the door.

Gil-su was whimpering in the dark with Eul-seon. The tune of songs from the theater flew by, covering the ground like dew. Eok-sun was about to call her kids but closed her mouth. She lay down, trying to forget her sorrowful mind like the crumpled and soggy paper money in a pot of long-stored rice. At that moment, songs from the speaker stopped and then Gil-su's voice was loud enough to shake the window.

"Mom, get my shoes back for me."

Eok-sun lit the lamp with a match.

"Hurry and bring me my shoes, please!"

Gil-su was stamping with his feet as if he were cockfighting. He was barefoot.

"Take them back from where?"

"The cinema."

She put her clothes on, entering the main road in a hurry.

"Was it a grownup or a child?"

"The one who collects the admission fee did it."

"That shameless thief!"

"I was sneaking."

He explained that he had no money but wanted to see the movie and tried to dash under the tent flap when the ticket clerk wasn't looking and he got caught.

"Next time I'll give you money. Don't you ever do that again."

"Ok, I will, so you promise to give me money.

Pulling Eok-sun's hand, Gil-su made a pinky promise with his mother.

"Swear?"

"I do."

"I will write you a letter", said the guy who had given her the first kiss and he vanished into the dark, leaving only those words. His face fogged her sight. That night way back then the sky had also been filled with stars.

Chapter 5

Rising above the horizon, Ieodo disappeared into the cloud once again.

Sitting in her diving suit while waiting to jump into the water, women divers were chatting to kill the time until the sea calmed down a bit more. On the days when Ieodo faded away, without fail the waves were strong or it was dark under water.

"I was going to swim but guess I should go home."

Sitting next to Eok-sun, Bil-rae raised herself, turning to the horizon.

"What kind of person swims in the autumn?"

"You must be still over the moon every morning, considering you still feel the heat in this weather."

"No wonder because both you and your hubby are healthy and fertile."

"Has it been two years or three since he moved in?

Squeezing in talk about having red bean porridge, all of the women chatted about Bil-rae and her husband.

"Bil-rae, he is a big guy so is it big, too?"

"Sure, just as big as this like a stallion's."

Disregarding the talk in dead silence, Bil-rae spread her arms towards the people.

"Then you don't have to worry about swimming in the middle of winter."

A high west wind blew their laughter away. Married women laughed loudly with hands slapping the ground and the others covered their faces with their hands, chuckling.

"You should've brought Big Guy along to wash your back so he can prove what you said."

"Now you also want to make fun of me?"

Bil-rae's face dimpled with a smile, pinching Eok-sun's shoulder. Eok-sun hung her head in shame. She felt flushed in the face. Others gave them awkward looks without saying anything. That was so relieving. Eok-sun said nothing about what had happened during the day to her yet.

It was the day to sow millet seeds. When finished plowing, Big Guy sowed the seeds with a mesh bag on his shoulder. She was about to insist on doing it on her own but she kept silent. Some fifty horses flocked to the field for trampling the ground. Like a school playground, the hard-packed earth helped the seeds grow properly and ripen well.

After a rice wine cup was passed around, a packhorse driver started talking.
"What a match made in Heaven! The chemistry is perfect between the two."
"Well, take a look at them. They go together like matching parts of a door hinge."
"The husband is horizontally-challenged while the wife is vertically challenged so they are meant to be with each other, right?"
"Ma'am, come here and stand like this."

The youngest looking guy pulled Eok-sun's chubby arm next to the Big Guy. On top of that, Big Guy took Eok-sun's wrist.
"Please, don't do this in front of people"

Eok-sun pulled back her body in surprise. What had been said couldn't be taken back. It was spontaneous, so embarrassing her more. Luckily, she was tanned by summer days and covered with sweat and dust. Returning from the field, Big Guy finished a kettle of rice wine and stood to leave.
"Dinner is ready. Why don't you eat before you go?"

All of sudden, he seem to be deaf and went over the stone wall to his home. Eok-sun leaned her head on the banister.

The full moon on the sixteenth night rose above the thatched roof. The gourd flowers covering the roof and the chirping of insects were distracting her. As it was late, the moon was high up in the sky, and she headed for the sea with some clothes. She walked to the wharf for a swim. Going round to a spring gushing out between rocks, Eok-sun slowed down.

"Who says diving is the only way to make a living?"

"Still⋯."

She heard the sound of spring water dashing against bare skin.

"Stop talking nonsense and give birth to another boy."

"Oh, that tickles!"

Leaving behind the scene of Big Guy washing his wife's back, Eok-sun mumbled like one possessed, as she was walking away black quartzite is good for stone walls, a dumb cow for meat, a bent tree for firewood, a bonehead rockfish for roasting, but what's the use of someone who is stupid?

Chapter 6

Two fishing boats left the port. Eok-sun stepped down to the waterside with the others. Except for nine, all had gone home one by one. The only people left were those who wished to see Ieodo emerging over the horizon. It only appeared between the sky and the horizon on clear days. The cold winter hardly gave a chance for people to enjoy seeing the isle.

The isle was a gourd, a lifeline for women divers. On Yeongdeung Day, the first day of February in the lunar calendar, Granny Yeongdeung visited Jeju, drifting about at the mercy of the wind, sowing seeds of seafood in the sea. The next day the mystical land of Ieodo could be seen from anywhere. People called it the Treasure Island with plentiful seafood. And none had set foot on it yet. Numerous people had gone there never to return. Some said that the more one sailed towards it, the further it receded from sight.

Ieodo was known for its raging waves which fascinated divers and made them want to go there even more. Perhaps there might be mountains of abalones and conchs and forests of seaweed because of inaccessibility. Ieodo drew sighs from people watching it in the distance. It could only be reached in a dream. That was why people would sing the song of Ieodo when sitting before a millstone, when holding a pestle or weeding between furrows and sweeping the yard.

Eok-sun picked up a rock as big as a block of fermented soybeans to attach to the string of her mesh bag. Rough waves required anchoring. If not, every time one came to the surface, one would find that the bag had drifted here and there far away from the gourd.

Holding her gourd to her heart, Eok-sun cast herself into the sea, and soon started chanting a melancholy tune. "When mom gave me life, was the day without the sun and moon? Ieodosan ieodosana···"

She kept on swimming forward to the tune. Perching on the island far from the seashore, seagulls flapped their wings, soaring high. Wild ducks moved along with her side by side.

"Ho-ho-y"

"Ho-oh-it"

The sound of other divers' labored breathing could be heard everywhere over the sea. Leaving behind the sound, she swam quite far away before starting to dive.

"Ho-oh-it!"

Rising to the surface, Eok-sun piped out the deeply stifled breath in a whistling way. White bubbles scattered around the water. Again she gave a kick at the sky. She went under the water like doing a handstand. As if running across the fields, she groped around the bottom. Her windpipe started aching. The King of the Sea had been said to live somewhere under the sea so he had to have a place to breathe but only a thicket of seaweed and some fish;

The abalone was so big but she didn't know if it was a male or female. The shell was large and round, suggesting it might be female. The male had a dented shell. She went up for air and came down again for just one abalone. Breathing out in short gasps, she kept falling headlong. It was hard to pick it up because the path was entangled with seaweed and rocks. After only five or six times of diving with a chisel, she finally grabbed one in her hand.

Chapter 7

She felt chilly all over her body, having apparently spent about two hours in the water. The only one there was Eok-sun herself. She could see the blurred shape of people warming themselves by the fire on the shore.

The mesh bag was quite heavy. There were even three abalones. She thought the abalones would be a roasted dish for her deceased husband's memorial service and the others, like conches and agar, could be sold for the kids' tuition. She hadn't been able to spear even one fish for the soup next to the steamed rice for the service. However she changed her mind and decided to prepare conches for the service and sell the expensive abalones. Eok-sun moved her legs quickly but something was strange. Keeping her legs moving made her sink slowly under the water. She lifted her goggles to her forehead and checked the gourd.

"Oh my Lord!"

Suddenly she remembered the sound of the gourd clattering to the ground and snapping last time. The one grain-millet sized crack had become the size of a red bean on the stalk.

It was too far to cry out towards the people around the fire. She looked around to see if there was anything that could help her by any chance. Only wild ducks were casually swimming in her sight. Taking off her white headscarf, she put it on the harpoon.

"Help!"

"......"

"Somebody help me!"

With the harpoon in the air, the echoes of her shouts dissipated into the air. Had she been on the land, she could have reached the shore while smoking one or two cigarettes. The wind blew the SOS scarf away. The mesh bag was falling down but she couldn't bear to throw any of the hard-earned sea produce from the bag because she had harvested it despite the burning in her windpipe. She was firmly determined to go on swimming even if the water-filled gourd tried to submerge her. She just decided to let the King of the Sea determine her fate. Buffeted by sea winds, the dark rain clouds smothered her. There are so many worrisome things in this world but let's try to enjoy our lives and have a good time. *Ninano nilliliya nililiya ninano eolssa joa*...

The beautiful melodies gushed into her gourd from the roadside where the cinema was set up. It was said that the clouds from Ieodo could ward off misfortune. The waves of Ieodo were said to wash sighs away. The wind from Ieodo was supposed to blow troubles away.

Eok-sun continued paddling her legs, holding her spirit box, the gourd in her arms. *Ieodosana iodosana.* Is there a rock to rest on in the sea or a stone wall to lean on in the fields among the hills? *Ieodosana iodosana*...

Sung-Chan Oh

My Hometown Where The Moon Rises

Writer's Introduction

Born in Seogwipo, Jejudo.
Awarded in the Spring Literature Contest by Shinah Daily Newspaper (Division: Novels). Former newspaper reporter and museum curator. Currently president of the Jeju Branch of P.E.N. Korea, runs a publishing company, the Panseok Yosan Literature Award, the Korean Novel Award, the Korean Literature Award.
Publications: *Halla Mountain*, *Portraits of a Dark Era*, *Reborn as a Butterfly*
Phone: (064) 721-1202, 011-9589-2134 E-mail: ohsungchan@hanmail.net

My Hometown Where The Moon Rises

Sung-Chan Oh

To someone like me, now over sixty, what on earth is the meaning of 'hometown?' This question occurred to me after waking from my slumber leaning against a bus window. Just then a long bridge appeared. Crossing the bridge, there was a forked road. The left lane lead down to the port and to the right was my hometown, Wolchul-ri[1] Village. It was so named because. Wolchul Hill sat at the back of the village. I abandoned the bus while watching the hill. I repeat this route whenever I come to my hometown. At this moment, my heart flutters just like it does when I see my mother. However, this time as I got off the bus and stepped into the village, I felt devoid of emotion. That was because high buildings stood here and there in the village making it look unfaniliar to me.

I slipped under the bridge and saw the sea spreading next to my right hand like a lake. But, I couldn't see any of the migratory birds such as seagulls, swans and cranes which used to come and sit there in flocks. The hill over the

---

1) Wolchul is a Korean word meaning 'moonrise'

way and the empty, ashen lake covered by shadows of clouds looked calm and cold. I started walking slowly along the asphalt road by the lake.

'Oh, this was it!'

I was startled when I looked down at the surface of the lake. It wasn't the same water that my friends and I used to skip stones on. The water used to be so clear that we could count pebbles like grains of sand. Waterweeds were growing there for the first time. They swayed gently with the waves deep in the blurry bottom that looked as cloudy as water from the first washing of rice. Between the waterweeds, small fish that I had never seen before were swimming slowly. I wondered where all the mullet had gone that used to swim there when I was young because I couldn't see any of them. It would be better to say that the water was dead.

I don't know when the village was built, but at first it must have been a fishing village where fishermen gathered together and lived. During the Japanese colonial era, Japanese people had an eye for the fish, shellfish and other marine products which were abundant along the coast. They settled fishery-related people there and started to develop this village into a fishery base. This history is evidenced by the fact that such a small village once had three pubs where young women served drinks. However, by the time I grew up, the country was already liberated and the once-popular pubs were deserted. Only the conch canning factory put up by the Japanese remained. My mother said that our family came here because my father worked for the factory as a factory manager. But after the factory closed down, my father built an inn in the village by selling some land in his parents' hometown. That's why I was called "son of the innkeeper" when I was little.

My father opened the inn here because he had often seen many people who had to go to nearby islands such as Goat Island and Rabbit Island through this port suffering because there weren't any inns when there were storms or when something just came up. In my boyhood, I also saw how my warm-hearted father brought those people home, took them in for the night and fed them before he set up the inn. While I was living in my hometown, business didn't go well and we were just able to make ends meet. My father once found a job as a chief engineer for a Mergoori[2] boat, but he quit because my mother strongly dissuaded him from doing it.

Passing by where the rice mill once stood I looked for the steamed bread shop where a short old lady baked bread. The shop was a thatched house, so low that people had to bend down to enter. However, the bread shop and the rice mill were now gone and an unfamiliar new building was standing on the land where those two buildings used to be. I had many memories of those places, so it was a pity to lose them. As I walked to the center of the village, feeling sorrowful, I found a three-story building named Dalmaji[3] Restaurant which seemed out-of-place next to the low, tile-roofed house, Wolchul Diner, where I used to go with my friends a long time ago. Now the Wolchul Diner looked even shabbier under the shadow of the three-story restaurant than it looked a long time ago. However, I found a more shocking scene at our family's Wolchul Inn. There was a huge tourist hotel, which looked to be ten-stories high, right next to the one-story, thatched roof of the Wolchul Inn. It seemed that the sparking gold letters of the. bright sign 'Dalmaji Hotel'

---

[2] A Korean word meaning a diver equipped with a diving helmet
[3] A Korean word meaning 'greet the moon'

were ridiculing me. I was dumbfounded. I then realized that this was the reason why big things and small things don't go well together. Relative poverty is not exclusive to the cities any more. It was not until that moment that I looked at upon my empty hands. The alpine hat that I was wearing and the worn mountain-climbing shoes with hastily tied shoelaces came to mind. Now my heart ached and the faces of my parents, which must have gotten older, flashed through my mind. My mother and father gave everything they owned for their excellent son, and even felt proud of themselves for doing it. But now I wonder what it all means.

In addition, I will soon be kicked out of my company. Technically, it's 'honorary retirement' but what kind of treatment is this, push out someone who has spent half of his life for the company. There is an old saying that one's hometown is the place for a glorious homecoming. I had times like this, too. When I came home for the first time right after graduating from one of the most prestigious universities and got into a conglomerate, not only my parents but also all my relatives and neighbors envied me so much.

"You are the most successful."

"When I went to Seoul, I saw the building while passing by in a taxi. I am so proud that you work in that building!"

Everyone I met patted me on the shoulder and praised me. It honestly would be hard for me to answer, if someone were to ask me whether those days when I worked in that high building made me proud or were worthwhile. Rich people always want more, so they are always nervous and have difficulty dealing with it.

In my prime, I worked for a while as a secretary for the great chairman.

I traveled around Europe and America with him and I got to know every detail of the chairmanship of an enormous company and the kinds of false images it has. Wherever he went after arriving at the hotel, his first job was to phone headquarters before even taking a shower.

"Hey, President Jeong! What's going on with the ten billion won I talked about?"

After listening to the long explanation at the other end, he suddenly lost his temper again.

"What are you gonna do? You still haven't done it? You've got to show me that money!"

The next day, he kept calling even in the damned early morning. This time he called a president of another subsidiary.

"Hey, President Han. I told you then. What did you do with the twenty five billion won?"

That's the way he worked. While I was traveling with him, I thought to myself that the rich are nothing special. I became disillusioned to the bone with the rich. After the hard trip, I lost interest in everything and tried to get an easy post if possible. And so I got pushed and pushed until I was finally pushed off the cliff.

My parents were changing a quilt cover together on the large floor of the empty inn when they saw me. They got up and came up to me with a sudden start.

"What's the matter? Why didn't you tell us you were coming in advance?" I saw concern on the wrinkled face of my mother. She was standing up with a threaded needle in her hand.

"Why didn't you call us first?"

Father's face also looked much older than before. Perhaps they could already guess the reason for my homecoming.

"You know, I was in Busan for business and I just felt like coming home." I couldn't finish what I was saying and so cooked up an excuse. On the other hand, it was great to be speaking the hometown dialect again without realizing it. How great it was.

"That's ok. You did well to come home. How about lunch?"

"I ate it with my friends on the way home."

"Then I'll get you a cup of coffee."

"He drinks coffee everyday. Why don't you bring something else?"

When mother was heading to the kitchen, father talked to her back. Since I had to drink something anyway, I said nothing. Before taking off my shoes, I looked around the backyard and everywhere inside the house. The private house my family had lived in was renovated and was now used as an outhouse. Everything was so old. It seemed as if everything would fall apart if I only touched it. Not only time, but the brine that typhoons drove in must have helped wear them out. Now these kinds of things were too unfamiliar for a city slicker like me.

We sat together around the table and drank tea mother had made. Coffee for my father and mother, and ginseng tea with honey for me. Had the brilliant cooking skill of my mother worn out too? The tea didn't taste as good as it used to.

"You must have fewer guests because of the big hotel next door," I cautiously said, turning my face and pointing to the hotel.

Mother said, "Have we ever made big money before? But there are still some people who can't go to hotels. Your father is not a grasping person, is he?"
Father was just drinking coffee and mother answered instead.
I briefly said, "Right, father isn't greedy. Being rich is nothing special."
Even in this short answer, I was already speaking my mind. If we continued to talk, I might have blurted out my true situation.
Finally father opened his mouth and said, "And there are still some rich people looking for inns or guest houses like ours, too."
I appreciated the positive attitude of my parents.
"Of course, there should be." I thought it was fortunate that at least they could still keep their chin up.

Mother went out to go buy some sea urchins and turban shells for dinner and I followed her. The road had been widened and I wondered when it had happened. It was about twice the width than it used to be in my childhood. At that time, it was too narrow for two cars to roll by in different directions. But now it had four lanes so that it could comfortably accommodate four cars with room to spare. There was an intersection four minutes walking distance from the inn where an advance fishery base used to be. Now that building had became the Fishery Cooperative (FC) Bank. There was the Agricultural Cooperative (AC) Bank in front of the FC Bank, a police station next to the AC Bank and a Family Mart across from the police station. Where the theater-like Family Mart now stood, there had once been a shop I often used to go to for buying torreya nuts. I was thinking of going into the store but I didn't. I've heard that it is called the era of consumption now, but this small village and big marts like this one don't go well together. When even the country has places like this to stimulate consumers, it is not an exaggeration to say the whole nation can now keenly feel the gap between the haves and have-nots.

A little way from there, there was a new Post Office right behind a red postbox. There was also a red postbox in that place when I was a high school student. In those days I liked a girl in my class who had an oval face. A memory flashed through my mind. During winter vacation when I was a second grade high school student, I wrote a letter to her with my heart fluttering. I came outside, wrapped in a coat on that day when the snow was gusting diagonally, and put the letter into the box. That's it, all right. There was also another girl called J. I have often heard that girls are more mature than boys, and now when I look back on those days, I am sure that that girl was much more mature than I was. Because I was a son of the innkeeper and smart to boot, I must have been an object of envy among not only the boys but also the girls.

Was it early spring just like now? No, it might have been autumn. Anyway, it was during a season when one doesn't feel cold near the sea. In those days, my uncle on my mother's side had bought me a harmonica on his way home from Japan. I practiced playing it for a while and could play the harmonica well. One night that season, J took me to the sands under the cliff of Wolchul Hill where the moonrise could be seen, and asked me to play the harmonica.

Just like that night, as if possessed by something, my steps were spontaneously taking me through the village roads to the beach under the moonlit sky. At that time, her house was at the mouth of the sea, maybe somewhere around here. But the old houses around here were now all gone and new buildings stood in their place, confusing me as to my whereabouts. However, the back street pubs where deep-sea fishermen often went during the Japanese occupation had not changed, and the buildings were getting old, due to the passage of time, and covered with dust. They were like retired *kisaeng*[4]. While passing by that back street on the way to the beach, I found out that the sands were completely gone because of the rising tide. Was it like this when the tide was rising? I couldn't remember. That was another unfamiliar experience.

Also the sea was not the way it was. Near the beach, the sea was filled with Styrofoam, cardboard, wooden planks, and broken pieces from boats, all floating in the surf. The blue sea turned dark even on the surface. I could not see any of the countless seagulls that used to fly, or any ducks floating on the surface, diving deep into the sea to catch fish.

I wondered where the sands we sat on had gone. On that night, she took out a handkerchief and laid it down on the sand for me to sit on. I strongly declined her offer, but she sat down next to the handkerchief first.

"To make up for sitting on my handkerchief, you can play the harmonica for me." she said.

She made me consent by causing me to feel sorry for her. I played songs that adults would have liked, such as 'Hometown Spring' and 'My Hometown, the South Sea'. I also liked to sing these songs at that time. Later, she sat close

---

4) A Korean word meaning women whose job is entertaining men at parties or events by dancing and singing during the Goryeo Dynasty and the Joseon Dynasty.

to me and whispered. "Do you like me, or what?"

Because she was pretty, good at her studies then, and one of those popular girls, I couldn't say no. But even when I was with her, I sometimes thought of another face, the girl with an oval face. But I answered, "Yes. I like you."

"What kind of answer is that? If you like me, you should hold my hand, don't you think so?"

I grasped her hand with my trembling fingers. Then she asked me again, "My hand is warm, isn't it?"

We had been outside on the beach, so how could it possibly be warm? It would have been more accurate to say they were freezing. But I couldn't say the truth.

"Yes. Your hands are warm."

Yet again I said something that I didn't mean. At that moment, she suddenly turned and hugged me. It happened in a moment of bewilderment. She was my first girl.

But, now I confess that she was not the one to whom I sent a letter on that day when the snow was gusting sideways, and I had put on a winter coat and put the letter in the mailbox. In those days there was another girl who stole my heart. Maybe J's rashness was a burden for a young boy. I was loved by one girl and I loved another girl. But I couldn't say anything to both, and I went to Seoul where I immersed myself in studying for a while. Was it the distance that set me apart from these girls? No, perhaps it was time that drew us apart. Now it covered everything just like the way the rising tide beats upon the shore and erases words written on the sand. Now where are they and what are they doing in their middle age? All of a sudden, I missed them.

After coming back from the sands of memories, I turned to the path that leads to Wolchul Hill. In my childhood, that lofty peak was our hope and symbol. Moreover, everybody climbed to the top and waited for the rise of the full moon in August, according to the lunar calendar, when Chusok[5] came. In the path to the top, there were one or two spots that were difficult to pass because of landslides from the last typhoon, but people went up by pulling each other from above and pushing each other's buttocks from behind. But when we reached the top panting, the white moon was already above the peak and looking down on us even before it became dark. That moment's disappointment···However, we climbed to the top again the next year, because it was traditionally said that one's dreams came true only when one went up to the peak and saw the moon.

I came here for sightseeing with my boss a few years ago, and I worried that the path up Wolchul Hill might be too difficult. However, I found that there were now steps made of stone and cement on the hill so that even young children could go up. There I actually met a middle-aged woman who climbed the hill wearing high heels. Mountain climbing should be a little challenging, but nowadays people seem to prefer easy ways.

When I got into Seoul National University after finishing high school in my hometown, people said that it was because I went to the hill and watched the moon often. I still remember that the Village Development Council put up a placard at the entrance of the path, celebrating my university admission and

---

[5] Its literal meaning is harvest moon day, and it is the Korean version of Thanksgiving.

saying that it was all thanks to the spirit of Wolchul Hill. But I heard that nobody goes to that peak any more. Instead, tourists were flocking around well-paved trails. If anyone from the village goes to Wolchul Hill, they are usually just there to show tourists around. Just as the port and the sea were taken over by the Japanese during the colonial period, the owner of moonrise peak has changed now.

I left the mountain trail and headed for a marine products flea market which is only open for tourists when the weather is good. If I went down to the shore, I might get to eat raw turban shells or sea cucumbers there.

"Hey, you must be Changhyeok!" A husky voice stopped me at the entrance to the market. I was wearing an alpine hat and sunglasses on purpose. I wondered how he recognized me.

"I'm right. You are Changhyeok. It's me, Taebu!"

His slim body had gotten so fat that it was hard to recognize him, but it was Taebu Park for sure. During our school days he ran track and was good at all kinds of sport. He swept all the medals at the township and province-level competitions and it was thought that he would be a professional athlete in the future. He learned Taekwondo and when he was in high school, he was in charge of the discipline of the school. Everybody was afraid of him. One time this guy squeezed me for one thousand won to buy cigarettes. After he graduated from high school, he couldn't go to college because of his family circumstances. I had heard rumors that he became a coach at a middle school in town, and now I could see that his slim body became fat like a Sireum[6] man or a flightless bird.

---

6) A Korean traditional wrestling

"Hoon's mom. Hey, Hoon's mom. This is my schoolfellow. Why don't you come and see him?"

She only cast her eyes upon me while bending over, handling squid with huge tentacles. She just looked like a market place woman and didn't seem pleased to see me. In just one glance, she seemed to notice that I wouldn't buy anything from her. In addition to that, he probably made pretexts of one kind or another to his wife about visiting friends.

"This fellow is an executive director of a big company. He is not like the other friends of mine."

I bent down and looked around but I couldn't find anything to buy.

"Hey, why don't we go down there and have some soju[7]. Wow, how long has it been since we last met?"

As I walked down the slope following his fat body, the woman's high, harsh voice seemed to hit the nape of my neck.

"Don't drink too much and make it snappy, got it?"

"As you know, I have many friends. So I often have company and have to go out to drink with them. That's why she is acting like that. Don't bother."

At the bottom of the slope, divers were selling soju and side dishes such as turban shells and octupi. After we ordered a dish of them, he carried on as before, filling my glass with soju. Instead of answering, I just chuckled and picked up one piece of turban shell and put that in my mouth. Ahhh, this is what I had been missing! For me, my hometown and the image of turban shells were intertwined. I asked him, while still chewing. "How are all our schoolfellows?"

---

7) Korean alcohol

"Oh, Actually almost half of them are dead. Dooman, Manho, Changsik, all of them are gone. To be honest, there are no more good days left for us, don't you think so?"

Holding the glass, I tried to remember their faces in the transparent soju. But no matter how hard I tried, those faces were misty and I couldn't remember them. Instead, there was one face I remembered. That was Hyeongman's big and round face. But soon I erased him from my mind. He and I attended the same schools from elementary school to high school and we always competed for first place. In those days, maybe I studied so hard in order to beat him.

"How is Hyeongman doing?" After drinking a few glasses, I couldn't help but ask out of curiosity.

"Just like in the old days, he is having a good time, making money from excursion steamers and canola flower fields. Why don't we have just one more drink and go see him?"

"OK." I agreed with him. We finished two bottles of soju as well as a side dish of turban shells and sea cucumbers in no time at all.

"Look, over there! That's Hyeongman's excursion steamer." Taebu told me, pointing to a small ship under the cliff which was turning around.

"People are already making a fuss because he is running for the township council."

That's right. People are supposed to pursue reputation after money, I muttered to myself.

"Oh, yes. You liked J? Have you thought about her?"

Again I made a slight chuckle.

"She cleans the hotel next to your inn."

"What about her husband?" I asked him abruptly, while drinking soju.

"He is a womanizer by nature. Nobody knows where he is."

I didn't ask anymore. I held up the glass and looked at the clear liquid inside. Inside the glass I could see, J wearing a sailor suit, smiling at me. I emptied the glass in a gulp. Suddenly I felt sad. If I had kept seeing her until today, would we have been happy or not? As the tide was rising, the waves came surging up to our feet where we were sitting while we weren't paying attention. Every time when the waves came in, they appeared to whisper in my ear. Pointless, pointless. Everything is pointless.

After having two bottles of soju in broad daylight, we went to a parking lot while avoiding Taebu's shop. The parking lot was filled with lots of cars, and there was one lone dusty jeep parked far away from the others. My face appeared to be burning and his face had also turned red. He forced me to get in the car and he sat in the driver's seat.

Honestly I was worried and said, "Hey, is it alright for you to drive after drinking?"

Taebu replied, "It's ok. My license is a drunk-driving permitted license. And besides, I'm not dead yet."

"All right. Ok. Just hold on fast to the steering wheel."

Hyeongman's field was so close that it only took five minutes by car from the village. The field, which stretched in a long line by the road, was right on the way to school. During the radish-harvesting season, we kicked at delicious-looking radishes, peeled them briskly and ate them, and during the sweet potato season, we pulled up little sweet potatoes, just starting to grow, scrubbed the dirt off in the grass and ate them. Since Hyeongman used the field's crops as a means to make friends, I also had stolen and eaten radishes or sweet potatoes a few times for fun. However, his unrelenting and impatient father didn't seem to like it at all. So one day he gathered thorny bushes from a mountain and put them up like barbed-wire entanglements, but it was not enough to stop us mischievious children. When sweet potatoes were about to ripen, we pushed aside those bushes one by one, put deep red sweet potatoes on the bushes, and lit a fire with tinder to cook them, after which we ate them. That's right. In spring, the field had canola vegetables, so yellow flowers were in full bloom.

By the way, I noticed something strange as we were going to Hyeongman's place. Now it was March, so how come canola flowers, which are supposed to bloom in May or June, had bloomed already? I asked Taebu.

"Taebu, how come canola flowers have bloomed already in March?"

"You'll see why. In this weird world, what's wrong with early blooming flowers?"

Taebu gazed drunkenly ahead while driving. There really were yellow canola flowers in bloom in Hyeongman's field. Even though these flowers were greenish rather than yellow and shorter than those blooming in the right season, these flowers were flowers, too. I also saw sentry boxes built just like old lookout sheds at either corner of the field.

"This is Hyeongman's car. He made a fortune," Taebu said, parking his car hurriedly behind a shiny, pitch-black Benz.

There were several entrances into the field in which people could freely go in, but at each entrance there were little signs that said the following.

"One thousand won per shot."

Now I figured it out. I shook my head forcefully from side to side and I thought to myself that this was wrong, so wrong.

"During the wedding season, nearly five thousand couples come here in just one day."

Taebu, who was walking ahead of me, said this as if he envied Hyeongman. But looking around the canola field, I felt gloomy in the same way as when I saw the filthy ocean under the cliff where the moon rises. Yes, that's right. Hyeongman was a smart boy. Didn't he always study with summaries rather than textbooks? In this way, he had beaten me before.

"Hyeongman! Come on out. Changhyeok has come." Taebu shouted in front of the sentry box, but there was no answer from the inside.

Bending his body, he squeezed into the sentry box. After finally squeezing in, too, I felt awkward. As a matter of fact, looking at these flowers, which were sown in the wrong season and bloomed in cold winter to help make money for their owner, I couldn't help but think of the flower-like, nameless young women that I had met at hostess bars in Seoul and whose hometowns were never known.

"Oh, what a cruel age we live in!"

Inside my heart, I sighed while looking at the canola field where honeymooners took various poses and took pictures with the flowers. How would anyone ever think of taking money for this kind of thing in the past? Because it was Hyeongman, it was possible to come up with such an idea. In the end, tourism makes peoples' hearts cold.

Hyeongman suddenly arrived and said, "Hey, Come in. What's up? What brought the executive director of the conglomerate to a place like this?"

Entering the hut, I shook hands with an unfamiliarly fat Hyeongman. I was surprised one more time when I saw the inside of the building which looked like a sentry box. While people usually decorate the exterior rather than the interior, this building was totally opposite. There was a luxury, foreign produced log table on the carpet, which he had obviously bought abroad, and a tiger skin laid on the back of his chair. He looked at me complacently and I blurted out, "You've made such a fortune."

I said only this.

"It's practically nothing compared to conglomerates." Hyeongman answered as if he ignored what I had said.

Without a doubt, this guy had already picked up the attitude of a parvenu. Soon after he called someone with his cell phone, a female employee quickly came in.

"Miss Jung, make some good tea for our esteemed guest from Seoul."

"Yes, sir."

The lady obediently started to make tea, taking out cups from the display. After she put tea in front of the three people and went out, Hyeongman said. "She is the daughter of Sungdoo, one of our alumni. She works here because he asked me to take her, but …"

"Right, what does Sungdoo do?" Although I couldn't remember his face, I asked anyways.

Taebu said, "What can he do, he is a sailor."

"Hey, Taebu. Now that Changhyeok is here, why don't you gather our friends? I'll buy dinner tonight." Hyeongman said magnanimously.

"Wow, do you mean it?" Taebu asked incredulously.

"You talk as if I always lie to you."

Hyeongman scowled at Taebu. But Taebu was in high spirits because he had drunk earlier so he couldn't say anything.

"Whom should we call?"

Taebu did not forget to get approval from Hyeongman in advance.

"Kyoungsik, Ilman, and call Daeho, too. At six. And let's go to Wolchuljung Restaurant. Changhyeok made a career and came home. Honestly, isn't this a happy event for us?"

Caught in this atmosphere, I couldn't say anything and I couldn't raise my face, either.

According to schedule, we got together at Wolchuljung Restaurant at six. Kyoungsik, Ilman, Daeho and Taebu made it. They greeted me perfunctorily and I noticed right away that they felt more uneasy in front of him than they did in front me. As if someone had made a reservation, there were two large tables which were covered with white paper, and set with glasses and hand towels matching the number of guests. Hyeongman, Taebu and I sat on the side by the shelf and our other friends sat opposite us. Hyeongman appeared to be a regular customer here and he ordered something from the female manager of the hostess bar, who dropped by to say hello.

"We don't need many girls, so just send us three of them. And bring the same alcohol and side dishes as usual."

"Yes, yes."

Alcohol and side dishes came in, and girls, too. Hyeongman had them fill our glasses, and then holding up his glass, he did not forget to make a toast. "We are all graduates of the same class and you know, today is a very happy day for us. Our friend Changhyeok went to Seoul to study and got promoted to executive director of a conglomerate, right? He will probably be the president of that company the next time we see him. What could be more pleasing than this? Let's drink a toast to Changhyeok to welcome him. Cheers!"

"Cheers!"

It seemed that they had done this kind of things several times before. At first, these fellows looked uncomfortable as if they were mobilized reserve troops. But after having some drinks, they started to get back their own facial expressions.

Hyeongman said, "Well, when people eat, people should eat to the fullest. Likewise, people should work hard and play hard. Don't you think so?"

Taebu was the first one to flatter Hyeongman.

"Why not? You are absolutely right."

"Pass me the beer glass."

Hyeongman almost filled the glass with beer and poured whisky into a smaller glass. Then he made a boilermaker, putting the whisky glass into the bigger beer glass. I couldn't believe my eyes to see that the bad drinking habit, which had started to spread in Korea after becoming popular with greedy soldiers of a particular era, had become popular in this remote area. Since I was the invited guest, I had to drink first.

I protested weakly, "I'm not a strong drinker."

Although I said so, I could not refuse the first glass from my old friends who had gotten together for the first time in many years. Also, I had to be careful not to get dead drunk or embarrassed in front of these friends. To do so, I had to be able to manage this kind of situation well. This was actually quite similar to the situations that I had to handle whenever I met people for business. Maybe it's not an exaggeration to say that this is the one thing I learned while working for the conglomerate. But I couldn't fake even the first glass. And to be honest, I was strongly craving a drink. I took that glass and quietly emptied it. All the women in the room clapped their hands. So did my friends.

"Everybody saw it, huh? That's the way you drink."

Hyeongman took that empty glass and was filling the big and small glasses with two different kinds of alcohol again. And then later a karaoke machine came in. It was time to sing by turns. Since I was the invited guest, I had to sing first. Wondering what to sing, I decided to sing 'Waiting heart' by changing its lyrics.

Please, call me. When the moon rises over Wolchul Hill.
Please, call me. When the sun rises over the Ilchul Hill.

I barely passed this test. People used to hesitate to sing when they were asked, but nowadays everybody fights over who will sing first. It seems that nobody is bad or has difficulty with singing. It appears that the so-called drive to 'spread karaoke across the country and make the whole population singers', which had occurred in a certain era, had succeeded. I went outside pretending to go to the restroom. It was already dark. I suddenly thought of my mother, who had gone to the seaside market to buy turban shells and sea urchins. While I was wavering over whether to return to the room or to go home after dropping by the restroom, a woman, who had just finished piles of dishes in another room, came out, and saw me. She suddenly scurried away while carrying dishes in her arms. She looked familiar from behind.

"Excuse me." I called to stop her in a low voice.

No, probably the alcohol did it. Oh, God. She definitely recognized me. She lifted her downcast face. Because the dim light of the almost-full moon hanging over Wolchul Hill was shining down, I could recognize the woman's face. It was poor-looking J in her early sixties. I didn't dare call her name. But she hesitatingly stopped and rushed to talk as if bidden.

"Yes, it's me, J. I clean at the hotel during the day and I work here doing odd jobs at night. I have to make money to send my children to school." Saying only that, she scuttled away.

Hyeongman might have brought me here on purpose to make fun of me. I wouldn't put it past him. Ah, what should I do? What I had done and seen in my hometown that day was like a nightmare. I turned my head and looked up at the full moon hanging over Wolchul Hill again. Maybe I couldn't see any stars because of the mist. Looking up at the moon, just like the good old days, I promised to myself that I'd do something for this spoiled hometown. When the moon peeked out of the clouds as if to say 'hi', I was walking out of the yard of the hostess bar echoing with sounds of singing.

Brief History of the Writer
- *The People Who Try To Gather Stars*, a prize-winning entry in the category of medium-length stories in the spring literary contest sponsored by Sin-a Ilbo in 1969.
- Filled the following posts; reporter and editorial writer for the local newspaper, museum researcher, representative of the Jeju Literary Men's Association and the Jeju Branch of the Federation of Artistic, Cultural Organizations of Korea.
- The writer chairs the Jeju PEN now.
- Author of *Halla Mountain, A Portrait of the Dark Period, Requiem Arirang, Wrapping Clothes Leave At Night, Growing Mountain, Saehando, Give the Bell A Ring* and 26 other pieces
- Recipient of the Yosan Literary Award, Korean Novel Literary Award, Korean Literary Award and many others.

Children's Literature

New Ramie Clothes in the Dresser
Mr. Crow Oh

Soon-Bok Kang

New Ramie Clothes in the Dresser

Writer's Introduction

Member of the Korean Writers' Association, P.E.N International, the Korea Children's Literature Society. President of the Jeju Branch of the Korea Skin Care Association.
Publications: *Paper Piano, Growing Magic Glasses, A Child Walking on Four Feet*
E-mail: ksb1234@hanmail.net

New Ramie Clothes in the Dresser

Min-suh's mother is worried about something lately. Min-suh's grandfather, who was so energetic and never got tired until recently, seemed to be getting weak, and he now looked like a totally different person because he rarely drank, a pastime which he used to love, and now usually came back home before sunset.

One day my mother said to my father.

"Honey, don't you think something's wrong with your father?"

"Nothing's the matter. He's probably trying to be careful due to his age."

"He doesn't drink as often as he used to and he comes home from the old folk's home so early."

My mother worries over what seem to be trifles although she has had hard times because of my grandfather's daily drinking habits and his tendency to become a bad drunk. My grandfather is considered a man of sincerity and that he would not do anything against the law, but when he is drunk, he gets so stubborn that no one can stop him.

"Dad, what does 'circumspection' mean?"

"That means cautious behavior. You should look up words in a dictionary instead of asking me questions so often."

Every family member is on the alert when Min-suh's grandfather comes home drunk. 'Min-suh, come here'. 'Min-suh, I had a few drinks'. 'Min-suh, you should study hard'. 'Min-suh! Min-suh!' Perhaps he gets sleepless when he's drunk because he calls my name all night. On such days, Min-suh's family has to turn out all the lights and keep deathly quiet until my grandfather falls asleep. Sometimes I can't finish my homework because all the lights at home have to be turned off, which annoys Min-suh, but Min-suh also thinks that grandfather is the one who cares about him the most, frankly speaking.

When my mother and father went out to work early in the morning, it was Min-suh's grandfather who used to feed Min-suh milk when he was a baby, take him to kindergarten, bring him back home after kindergarten, and feed him rice with baked fish when he grew older. Min-suh's grandfather was full of affection for him, and that is why Min-suh couldn't complain even though his grandfather called to him drunkenly all night.

"Min-suh, you should understand your grandfather. He drinks because he feels lonely after your grandmother's death. You understand, right?"

That's what his father told him when Min-suh once complained that he could not finish his homework because of his grandfather. Min-suh still would have liked his grandfather even if his father had not told him so. His grandfather would've been beyond reproach if he just drank a little bit less. He used to get energetic when he got drunk, but nowadays something is strange with him because he rarely goes out or calls to Min-suh.

"Honey, I think he is getting old."

When Min-suh heard his mother murmur to herself as if she did not care whether she was heard or not, he thought about aging. He was curious what aging or getting old meant and soon concluded that it meant drinking and going out less and less often.

As time went by, his grandfather became forgetful, and whenever he forgot something, she muttered with a big sigh, "What shall we do? It just won't do if he gets like this…"

Min-suh asked her what she meant, and she told him that she was worried that his grandfather was getting old, and that his body and soul were wasting away. Min-suh learned that what she was really worrying about was not amnesia but dementia, a serious illness of the mind. Forgetting rather than aging was the thing to be worried about most, he also learned.

"Father! Why don't you wear something else when you go out? Why do you have to wear such old clothes when you have so many other clothes? People will blame me when they see you in those old clothes. Do you want me to buy you some if you don't like any of yours?"

It was one morning on a clear sunny day, and Min-suh's mother talked to his grandfather imploringly from behind when he was about to go out.

"It's not necessary. What's wrong with these clothes? I feel comfortable in these clothes. These are still new, and I have new clothes in the wardrobe. Min-suh's aunt also bought new clothes for me last time."

He quickly got out of the house and flew into a temper over what Min-suh's mother had said. He had no other special place to go except for the old folk's home.

Min-suh felt melancholy and sometimes shed tears when he saw the fallen leaves rolling on the street. He stopped by his grandfather's room on such days because he wondered if his grandfather got speechless and weaker when feeling lonely while watching fallen leaves. When Min-suh visited, his grandfather talked about what had happened during the day as joyfully as a kid who had been in the playground. While he was talking, he seemed to forget his status. Min-suh realized that forgetting was sometimes good, which proved that Min-suh was now an adult.

Min-suh's father and mother got worried about grandfather more and more.
"Min-suh, try to stop by grandfather's room when you come back from school. Old men easily get lonely."
"You don't have to worry about that since I do it anyway."

The first thing Min-Suh did before going to and after coming home from school was to visit his grandfather's room. He would buy cookies or red-ripe persimmons his grandfather liked.

His grandfather was so happy to receive those from Min-suh.
"Grandpa, why don't you throw this away? This one is too old. Why do you have to save it since you have other nice ones?"
"Leave it. It will be useful someday."

Grandfather, who always said yes and okay to Min-suh, lost his temper at him today. Min-suh felt sorry for his grandfather when he thought that his grandfather might be trying to consciously ignore the fact that he was getting old, which the old man knew. Min-suh suddenly got scared remembering what somebody told him; one of the characteristics of the elderly was that they tried to keep everything with them. Min-suh thought that people might forget things like desire, attachment, and loss upon death, and the thought sent a chill through him.

Last summer, a younger sister of Min-suh's grandmother severely scolded Min-suh's aunt, the younger sister of Min-suh's father, after happening to see the grandfather going out in a winter suit.

"You are so undutiful to your lonely father whose wife passed away a long time ago. Winter suits in the middle of the summer? It was such a shame to see my brother-in-law in a winter suit. Ramie clothes cost only twenty or thirty thousand won at most."

Min-suh's aunt did not know what to say while her aunt was yelling over the phone.

"Auntie! My father has enough clothes. The old man is just good at making his children feel shameful while he keeps his clothes in the wardrobe."

Min-suh's aunt was busy digging her grave with poor excuses.

"Have him change his clothes. I bought him a new suit of clothes just a while ago, but why does he still wear the old ones all the time? Another relative happened to see him in winter clothes and called me saying she was simply aghast. I got in trouble."

It was not that grandfather did not have other clothes. There were some new clothes in his old wardrobe that he had never tried on.

Pleading that she was busy, Min-suh's aunt bought grandfather good quality jade green ramie clothes. We later found out that Min-suh's grandfather had never tried them on.

"Father! Why do you wear the old ones all the time when you have new ones?"

Whenever his daughter-in-law said even one word about clothes, Min-suh's grandfather just held his old clothes in his arms stubbornly, adding that mother's nagging hurt his ears. Nobody could change his habits or his obstinacy.

"Grandpa! If you keep wearing your old clothes, you will bring shame on our whole family, so why don't you wear new ones? When are you going to try new ones if you just store them away in the dresser for future use? If you leave them like that, they will be worm-eaten and useless."

Min-suh also thought that his grandfather was unduly stubborn, but his grandfather was not stubborn at all. Grandfather thought that the clothes he was wearing were still new, and that it was a waste to wear newer ones. Nobody knew how many times he took out and felt the ramie clothes his daughter had bought for him. Sometimes, he even told Min-suh with pride about how many clothes he had.

"So try this and that. Now that grandma is gone, people will look down upon you unless you wear nice clothes." Min-suh reproved his grandfather as if he were a grown-up.

Min-suh's whole family just wanted his grandfather to drink less and take those old clothes off, but he kept wearing the old ones, saying he did not feel comfortable in new clothes.

"Leave him alone, Min-suh! Who can change his mind? Father, you are going to just cherish the clothes in the dresser that are from your daughter, aren't you?" Min-suh's mother said smiling, but the grandfather pretended not to hear her.

He was still an amiable and gentle grandfather to Min-suh. However, something terrible happened to Min-suh. The ramie clothes became grandfather's last gift from his daughter.

What Min-suh's mother was always anxious and worried about had become a reality after a party at someone's home. Min-suh's grandfather had to be hospitalized because of diarrhea he contracted after eating food served at an old folk's home. He passed away two days later. Min-suh could not believe his grandfather's sudden death at all. He was simply aghast to find out that his grandfather had died merely from diarrhea.

"He was in such good shape."

Min-suh's family as well as all the relatives said a few words about grandfather's sudden death, which they all could not understand.

The relatives arranging his personal belongings after the grandfather's death talked to Min-suh's aunt as if they were scolding her.

"How come he has no clothes nice enough to wear? What have you done? You should have bought him some clothes. It is lucky that these ramie clothes are somewhat new at that."

That was strange. As far as Min-suh remembered, his mother had bought some clothes not long ago and his aunt often had done so. He thought that those clothes were lying deep in the wardrobe, but now they were saying his grandfather had nothing to wear.

Now the rumors about Min-suh's grandfather were spreading through the village as the time went by after his death. A rumor had it that there wasn't anyone at the old folk's home who hadn't received help from Min-suh's grandfather. Furthermore, it was revealed that his grandfather had continued to take his clothes to the old folk's home up until even a few days before he died.

"They would gladly receive and wear my clothes when I am alive, but would they take them after I am dead?"

Grandfather's death made him think once again about life, death, and aging. Min-suh realized that how one prepares for death is as important as how one lives. His grandfather already knew that life and death meant release or a clean slate.

"How to live is important to human beings, but how to prepare for death during one's life is also very important. Life means, Min-suh···mm, releasing, emptying. We will leave with empty hands. It's like sharing everything except for my precious Min-suh."

Now Min-suh could somewhat understand what his grandfather had meant when he repeated the statements Min-suh could not understand then.

Winter is coming around.

His heart ached when he realized the ramie clothes from his aunt were the last gift for his grandfather.

"Your grandfather never tried on the new ramie clothes, which was his last gift."

Min-suh had tears in his eyes when he saw tears form at the corners of his aunt's eyes. Does Grandpa still wear the same old clothes in heaven? While he was asking himself this question, he thought he heard his grandfather's voice calling him from somewhere, "Min-suh".

Jae-Hyong Park

Mr. Crow Oh

Writer's Introduction
Former president of the Jeju Children's Literature Association, vice president of the Jeju Writers' Association. Kyemong Children's Literature Award.
Publications: *Searching for Gumdoongee, My Friend, Sahmrye, Sad Songs of Dahrahngshi Hill*
Address: 300-94, 3-Do 2-Dong, Jeju, Jejudo, Republic of Korea
Phone: (064) 753-1288, 011-694-1266 / E-mail: pa1429@shinbiro.com

Mr. Crow Oh

Jae-Hyong Park

It was last spring. While I was playing with jumping ropes with my friends, a postman approached us riding his bicycle.

"Hi, kids! Do you happen to know where Mr. Ji-Soo Oh lives? I can't find his house since the house number is not written." The strange postman took an envelope out of his bag and asked again.

"Mr. Ji-soo Oh?"

We all shook our heads at his question. For the life of us, we could not figure out just who Mr. Ji-soo Oh was. Mr. Ji-soo Oh, Jeonhang-dong, Sehwa-li, Gujwa-eup, Bukjeju-gun, Jeju Province. The address on the envelope clearly indicated that the man lived in our village, but the name, Ji-soo Oh, was unfamiliar to us.

"There is no such a man in this village," Mi-hee answered with confidence. Just then, Joo-hee's father was passing by, and the postman asked him. "Excuse me, do you know who Mr. Ji-soo Oh is?"

"Mr. Ji-soo Oh? Who can that be? Ah, that's Mr. Crow Oh! His house is over there." Joo-hee's father pointed out the house at the end of the village near the ocean.

Mr. Crow Oh is Ji-soo Oh? I was not really surprised but felt strange. I had never dreamed that Mr. Crow Oh would have such a classy name. Well, there was no rule that said that Mr. Crow Oh could not have a nice name, but it seemed that common country bumpkin names such as Man-bok or Dal-yong would suit him better. We thought that Mr. Crow Oh was the best name for him just because everybody called him that, yet it turned out that he had such a stylish name, Ji-soo.

We all found Crow Oh's real name to be funny, so we started cracking jokes about it.

"Mr. Crow Oh is the same person as Ji-soo Oh! The name does not go with his image, does it?"

"Of course not, it's like an ant with a nice pair of shoes!"

We laughed ourselves helpless. It was after a long laugh that I opened my mouth out of curiosity.

"Why would people call him by Mr. Crow Oh but not by such a nice real name?"

"Well, I guess that's because he's got a dark skinned face. Don't you think so?"

"No, that's probably because he doesn't wash his feet. My mother sometimes teases me by saying I will get crow's feet if I don't wash them."

"That can't be the reason because he is always clean."

"Isn't that because he is so forgetful? Sometimes he is called senile old man,"

We went on talking and talking about his nickname unaware of the passage of time. Soon we were busy playing with jumping ropes again, and totally forgot about Mr. Oh.

There were only a few days left before summer vacation, and one day Mr. Oh raised his head over the stonewall and called to us when we were coming back from swimming.

"Hi, kids! Stop by! Garden balsam flowers are in beautiful bloom."

I wanted to see the garden balsams but was not willing to enter his house. The house Mr. Oh lived in was an old one, with its thatched-roof crumbling away. Actually, someone from Seoul purchased that house to renovate it into a villa but did not take care of it at all. Yet we went in over the jeongnang (the bar at the entrance of the house) since Eun-jeong insisted. The house where he had lived alone since his mother's death was not strange at all, and that was probably because the house was bathed in sunlight. I had been afraid of that old thatched house as if it was haunted. However, the moment I saw flowers in bloom in the garden, they melted my heart and kept my mouth open wide in wonder. I did not know when they had been planted, and yet many kinds of flowers were in bloom in the large garden. Garden balsams, Indian lilacs, scarlet sage, and cosmos flowers were boasting their beauty. Tall sunflowers were smiling at the sun, and unknown wildflowers were all smiles in the corner of the garden as well.

"Guys, take some leaves of the garden balsams. Fingernails dyed with garden balsams look really pretty." Mr. Crow Oh spoke slowly and inarticulately while plucking the leaves. His little fingernail was dyed red.

"A grown man dyed his nail like a woman."

"That's why he is a senile old man."

We giggled at his nail. He, however, thought we were laughing because we liked his nail, and started showing off his dyed nail to us.

"If the color on the nail lasts until the first snowfall, your dreams will come true."

He was so proud of it and smiled like a kid. At that moment, he looked so simple and innocent that I could not help thinking to myself that the nickname 'overgrown kid' might be better than 'senile old man'.

All of a sudden, Mr. Oh raised his voice. "Don't step on the flowers! You should be careful."

"But I stepped on the grass." Joo-hee, who went into the flower garden to pick garden balsams, made an excuse.

"That is not just grass. Do you know the beautiful flower that will bloom there? Those are baby-oil flowers. Beautiful flowers will blossom in late fall."

Joo-hee protested, "But you can see these everywhere in the field."

Being displeased with angry Mr. Oh, she stepped on the little wildflower and trampled it.

Then Mr. Crow Oh's face turned red and he yelled. "You should not even step on the grass without good reason."

It seemed that Mr. Oh was really angry now.

"Why not? Is this a piece of gold? It's nothing but useless grass." Joo-hee flew at him trampling down the grass as if to spite him.

I could not understand why she was doing that. She might have acted that way because everybody in town looked down on Crow Oh.

Breathing heavily, Mr. Oh glared at Joo-hee and pushed her. Joo-hee fell down and blood trickled from a scratch on the back of her hand.

"Why did you push me? You bastard."

Joo-hee saw the blood spread on her hand and turned to Mr. Oh in a fury, shedding tears.

"Get out of here!" He turned us out of the house with his arms waving. We were afraid because he was angry, so we got out of his house in a hurry.

"He must be crazy to get so mad just because I stepped on grass. We were fools to enter his house to see the flowers."

"He was really scary when he got mad."

We went home blaming Mr. Oh although Joo-hee was the one who caused the incident.

"What happened this afternoon? Joo-hee's mother made a big fuss at Mr. Oh's home.

That night my mother told me that Joo-hee's mother went over to Mr. Oh's house and cursed him out loud. Although Joo-hee's hand was scratched a little bit, I thought it was a bit excessive of her to go over to Mr. Oh's house. I felt bad but decided to pretend that I knew nothing about it since Joo-hee was my friend anyway. Nevertheless, a rumor that Mr. Oh beat her up until Joo-hee shed blood was spreading, and everybody in town swore at him.

A few days later, Mr. Oh came to my house.

"Ma'am, don't you need me to spray herbicides?"

"We are not going to ask you to spray herbicides for us again."

"What's the matter? Have I done anything wrong?"

"I don't want any more excuses. How dare you hit a kid?"

My mother usually would have treated him favorably by buying him a pack of cigarettes, offering him lunch, or asking him to help spray the pesticides, but she refused his request obstinately this time.

"I HIT her? I never hit her. I only pushed her a little bit."

He tried to explain himself in his mortification.

"It really makes no difference. You returned evil for good."

Her heart did not go out to him and refused his request.

He trudged home with heavy feet. I felt pity for him but did not want speak for Mr. Oh.

After that, he was entirely left out in the cold by the people in town. They did not ask him to do anything. People now let Mr. Kim, whom they used to accuse of laziness, clean cow barns or spray fruit trees instead of Mr. Oh. He now came out of his house less and less often. Walking down to the sea, I sometimes saw him standing and watching flowers or a mountain in the distance, and felt that his shoulder, looked tired and narrow, which made me feel sorry for him.

One day towards the end of the summer vacation, I visited Joo-hee's and saw that she was weeping her eyes out.

"What's the matter, Joo-hee? Are you sick?"

"No. It's nothing serious."

She replied with a sorrowful countenance and then went into the house.

I left her house thinking that something was wrong with her.

When I came home, my father and mother were standing in the yard saying something about the hospital.

"Is anybody ill or something?"

"That's none of your business. Just get in and study. It will be the ruin of them. They have just emerged from poverty, and all of a sudden he came down with a disease."

My mother went into the kitchen with a sad face. I was so curious that I had to ask my father.

"Dad, did you go to the hospital today? Are you sick?"

"It's not me, but Joo-hee's father was found to have a kidney problem. If he doesn't have surgery soon, he might die."

"Is it so serious?"

"Sure is. He will get better if someone spares him a kidney, but who will be willing to do that?"

My father said this with a very worried face. Joo-hee's father had to stay in the hospital for a long time. It would have been best if one of his family members could have donated him a kidney. However, he had to wait until someone who had the same blood type could donate since none of his family members had the same blood type as he did. Meetings among the people in town were held to find a way to help him, and the people visited him in hospital. However, they still could not find anyone who was willing to donate a kidney. That always made Joo-hee blue. I wished her face would brighten up as before.

"Hello! Don't you want to take some flowers?"

On a sunny day in autumn, I was returning from an errand carrying a pumpkin that my mother had me pick and bring home when Mr. Oh raised his head over the wall and spoke to me.

"What flowers?"

I felt awkward when he talked to me, but I was somewhat glad that he was going to give me some flowers. Besides, I knew that he was not a bad person, and so entered his garden without fear, which made him happy. He pointed at the flowers in the garden with a big open face.

"Let me pick some flowers you like"

"Are you sure?"

"Of course! I will give you enough so that you can put them in the vase." He brought a pair of pruning shears and cut some of the flowers for me. Scarlet sage, petunia, cosmos, cockscomb, and some other flowers that I did not know the names of. I wondered why he cut those flowers, his most prized possessions, but I kept pointing at different beautiful flowers since I was just happy to get them.

After he finished cutting them, he talked to me in a quiet manner.

"Won't you take care of these flowers instead of me? I know you like flowers."

"I will do it. Do I just need to water them?"

I agreed to his suggestion without hesitating because I only thought he would just be gone for a while to get a job and also because I liked flowers myself. Mr. Oh beamed at me and said,

"Yes, you just need to water them."

"Do you want me to pull out weeds, too? I can see lots of weeds here." I said to him looking at the weeds in one corner of the garden. More weeds were growing than the flowers.

"No. All of them here are flowers. They are such beautiful flowers that you should not pull them out."

"The ones here are weeds, I am sure." I told him, taking a look at sow thistles and clovers.

"Probably you are right. However, they become weeds when you think they are weeds, or they become flowers if you think they are flowers."

I could not understand what he said, but I could guess that there was something more than I could understand. I gazed silently at his face. His face with high cheekbones was gaunt and haggard, but his eyes really seemed to sparkle. At that moment, I felt ashamed to have called him Mr. Crow Oh or 'senile old man'. I promised to take care of his garden and came back home.

However, I soon forgot about the promise that I made to Mr. Oh. I was so excited about an autumn athletic meeting that I could not even think of the promise. A few days later, I was writing a diary which I was supposed to have finished the day before when I heard my mother and Young-sook's mother, a neighbor, talking.

"Did you hear that Joo-hee's father can now have a surgery?"

"Yes, I did. It was really nice of Mr. Oh. It's not an easy thing to do, you know."

"That's what I mean."

"He really is a nice person. I regret saying such harsh words without realizing what a nice person he is."

"Me, too."

My heart was palpitating when I heard them. How nice of Mr. Oh to spare his kidney for someone who even used to pick on him! It occurred to me that Joo-hee would be so happy, and I thought that Mr. Oh was such a nice person. Suddenly the promise to take care of his garden lashed through my mind.

"That's right. He asked me to take care of his flowers."

I realized that I had not kept my promise to him, so I put on my clothes and I left the house.

"Where are you going? Why don't you sweep the yard?"

My mothers voice lingered in my ears, but I crossed over the threshold in a hurry and ran to Mr. Oh's.

Drama

The Choir Of Birds Which Makes Us Sleep

Il-Hong Jang

The Choir Of Birds Which Makes Us Sleep

Writer's Introduction
Born in Jeju in 1950. Recommended and first recognized by *the Modern Literature* in 1985. Awarded in the Spring Literature Contest by Hahngook Daily Newspaper. Grand Prize in the Drama Contest by the Korean Ministry of Culture and Tourism. Korean Literature Award, Korean Playwrights Award, Monthly Literature Dongli Award.
Address: 102-1101 Huyndai Apts, Nohyung-Dong, Jeju, Jeju-do, Republic of Korea
Phone: 010-3119-4353

The Choir Of Birds Which Makes Us Sleep

CHARACTERS

CHEONDOL: A farmer from Bullokuk
PRESIDENT: Dictator from Kirokuk
SECRETARY: An aide to the president
MADAM: A waitress of a luxury hostess bar
SECRET SERVICEMAN: An intelligence agent
INVESTIGATOR: A military investigator
REPORTER 1, 2: Newspaper and broadcasting station correspondents
MILITARY GUARDS 1, 2: Border guards

The emptier the room, the better. Two spare chairs and one simple bed are enough. The crucial stage settings in this play are all horizontal. The entire backdrop is a large screen and the background scenes throughout the progress of the play will be reflected on the screen. When the curtain is lifted, the President's office with Kirokuk's flag overwhelms the atmosphere. The President, pipe in mouth, is thinking about something.

SECRETARY enters.

SECRETARY (*with a big smile on his face*): Your Excellency!

(*The President glances briefly at the secretary, then turns his head away again.*)

SECRETARY: Sir, there is good news.

(*PRESIDENT just stares blankly.*)

SECRETARY: An emergency report has come through the hot line from the head of the border guards. He says one farmer of Bullokuk defected across the border to Kirokuk.

PRESIDENT (*taking the pipe from his mouth*): Defector? Not a spy?

SECRETARY: It's a defector, sir. It is our first brilliant feat since our nation was liberated from the chain of suppression and disgrace of being a colony of Bullokuk.

PRESIDENT: Mm, How many people defected from our country to Bullokuk?

SECRETARY: Yes. 5,000 people went across the border the year before last and 10,000 people fled last year. Although we have been reinforcing the border with extra guards, the number of illegal defectors is annually on the rise. (Head drooping) I'm sorry, sir.

PRESIDENT: You don't need to say sorry. It's all my fault.

SECRETARY (*waving his hands in protest*): No, It's not true. You are the father of this country and the people of this nation shed tears of gratitude for your unlimited grace.

PRESIDENT: Do you mean that the nation is really following me?

SECRETARY (*bowing with gratitude*): I shall never forget your kindness. If you did not devote your life to the independence of Kirokuk, our nation would still be Bullokuk's toilet paper.

PRESIDENT (*nodding his head*): The host of heaven knows my patriotism and love for my people. However, what does the current situation mean? There are constant student protests, labor strikes, and the politicians slander and connive against me.

SECRETARY: Don't worry about that too much. I intend to disrupt the plots of the labor movement and a few students who espouse evil ideology. Dissident politicians are under strict surveillance and censorship and house arrest also help keep them in line. (*Sneering.*) The prison is large and the rope of the scaffold is still strong.

PRESIDENT: I heard that the Minister of Home Affairs and Defense declared martial law across the metropolitan area.

SECRETARY (*forcefully*): Your Excellency! Martial law is the last resort of the regime. It's the same as administering powerful medicine to a dying patient who has no hope of recovery. In my judgment, the present political situation is not so hopeless yet. If we overcome this crisis wisely, the security of this country will be as solid as a ten thousand year old rock.

PRESIDENT: So···do you have any alternative measures?

SECRETARY (*confidently*): Yes, sir!

PRESIDENT: What's that?

SECRETARY: The timely defection of one farmer from Bullokuk has great political significance for us.

PRESIDENT: ···?

SECRETARY: As you know, the reason for the current university student and opposition party uproar lies in the constitutional amendment giving you a lifetime term in office. They argue that the constitutional amendment is unjust, so the most urgent work we have is to justify the amendment.

PRESIDENT: How?

SECRETARY: By showing the inevitability of a lifetime term in office,···that is, persuading people that we can prevent social disorder and invasion by enemies through your strong, continuous leadership. By exploiting the defector···

PRESIDENT (*incredulously*): Isn't he a farmer? What on earth can this silly and ignorant peasant do?

SECRETARY (*flatly*): He's not a farmer.

PRESIDENT: He's not? (*After staring him in the face.*) You are plotting something.

SECRETARY: We must make him a field-commander of Bullokuk.

PRESIDENT: What? Commander? Ha ha ha···(*laugh-cough-laugh.*) Ha ha ha···You are crazy, really crazy!

SECRETARY (*looking serious*): Your Excellency, I want you to consider my true motivation. This is the only way for us to get through this crisis. I'm sure that there will be great repercussions if the enemy commander himself discloses that Bullokuk has prepared for an attack against Kirokuk.

PRESIDENT (*groaning*): Hm···You're saying that we threaten the people, citing war as an excuse? Are they going to believe the words of the farmer?

SECRETARY (*sharply*): I said he's not a farmer! I'm determined to change him into a commander brimming with martial spirit. (*Brief pause.*) When I was young, I was the puppet master of a local theatrical troupe. I'm very confident of my profound puppet mastering skills. Please allow me to do this!

PRESIDENT (*after pacing restlessly with pipe in mouth*): The students will not be taken in by your puppet master tactics. They have genuine passion, which gives one the power to see the truth through the lies.

SECRETARY: I have a clever scheme. I'm planning to provoke internal strife amongst the students.

PRESIDENT: I sometimes feel that you are insufferable.

SECRETARY (*engrossed in speech*): I've already won over the moderate students from the Religious Group Council.

PRESIDENT: I feel uneasy about exploiting naive youngsters, though.

SECRETARY (*jeeringly*): Your Excellency, the politicians should know how to use Jesus and Marx at the same time if needed.

PRESIDENT: What if you fail?

SECRETARY (*showing a tragic resolution in his face*): This operation will probably put your political life at risk. The chance of success is about half. But the possibility was about half when we had the war of independence. Brave people are never afraid of a 50% chance of success.

PRESIDENT (*opening his eyes after closing his eyes*): There were times when I did not fear the impossible. I'm too old—

SECRETARY (*firmly clenching his fist*): Sir! Now is the time to recover from calamity and reverse the unfavorable situation. Even though the students and the opposition party are opening champagne bottles to celebrate their victory, just wait and see. The war is not over. The one who smiles at the end is the real winner. (*While holding his pipe, the President raises both arms and slowly takes them down again. It's a sign of acceptance.*)

SECRETARY (*standing at attention*): Thank you sir! I shall fulfill my mission at the risk of my life.

(*Both of them exit. The scene changes into the press conference hall. The national flag disappears, replaced by the portrait of the President. Enters SECRETARY*)

SECRETARY (*towards the audience*): Hello, everybody. We will now begin the press conference for Bullokuk's first field commander General Um Cheon-Suk, who defected to Kirokuk. Please welcome General Um with warm-hearted cheering and applause. He escaped from the 'empire of evil', seeking freedom (*applause*).

(*Enter* CHEONDOL. *Despite his dignified entrance in gay military uniform with abundant decorations, he looks funny and awkward. As* CHEONDOL *sits, flashes pop up here and there while television cameras gather right up against the stage.*)

SECRETARY (*after clearing his throat several times*): Well then, reporters from the media! Please ask a question of General Um without hesitation.

REPORTERA (*standing up from his seat*): I am Gap-Su Park from Sudo Newspaper. Would you please tell us your name, age, rank and position?

CHEONDOL: CHEONDOL Eom- no, I'm Cheon-Ssuk Um. (*Flustered, he trembles with nervousness.*) I'm 48 and my rank is major general. My position is- (*turns his head behind and looks anxiously at the* SECRETARY. *He looks behind whenever he's at a loss for an answer.*)
SECRETARY (*smiling calmly*): Position. (*He gives hand signals like baseball coaches give to their players.*)
CHEONDOL: My position is-first division field commander.
REPORTTER1: You were a field commander of Bullokuk, a high-ranking position- is there any special motive for your defection to Kirokuk?
CHEONDOL: Yes — You may already know this, but Bullokuk is a living hell where 40 percent of the people starve and beggars overflow. The whole nation has fallen into extreme distress and suffering, however, the executive members of the green party and senior officials of the government spend days feasting sumptuously. Some commanders in the front and the younger officers who resented the ruling class resolved to fight to save the nation and plotted a rebellion. However, in the process of plotting the coup, information leaked out, resulting in a purge of the army. I became aware of my personal danger and decided to defect.
REPORTER 1: As we understand it, Bullokuk's GNP and per capita income are three times that of Kirokuk's. You claim that 40 percent of the people are starving, I'm not convinced. What is this statistic based on?
CHEONDOL: Yes, that is- that is- (*When he looks back, the* SECRETARY *gives a hand signal.*) I learned this fact after reading the book, *The*

International Economic Trends and Issues, which was published in the third world.

REPORTER 2 (*standing up*): I am Seong Joo-cheol from Jungang broadcasting company. I believe that you, as a field commander, would know in more detail than anyone else about the military power of both countries and the state of confrontation in the border regions. Currently, the people of Kirokuk are sleeping badly due to the threat of invasion from the puppet state of Bullokuk, a group of the most belligerent war maniacs in the world. Can you tell us about this? Are they going to attack us for sure, or what? (*A burst of laughter erupts from those seated.*)

CHEONDOL (*with a confident attitude*): I'd like to make it clear that the enemy is vigilantly watching for a chance to attack. In particular, the anarchic chaos caused by student protests and labor strikes in Kirokuk will make military provocation by the enemy more likely, as the enemy might misjudge this time to be the decisive moment for their preemptive attack.

REPORTER 2: Don't speak ambiguously, but please suggest any specific cases and evidence you have that Bullokuk will invade us.

CHEONDOL (*As he looks back, the secretary sends a sign*): Bullokuk's general field command headquarters ordered the deployment of five corps and twenty divisions to the border areas some time ago.

Armored vehicles, artillery, and missile units have been assembled all along the front line — (*He gradually speaks with more and more eloquence.*) They will occupy Kirokuk in a minute and will surge in upon us as soon as they receive orders! Ah- now the fate of this country is in dire straits and imminent peril. The enemy wills wallow all of your properties and lives like a pack of starved wolves falling on sleeping lambs. It could even happen tonight! (*There is deafening silence from the press as if someone cast a chill over them.*)

SECRETARY (*comes forward swiftly*): If there are no further questions, I hereby finish the press conference of General Um. Thank you.

(*The portrait of the president is removed,* REPORTER 1, 2 *and the seated media exit. The* SECRETARY *approaches* CHEONDOL, *who is wiping his brow.*)

SECRETARY: You did a very good job.

CHEONDOL: Yes. It was thanks to you — Did I make any mistakes?

SECRETARY: No, it was excellent. The PRESIDENT will be satisfied with what you've done after watching you on TV.

CHEONDOL: Thanks a lot.

SECRETARY: General Um. Although your debut was successful, the more important part starts from today. The public is focusing their attention on you. The words from your mouth will lead the people's hearts and minds. Thus, I want you to immediately leave on a lecture circuit all across the country.

CHEONDOL (*reluctantly*): Do I have to leave now?

SECRETARY: Yes. There's not much time left.

CHEONDOL (*pointing to his decorations*): In this suit?

SECRETARY: Yes, leave in that military uniform. The way one dresses represents one's status. The only evidence that you are a general of

Bullokuk is that uniform. That uniform is simply for show, and I think it will be very effective. Silly people tend to believe blindly what they see with their eyes.

CHEONDOL (*talking slowly*): What should I say during the speeches? I get nervous in front of people.

SECRETARY: You don't need to be nervous. Just do as you've been trained. Did you forget that you are the general?

CHEONDOL: Where will I hold my speeches?

SECRETARY: All over the country. First, you will visit provincial seats, next you will go to the cities, then county offices, and finally to the town and village level, *eup*, *myon* and *ri*.

CHEONDOL: How long will it take to tour all the places?

SECRETARY: It will take around three years.

CHEONDOL (*frustrated expression*): Whew~, what shall I do?

SECRETARY (*patting him on the shoulder*): Don't worry. You will make a fortune after this. You will get a large sum of money which you otherwise wouldn't have been able to earn in your life time, no matter how hard you worked.

CHEONDOL: What shall I do when I have nothing to say? I've only learned this script by heart- what if I run out of words?

SECRETARY: Haha — Not to worry. Just recite the scenario you've practiced with the script. Whenever you go to someplace new, just repeat the same story since the audience is new to it. In short, you become a parrot instead of a human being for three years. Do you get me?

CHEONDOL (*imploringly*): You will go with me?

SECRETARY: No, I won't! A SECRETSERVICEMAN will accompany you. (*Towards the audience.*) Come here, secret serviceman!!

SECRET SERVICEMAN (*standing up from the audience all of a sudden*): Yes sir! (*Comes up to stage in a hurry. He is a big strapping looking person with a megaphone on his shoulder.*)

SECRETARY: Please serve General Um.

SECRET SERVICEMAN: Yes, sir!

SECRETARY (*asks to shake hands with* CHEONDOL.): Then keep up the good work.

CHEONDOL (*He is trembling and on the verge of tears.*) (*The SECRETARY waves dismissively and exits*)

SECRET SERVICEMAN (*He takes his megaphone over to* CHEONDOL *and takes a seat*): Well, why don't you get on.

(CHEONDOL *sits on* the SECRET SERVICEMAN's *shoulders and the man threads his way through the audience in every direction while heading to the stage. All the while,* CHEONDOL *is on his shoulder. When* CHEONDOL *cries through the megaphone, the seasons change three times on the stage background and Vivaldi's 'Four Seasons' is played calmly in the background.*)

CHEONDOL (*towards the audience*): Dear countrymen! I'm Cheon-Suk Um and I was once the first field commander of Bullokuk. I defected to Kirokuk seeking freedom. Even at this moment, Bullokuk's leader Dorum Uok is nursing his greedy ambition to invade and is making finishing touches in his war plan. He boasts that he will "liberate" the citizens of Kirokuk within a week! Now, at this time when the two countries are on the brink of war, we need a strong leader to settle the social chaos and prevent the enemy's attack···Who else can lead us besides the president who is the sun of the people and the light of the nation! Dear citizens! The only way to overcome this national crisis is to revise the silly constitution which came from the West and adapt it to our needs. We must let the president rule this country until he dies. I earnestly believe that the constitutional amendment is the only way to survive.

(*Big applause form the crowd, cheering, sound of the chant: "Constitutional amendment, constitutional amend-ment" flows through the stadium speakers. At this point, the* SECRETARY *enters, applauding. The* SECRET SERVICEMAN *sits down, and* CHEONDO *gets off the man's shoulders.*)

CHEONDOL (*stunned*): Good heavens! Why, SECRETARY! What are you doing here-?

SECRETARY: Hahaha- you did a very good job up 'till now. Isn't this your last lecture? I came here for the double purpose of congratulating and seeing you.

CHEONDOL (*sigh*): It's been 3 years already?

SECRETARY: Yes. Anyways, you've worked very hard. It was a greater success than I expected.

I read the report by the intelligence agency, which collected and analyzed public opinion. The report says that your lecture circuit contributed a lot to national unity. It not only became an opportunity to give vivid information on the real condition of the enemy, but also acted as a catalyst, making people support the constitutional amendment. It's safe to say that all of these accomplishments are due to your hard work. The PRESIDENT ordered me to convey his congratulations and to give you recognition for your services.

CHEONDOL: I don't know what to do now. I have nothing special to do.

SECRETARY: Yes, you do. Frankly speaking, I was impressed by your eloquence in attracting and exciting people. (*To* the SECRET SERVICEMAN) Yes, you did a good job, too. Now you may return to your position in the agency.

SECRET SERVICEMAN: Yes, sir! (*salutes and exits*)

SECRETARY: Why don't you take a rest for a few days. I've got a house for you, so go there and take a bath. I want you to be relieved of your fatigue. Ah- I also brought a girl for you, she's waiting at home. She has amazing skill in this work.

(*Hands over an envelope.*) This is an imperial grant of 100 million won, a cashier's check from the president. With this money, you can buy ten tile-roofed houses.

CHEONDOL (*with his eyes wide open*): Wow! That's a lot of money-!

SECRETARY: Well, well······ what did I say? I said that you'd make a fortune, didn't I? Let's go home. The woman must be dying to meet you. She is a girl from a famous hostess club known throughout the capital. When she laughs, dimples appear on her cheeks.

In my experience, dimples signify good skill. Hahaha-

(*Both of them leave the stage. When the stage turns pink, a madam appears, covering her shapely nude body with a towel, still dripping wet just after taking a shower. She sticks a cigarette in her mouth. Enter* CHEONDOL.)

CHEONDOL (*looking in the direction opposite the woman, acting as if he doesn't see her*): Who, who are you?

MADAM: Oh! Our hero! You must be General Um, right?

CHEONDOL: Yes, I am······ that's right.

MADAM (*smiling*): Didn't SECRETARY tell you about me?

CHEONDOL (*peeps at her and then turns his head swiftly back again*): Yes, he did.

MADAM: Oh! Why are you standing there like a borrowed barley sack? How about taking a shower quickly so we can 'exchange the nuptial cups'.

CHEONDOL: Where is the bathroom?

MADAM (*pointing to the bathroom*): It's over there.

(CHEONDOL goes to the bathroom, shaking with fear)

MADAM: Hohoho- oh, my dear! It's so funny. After becoming a general didn't he even play around a little? By the way, what's wrong with him? He's like a boorish peasant.

(CHEONDOL comes out of the bathroom)

CHEONDOL (*swallows his saliva*): Mm- now that I think about it, I took a bath a few days ago at an inn.

MADAM: A few days ago? Don't you take a shower everyday?

CHEONDOL (*grins*): Well-when I was in my hometown, I took a shower just twice a year,-on New Year's Eve and Chuseok (the Korean version of Thanksgiving Day).

MADAM (*startled*): What? Is that true?

CHEONDOL: Yes, it's true.

MADAM: Oh my goodness, how dirty you are! How can I press the flesh with such a man?

CHEONDOL: Even so, my wife didn't have any complaints.

MADAM: Oh my god! I'm dumbfounded. Are the people in Bullokuk that poor? Don't they have tap water?

CHEONDOL: Everything is organized by the rations system, so getting a water ration ticket is like plucking a star from heaven.

MADAM: (*pretends to pour the liquor into an imaginary glass*):
Just drink it. I heard that you blistered your feet due to your nationwide lecture circuit- why don't you relieve your fatigue by drinking the wine. Well, cheers to the president and the republic of Kirokuk! (*clink their glasses together, madam drinks it in one gulp*)

CHEONDOL (*frowns after tasting the wine a little*): Oh My! what kind of liquor is this?

MADAM: It's the best quality foreign wine. The rumors have it that the president is fond of this.

CHEONDOL: I like makkeoli (rice wine) though- don't you have that?

MADAM: How boorish you are to want makkeoli! People like farmers like to drink it.

CHEONDOL (*displeased*): What's wrong with farmers who like mokkeoli?

MADAM (*flirting*): Well really, General Um. Are you playing with me?

CHEONDOL (*has a long drink of wine as if he were angry*): I'm very tired so I have to go to sleep early. (*Takes off uniform roughly and gets under the bedcovers.*)

MADAM (*speaking nasally, fully displaying her disposition as a whore*): Oh, Mr. general, you seem to be angry. Why are you so upset? That's unbecoming of a hero. You know, when people sleep together, the man must be gentle, soft, and pleasant. Oh, I don't want you to be angry···(*She throws off the towel she's wearing and gets under the covers.*)

(*Sound of laughing. A human double-deck bulges out of the sheets but suddenly becomes a single deck. Madam pushes her face out of the sheets first.*)

MADAM: Goodness gracious! Already?

CHEONDOL: −

MADAM (*unabashedly annoyed*): How can a man like this exist on the earth? Good heavens, do you call that thing a penis? (*She wraps herself in a towel and rises from bed.*)

How about cutting it off with a pair of scissors and throwing it to the crows?

CHEONDOL (*pushes his face out of the sheet*): I'm terribly sorry. I guess my thing has gotten rusty since I haven't used it for a long time.

MADAM (*getting angry*): Hey! I'm under orders to pleasure you all night tonight. Shit! Do you think I do this because I want to? Just try to perform half as well as the SECRETARY. (*Pours a glass of wine and drinks it swiftly.*) I give him kudos for his stamina. He teases me all night as if he'd drunk snake liquor (an aphrodisiac in Korea). (*Pause*) Anyway, don't you ever think that you can meet me later? Damn! What a stroke of luck!

CHEONDOL (*sneaks into the sheets and disappears*): —

(*Madam, standing voluptuously in a suggestive pose, puts a cigarette between her lips while sitting cross-legged, almost exposing her bare thighs. Onstage when the lights come on, CHEONDOL stands up, stretches, and then realizes that madam had disappeared and that he's only wearing his underwear. He looks for her. While doing so, he discovers the fallen envelope and picks it up. He confirms that the cashier's check is gone and his face turns pale. (He dials an imaginary telephone.)*)

CHEONDOL: By the way-what do you call it-well, is this the secretary's department? Can I speak to Mr. SECRETARY, please? Yes, this is CHEONDOL Um. (*Pause*.) Ah, Mr. Secretary? I'm CHEONDOL. I slept well thanks to you. Gee, It was so-so-that's the way things go, hehe-by the way, when I woke up this morning, madam had disappeared. Yes, she disappeared, and the money you gave me is gone, too. Ah, I mean it! I'm not in the joking mood right now. Then you can come here and confirm it directly. (*Pause*) Mr. Secretary-it's nothing to get mad about. Yes, well then, I'll wait for you. I see-(*hangs up the phone dejectedly*.) Geez, what's going on? That's really strange. Mr. Secretary certainly gave me an envelope, saying that there was 100 million in it —.

(CHEONDOL *opens the envelope and shakes it. He then fumbles in his suit pocket and looks under the bed and sheets. At that moment*, the

SECRET SERVICEMAN *enters quietly. He keenly watches what* CHEONDOL *is doing. When* CHEONDOL *stands up, he is startled to see the* SECRET SERVICEMAN.)

CHEONDOL: Ah, Mr. Secret serviceman! What brought you here?

SECRET SERVICEMAN (*coldly*): Mr. SECRETARY sent me here. The Secretary's direct order is that from now on, you must refrain from going out of this house. A sentry is on guard at the gate.

CHEONDOL (*in low spirits*): If that's the case, you mean that I can't go outside?

SECRET SERVICEMAN: Yes.

CHEONDOL: That's different from what he promised. He said that I could live my life feely when the lecture circuit ended-

SECRET SERVICEMAN: Things have changed.

CHEONDOL: Until when do I have to stay here?

SECRET SERVICEMAN: I have no idea. I'm just delivering instructions from head office.

CHEONDOL (nodding): You-yes, you-were watching me yesterday and you have been watching me since I began the lecture circuit.

SECRET SERVICEMAN: −

CHEONDOL: Haven't you? Aren't those orders from the head office, too?

SECRET SERVICEMAN (*nodding silently*.): −

CHEONDOL: Even so, how can I live since I have no food to eat?

SECRET SERVICEMAN: Food will be delivered at every meal.

CHEONDOL: Mr. Secret Serviceman. I have a favor to ask of you-

SECRET SERVICEMAN: What is it?

CHEONDOL (*pointing to his military suit*): It's too hard for me to walk because this uniform is too heavy due to all the decorations. Can you change it?

SECRET SERVICEMAN: There are extra clothes in the wardrobe. (*He comes out with some clothes*)

CHEONDOL (*wearing loose-fitting clothes*): Now that I've taken off the military suit, even though the clothes are too big, I feel quite well. I feel like I could fly away.

SECRET SERVICEMAN: Take it easy. (*Walks off the stage and exits.*)

(CHEONDOL *is sitting down with a miserable expression, but suddenly claps his hands. He takes a lighter out of the pocket of his military uniform and lights a fire everywhere, and then shouts "fire! fire!" towards the audience. He flees hurriedly to the opposite side. Red psychedelic lighting on the stage spins dizzily and when a siren goes off noisily. Blackout. After a while, the stage brightens, against the backdrop of long barbed wire.* CHEONDOL *appears and gets close to a chain link fence while snooping around.*)

CHEONDOL: Hmmm-That's strange, what on earth is this? What's this fence for? There wasn't anything like this back then — (*At this juncture,* MILITARY GUARDS 1, 2 *suddenly jump out from the audience while pointing their guns.*)

MILITARY GUARD 1: Freeze! Don't move or I'll shoot! Put your hands up! (CHEONDOL *raises his hands slowly.*) Turn around! (*He turns around.*)

MILITARY GUARD 2: Who are you? You must be a spy!

CHEONDOL (*absent-mindedly*): S — spy? What is a spy?

MILITARY GUARD 1: You punk! Stop messing around or you'll have a hole in your head if you keep talking nonsense! (*To* MILITARY GUARD 2.) Hey, tie him with the cord quickly. (MILITARY GUARD 2 *leaps on* CHEONDOL *and ties him up*.)
CHEONDOL (*trembling with fear*): Gosh, why are you doing this to me? I didn't do anything wrong.
MILITARY GUARD 1 (*kicks* CHEONDOL's *behind*): Hey you son of a bitch! Do you want to die? How dare you try crossing over the wire fence?
MILITARY GUARD 2 (to MILITARY GUARD 1): This crazy guy must have wanted to be pork for a barbecue.
MILITARY GUARD 1: It's impossible for a man who received secret training not to be aware of the fact that high-voltage current flows through the wire fence
CHEONDOL (*stunned*): Se — secret training? I'm a farmer. This land is mine. I farmed here. This land has been owned by my family since my grandfather's time.
MILITARY GUARD 2: Your land? Haha-You're talking bullshit! (*To MILITARY GUARD 1*) why don't we take him to the company office?
MILITARY GUARD 1: Why not? We'd better report this to the company commander and inform the Political Defense Company. (*Making a victory sign with his hand*) We have it made. We're likely to get a long vacation when our service is nearly up.)
MILITARY GUARD 2 (*hits* CHEONDOL's *back hard with the butt of the gun*):

Move quickly, you son of a bitch.

CHEONDOL: AHHHHH! (*He's dragged along with his back is bent like a bow*). (*When the three of them exit, barbed wire in the background disappears and in a short time, the investigator and* CHEONDOL *enter together.*)

INVESTIGATOR (*seated in the chair*): Take a seat. (CHEONDOL *sits down.*) I heard roughly about your arrest from the company commander-well, the thing has happened already, so just confide everything to me. It is in your interest to do that.

CHEONDOL (*blinking*): I have no clue what you are talking about. As I told the soldier, I farmed here-

INVESTIGATOR (*interrupting him*): No more acting! Nobody will be fooled by your clumsy acting!

CHEONDOL: Oh my! What acting? I don't know anything other than farming. Except that lecture circuit something or other, I've spent my whole life farming. I came back to my hometown a few days ago because the lecture circuit is finished-and you know, I unexpectedly found a chain link fence on the corner of my land.

INVESTIGATOR: Humph, you're hardcore, is that it? I've seen some political offenders like you. They don't confess before they get tortured. They tend to disclose everything after that. How about going straight to the torture room?

CHEONDOL (*hits himself on his chest*): It's really frustrating. I'm telling the truth. If you don't believe me, ask Mr. SECRETARY and then you will be able to know the truth at once.

INVESTIGATOR (*sarcastically*): Shit, the Secretary of the secretary department?

Why don't you say that the president is your old friend.

CHEONDOL: I'm General Cheon-Suk Um, who delivered the lecture circuit for the past three years! It's me!

INVESTIGATOR (*stunned*): What, General Cheon-Suk Um! (*Staring at him.*) Let's see, from what you've said, you look like him-

CHEONDOL (*a bit proudly*): Haven't you seen me on TV or in the newspaper? My face was on every three days-

INVESTIGATOR: Oh my God-I'm puzzled. Anyways, it's okay. To begin with, let's put this down on paper and confirm the facts again. (*Takes out pen and pad.*) Nationality?

CHEONDOL: What's the meaning of nationality?

INVESTIGATOR: It means what country you are from.

CHEONDOL: I'm absolutely a citizen of Bullokuk.

INVESTIGATOR: Your place of origin and home address?

CHEONDOL: They are the same, 380 Suro-myeon, Nackrang-gun, Garack-do.

INVESTIGATOR: Your name?

CHEONDOL: I'm Cheondol Um.

INVESTIGATOR: Age?

CHEONDOL: Fifty one.

INVESTIGATOR: I've watched General Um's press conference after defection on TV. At that time, the general said he defected to Kirokuk seeking freedom, right?

CHEONDOL: Oh no, that's a total lie. It's fake.

INVESTIGATOR (*yells*): What? A fake? Are you mocking me now?

CHEONDOL: I'm not General Cheon-Suk Um, but Cheondol Um.

INVESTIGATOR: If that's true-?

CHEONDOL: Mr. Secretary told me to play the role of General Um, so I did as he ordered.

INVESTIGATOR: Then what's the motive of defection?

CHEONDOL (*shaking his head*): Defection? I did not defect.

INVESTIGATOR: You don't seem to understand. Didn't you come to Kirokuk from Bullokuk of your own will?

CHEONDOL: That's right.

INVESTIGATOR: Then if that's not defection, what is it? You weren't abducted by someone either.

CHEONDOL: I must tell you the whole story-I guess it was early June at the time. One day while the cattle were grazing, one calf had gone missing while I was gone cutting fodder. As I went out searching for it, I saw thick grass near the stream. Because I had a sickle at that time, I got greedy and went down gradually mowing the grass. I was mowing hard, until all of a sudden, somebody pointed a gun at my back and dragged me away by force. It was a soldier of Kirokuk. I realized later that I had probably crossed the border unintentionally, but it is no use crying over spilt milk. (*Pause.*)

CHEONDOL (*nearly crying*): That's what happened. I didn't intend to come to Kirokuk. Because of that calf-If I had not been greedy for fodder —

INVESTIGATOR: Hmm, I think that kind of thing could have happened because there was no barbed wire at border at that time.

CHEONDOL (*rubbing his hands*): Anyway, It's all my fault. Please forgive me.

My parents, brothers, wife and children in my hometown must think that I'm dead. (*He feels his heart getting warm.*) I haven't kept in touch with them since coming to Kirokuk three years ago. My own land is just over that fence. (*Thinking of his remote hometown*) Since the barley harvest season starts the day after tomorrow, the barley on my land must be ripe and golden by now. In the furrows, we have wild garlic, shepherd's purse, wormwood, wild berries, beans, and vegetables-we have a lot of things to eat. When we have a bad harvest, we pick and eat different kinds of herbal grasses such as tungecle, gehjari, haneullegi, and baecheggi-Yes, you can even cure diarrhea by eating boiled baecheggi. There are lots of grasshoppers in the furrows as well. In autumn, we tie up fatty grasshoppers like we tie dried radish leaves and then when we roast them over the fire and eat them, hehe-It's absolutely delicious! In addition, there are many frogs in the mud puddles by now. The way they croak sounds like the cries of Heungbu's children wanting rice.

INVESTIGATOR (*interrupts him by raising his hand*): I see. If you are really general Um-you were probably treated as a national hero. Did the government dump you without any compensation?

CHEONDOL: They gave me a home and large amount of money.

INVESTIGATOR: Then, It would be good for you to get married again to a pretty, young woman and settle down here. Why do you want to go back to Bullokuk?

CHEONDOL: Because I miss my hometown.

INVESTIGATOR: Kirokuk is a much freer country than Bullokuk.

CHEONDOL: What is more important than freedom is blood. I miss my old parents, brothers, and wife. The faces of my children are still fresh in my memory. I've never forgotten them since I came here-(*Tears in his eyes*) I miss my children badly. You might know how I feel.

INVESTIGATOR: If you wanted to go to your country, you should have let the Secretary know earlier.

CHEONDOL (*with a displeased look*): He wouldn't have consented even if I'd asked him.

(*Speaking hesitatingly*) and —

INVESTIGATOR: And what? Tell me frankly.

CHEONDOL: If I had stayed in that house like a jail, I would not have survived.

INVESTIGATOR (*with curiosity*): What does that mean?

CHEONDOL: The Secretary and the Madam fled together with the 100 million won the president granted to me.

INVESTIGATOR: Really? Is that true?

CHEONDOL: Sure! I smelled a rat. Although I'm only a peasant, I have that much sense. The Secretary conspired with that sly woman and tried to get rid of me to take my money.

INVESTIGATOR (*feeling pity for* CHEONDOL): You'd better not return to your country.

CHEONDOL: Why?

INVESTIGATOR: You slandered Bullokuk during the lecture circuit. Do you think they will leave a collaborator like you alone? (*Makes a gesture of cutting his throat*)

CHEONDOL: The person who did the lecture circuit was Cheon-Suk Um, not me. I'll live by myself in the country by farming, so no one will ever notice me.

INVESTIGATOR: Even though we let you go, you will be caught by the guards of your country. As the tension between the two countries heightened, the defenses have been strengthened.

CHEONDOL (in low spirits): If I will die no matter where I go-I will die in my hometown. Even the animals go to their homes when they are near death-

INVESTIGATOR: You will be safe here. Did anyone say that they would harm you?

CHEONDOL (*kneels down and seizes the pants of the* INVESTIGATOR): Please, let me go home! I have to go no matter what! Sir-! Please, I'm begging you-let me go!

INVESTIGATOR (*stamps out of the room*): No! You came here of your own will, but it's impossible to go back to your country! (*Pauses*) Hey, look-you are just like an unlucky wild animal that was caught in a trap. The hunter decides how to handle the booty. Well, just go inside and take a rest until I call you again. (*The two of them exit and the secretary enters with the investigator.*)

SECRETARY: Well, so are you saying that you believe what he said to you?

INVESTIGATOR (*bewildered*): No, no-no, sir. I'm just reporting all the circumstances in detail because I heard you took care of him.

SECRETARY (*contemptuously*): He is a lunatic.

INVESTIGATOR: What?

SECRETARY: According to the report from one agent who observed CHEONDOL, he says that CHEONDOL has a delusion of persecution.

INVESTIGATOR: Yes, I've heard about that from Cheondol Um

SECRETARY: What have you heard?

INVESTIGATOR: He says he feels like he might be killed. I also felt that he was extremely obsessed with the fear of being killed by someone.

SECRETARY (*proudly*): Haha-see? From the get-go when he crossed over to Kirokuk he was abnormal. If he had been normal, he would not have crossed the border.

INVESTIGATOR: I think the immediate reason why he felt threatened was he thought he would be murdered for his money.

SECRETARY (*turns pale*): Money? What money-?

INVESTIGATOR: The money granted by the president-

SECRETARY: Right, that money. Thus, I've arranged to search for her as a most wanted criminal nationwide. She's a boldfaced robber! 100 million won for one night! Does she think her equipment is framed with gold?

INVESTIGATOR: Mr. Secretary-How should I solve this problem?

SECRETARY: What? Are you really asking me? (*Cold-heartedly*.) He is no longer useful. Not only that, we will be in trouble if we go around talking about it. Therefore, in particular, pay attention to maintaining security and take care of this problem in secret. The fate of the regime hinges on this issue!

INVESTIGATOR: So are you telling me to refer this issue to court martial?

SECRETARY (*abruptly*): You idiot! How can we condemn him after treating him like a national guest? After all he's traveled about the nation for three years!

INVESTIGATOR (*looking perplexed*): —......

SECRETARY: He didn't come here as a soldier so we should let him go to his country regardless of the law.

INVESTIGATOR: You are ordering me to send him to his country as he wishes?

SECRETARY (*with an angry glare*): What? How did you become an investigator with your rotten brain? You idiot! You pea-brain!

INVESTIGATOR (*looking more embarrassed*): —

SECRETARY: He knows a lot of confidential information about our country. In addition, it's certain that he will be used for counter-propaganda when he goes to Bullokuk. CHEONDOL says he's leaving because he can't stand the sight of me, so we should let him go peacefully, right? (*Pausing, speaking quickly now.*) Under what crime category do they classify citizens who cross the border?

INVESTIGATOR: That comes under the crime of escape.

SECRETARY: The punishment for that crime?

INVESTIGATOR: Of course it's......

SECRETARY: Now, do you understand? Then, go out and do it. (*He brushes the investigator off.*) Why are you dawdling? Beat it!

INVESTIGATOR: Yes, sir! (*He makes a military salute and exits.*)

(*The* SECRETARY *makes a satisfied laugh and exits. An iron curtain is draped as the backdrop,* CHEONDOL *and* MILITARY GUARDS 1, 2 *enter.*)

MILITARY GUARD 1: Mr. Cheondol Um, good-bye.

CHEONDOL (*continues to bow*): Good-bye.

MILITARY GUARAD 2: You must be happy because you are now allowed to go to your country, where you really want to go.

CHEONDOL (*shows his yellow teeth as he laughs*): Of course, it's the happiest day of my life. I feel like I'm dreaming.

MILITARY GUARD 1: Don't forget that this was the special consideration of the president.

CHEONDOL: Of course. How can I forget that? He gave a large amount of money. He even offered me his hand.

(MILITARY GUARDS 1, 2 *walk over to the barbed wire and pretend to open the iron door before they exit. When* CHEONDOL *passes through the door, the barbed wire disappears from the backdrop and the field with ripe, yellow barley unfolds. At that moment, the evening glow is on the horizon.* CHEONDOL *turns around towards the audience and shouts, waving his hands charmingly.*)

CHEONDOL: Hey you guys, Good bye-! Thanks a lot-! I really appreciate it!

(*After turning around and taking one step, bang!, the sound of a gunshot rings out, startling* CHEONDOL, *who tries to move his shoulders. This is followed by the sound of continuous machine-gun fire that rings out through the speakers in the hall.* CHEONDOL *falls to the ground and the dismal sound of a crow is heard. The crying sound of the dark birds is coupled with the fifth movement of Berlioz's "Symphonie Fantastique" and the color of the field of yellow barley changes to the blood-red glow of sunset.*

Essay

It Takes Two To Hatch (Jultakdonggi): The Moment of Enlightenment
My Heart Is A Flower
The Traveler's Teahouse

Tae-Gook Kang

It Takes Two To Hatch (Jultakdonggi): The Moment of Enlightenment

Writer's Introduction
Member of the Korean Writers' Association, board member of Modern Essays, Professor Emeritus at Cheju National University.
Publications: *Pieces of Scribbling, Pieces of Memories, How Dare You?, Essays or Novels,* etc.
Address: 79-9 Donam-dong, Jeju, Jeju-do, Republic of Korea
Phone: (064) 758-8817

It Takes Two To Hatch (*Jultakdonggi*): The Moment of Enlightenment

Tae-Gook Kang

The broad, sizzling sun is glaring. It seems quite threatening. Every door in the lab is swung open, and it is 2 o'clock with no breath of fresh air. Even though it is a vacation, I idle away my time in the lab since there is no special place to go nor is it easy to wander about in the street. I am not so hungry but I still perfunctorily open my lunch box feeling this is the matter I have to settle.

There is a knock on the door, and a young man comes in before I can even ask, "Who is it?" He bows deeply to me and approaches me with a joyful appearance. I am wondering who he is when he begins to introduce himself. At that moment, I dimly recall his name.

His name card indicates that he works for a fairly good company in Seoul. I ask him what brought him here, and he says he wants me to officiate at his wedding.

A few years ago this young man paid a surprise visit, knocking on the door just like today to consult with me. He was not one of my students, but I did not mind and listened to his troubles. He said he was the third child of five children with an elder brother and elder sister, a younger brother and a younger sister, but his parents were indifferent to his existence. He assumed that his parents would have preferred it if he had failed to enter the university.

He added that he always felt alienated since he was recognized only when hard labor such as moving big furniture was needed to be done or the relatives needed an errand boy to help with a big event such as tending to the ancestral graves, weddings or funerals.

He said that recently he did not want to come to class, and seeing his worried school seniors who faced uncertain job prospects bothered him, which was why he was in the depths of despair when he visited me the first time. I earnestly listened to his worries. We kept silent for a minute. I was trying to pull my stream of consciousness together.

Looking back at history, I thought about the lives of the people who had been born and died in different eras and the challenges they had faced. It was too complicated to be solved in a limited space of time. I wondered how people could be so despicable yet noble, foolish yet wise, all at the same time. Perhaps people put themselves in unavoidable crises through their desires, knowledge, beliefs, and fixations, or maybe people have fully digested these things and have moved past this stage to create and protect their own civilization and culture.

It does not seem right, though to think that it is only the people of today upon whom the distress and crisis of culture rests. Everybody has their turning point, reforming stage, or transition period in the process of character building, and we need to be able to tackle the present challenge with wisdom.

There are no reference or answer books that provide solutions for our problems. Instead, we must rely on a thorough grasp of sound and realistic principles to take us on adventures in deep thought and exploration.

The young consider mental illness a more serious problem than physical illness. It is not easy to be aware of mental illness as the condition worsens. This kind of threatening situation can result in a total breakdown, and the patient's condition becomes chronic and it is hard for the patient to recognize him/herself. To the patient, every situation looks unstable, and symptoms of this condition manifest themselves in anger, violence, and a disdain for human life.

A determined work ethic and enough presence of mind to plan ahead seem to be scarce these days. As such, there have been more and more young people suffering from anguish and skepticism. Sometimes, a nervous disease, which can come from living either in the grip of poverty or in too much abundance, can paralyze one's soul, causing the severance of internal and external communication. This can ultimately ruin us.

When self-destructive symptoms are serious, a sense of unity and balance is lost, and a conflict of opinions between the inside and outside develops. This conflict possibly goes out to other people in the form of violent, destructive behaviors.

Favoritism, lack of love, or indifference from parents interrupts certain parts of children's characters and may even lead to murder among family members in extreme cases.

I broke the silence when my thoughts had gone this far. I told him quietly, "Join the army, and serve on the front line." "Why?" He asked me, looking surprised to hear a totally unexpected answer.

"You are not majoring in the same subject that I majored in, but if you consider me your mentor and seriously want advice from me, just join the army without questioning."

I don't know if it was my sincerity that calmed him, but he lowered his eyes and appeared to be deep in thought. I, in my own way, imagined him in the army, standing firmly with his eyes wide open, watching intently to the North in the dark on the front line.

We go to bed with ease since we trust the soldiers. This is a simple fact in this divided nation. It seemed that he should be standing there like a giant. Maybe thinking the same thing as I did, he said, "Yes, I see." and went out giving me a deep bow.

Later, he enlisted in the army and sent me a letter. He visited me after his discharge from military service and made a military salute. He was reborn as a man whom others could depend upon.

In *Jul-tak-dong-gi*, *jul* means to peck while the little bird fights its way out of the egg. *Tak* means to peck when them other bird tries to break the egg from the outside as the little bird does from the inside.

If they cannot do it at the same time and lose the opportunity, the little bird will die from suffocation inside the egg. In the dictionary it says dong-si, the same time, but I changed it to *dong-gi*, the same opportunity. *Jul-tak-dong-gi* could be called the key to relations between father and son, teacher and student, and seniors and juniors in the process of development from childhood to adulthood.

"So what did you find out while you were in army?" I asked the young man giving me a salute. He answered gallantly. "Yes, I found myself."

I smiled at the boy who was now a grown-up. He smiled, too. I am looking forward to autumn.

Ga-Young Kim

My Heart Is A Flower

Writer's Introduction

President of the Jeju Essay Association, Korean Writers' Awards, Grand Prize.
Publications: *When a Women Loves a Man*, *Women with Good Luck with Men*, etc.
Address: 1001 Jaehyung Park Ville, 914-1 Nohyung-dong, Jeju, Jeju-do, Republic of Korea
Phone: (064) 745-2101, 018-693-6512

My Heart Is A Flower

Ga-Young Kim

I was absorbed in the beauty of flowers while planting hollyhocks, marigolds, royal azaleas, and roses in flowerpots when suddenly I thought how lonely the world would be without flowers.

How would we teach our kids about spring if all the flowers disappeared? What would the kids put on paper to draw spring scenery? Kids used to draw flowers and butterflies for spring scenes before. Without flowers, it would only be possible to draw a spring scene with just the color of the sky.

If flowers disappeared, then the old would tell children, "There used to be things called flowers. They were beautiful. Flowers had different shapes and colors. Different flowers come into bloom and lost their petals in different seasons, so we had flowers all year around."

The kids, however, would not really understand what bloom meant. They might ask a question like, "Is bloom like appearing?"
Then, appearance and extinction, or the idea of flowers blossoming and leaves falling would not be understood. For instance, they would not understand the

sentence, 'the beauty of cherry blossoms coming into full blossom and falling the next moment is sorrowful'. Death would be nothing but vanishing, neither beautiful nor ugly.

Flowers are beautiful because they fall. They would not appeal to people at all if they did not fall. I think the fact that flowers fall or wither appeals to people's sentiments and gives them peace.

People love flowers because they fall. People try to take care of flowers by watering them and exposing them to fresh air. This tenderness helps give serenity to people in their everyday lives. If flowers did not exist, different seasons might have been expressed using fruit instead. In the past, every season had its own characteristic fruit and vegetables.

This is not true anymore. There are all kinds of fruit and vegetables available all year regardless of season, which might confuse people's senses.

The same is true of children's songs; "My hometown I used to live in was a mountain village full of flowers; peach blossoms, apricot blossoms, and azaleas."

How could we explain this without flowers? I stopped my car on the way to Seonheul. Wild roses were in bloom entangled by a thick vine. Charmed by them, I was wondering how I could pluck a flower. Wild roses had more thorns, and the thorns were sharper.

A purple wild flower could be barely seen among the tangled stems of the wild roses. If I had not taken a close look, it would have bloomed and faded without anybody noticing it.

The beauty of flowers lies in their modesty: they bloom without fanfare, struggle against the wind, bask in the warm sunshine, and finally wither after a short while.

People would be miserable if there were no flowers. To buy and plant flowers is not the only thing that makes people's lives rich. People feel joy in appreciating flowers quietly and reverently without knowing who planted them.

I thought about this while planting flowers in flowerpots and I wondered if perhaps flowers might possibly disappear one day.

Myung-Chul Cho

The Traveler's Teahouse

Writer's Introduction
First recognized in the monthly *Essay Literature*. Board member of the Korean Essayists Association and the Korean Literature Association.
Publications: *Wife's Smile Woongnyeo's Smile, Traffic Lights and Dolharbahng, Going Wind and Coming Light*, etc.
Address: 701 Seobahn Apts, 132-44 1-Do 2-dong, Jeju city, Jeju-do, Republic of Korea
Phone: (064) 757-3535, 011-665-7656

The Traveler's Teahouse

When my head is cluttered with thoughts and I feel stuffy, I temporarily stop what I'm doing and go find 'The Traveler's Teahouse'. If it's a pleasant, refreshing day, that's even better, but rainy days are fine, too. It doesn't matter whether the sun is shining or not. The cold wind streaks across the landscape and takes all my worries away. When I return to my work and sit down in the company of an agreeable female, I couldn't ask for anything more.

If you're in Jeju, take the Eastern Industrial Road at a good speed for about 20 minutes or so and you'll reach the exit ramp for Namjo Road. Take this road a little ways to the east, and on your right side you'll be greeted by a brown sign indicating the entrance to 'Sangumburi'. If you go to the end of the road, you'll see a shabby yet quiet-looking house. This is 'The Traveler's Teahouse.'

At the entrance to the yard, there's a pile of rocks resembling a pagoda that looks as if it's standing there to ward off evil spirits. Opposite this are two hills, one to the right and left, which appear as if they're making room for something. These hills are not so remarkable, as is the characteristic of all such hills in Jeju. However, they could be trusted to act as wind breaks in the case of strong winds. They look like they were ready to stand upright to block any wind gusts. The hills appear to be bent over, breathing slowly.

If one turns one's gaze to the southwest, the peak of Halla Mountain seems to connect with the gentle ridge line of *Gwagori Oreum* spreading out to the southeast. It seems as if the hills around 'The Traveler's Teahouse' were poised to engulf the teahouse at any time. The place is perfect for enjoying peace and tranquility or just for taking a rest.

Upon entering the house, one is greeted with the sound of quiet meditation music and the shopkeeper wears a simple smile for all guests. From the appearance of the shopkeeper, she is a middle-aged woman who might be trying to follow the path of a Buddhist nun. Perhaps because she hasn't been able to wash away the afflictions of the world or something, but from time to time, her countenance appears dark. The fate of all human beings for eons has been nothing but suffering, so it's no surprise that one can't escape affliction and pain so easily.

As the seasons change their clothes, the mountains change their appearance like one who has picked their own outfit. The winds whistle by, carrying the news of fate. The moon chats with the wind and shines down on the whole world without regard for who might be below. The beautiful bird songs of the birds flying from Gwagori Oreum are associated with the house servants of yore.

The sound alone is sufficient for washing away the filth of this world. The path to enlightenment lies here, so take your time.

Ah, the Traveler's Teahouse! Every time I go there the fragrance softens my heart. If you go there in the winter, you will find a rustic, old country atmosphere complete with the scent of firewood burning in the fireplace. In the spring, you can see picked wild flowers put in a vase, evoking childhood memories of flowers lining country roads. In one corner of the room, a candle and incense is burning, from which the profound fragrance of incense fills the room. It seems as if the fragrance could soften the harshness of this world of pain and suffering. My body feels like it was on fire and I could feel my mind at ease.

The fragrance of the tea poured from a roughly-textured tea bowl contributed to the tranquil atmosphere. Also, the sesame seed sujaebi (a Korean pasta shell soup) I ordered to satisfy my hunger had a delicious aroma that further heightened my senses. In an environment where all the smells and aromas come from nature, I couldn't help but feel meditative. I felt like nature's magical healing power was soothing my soul.

I sat down and remained motionless while looking around the room. My gaze rested upon the many pieces of pottery lying all around the floor, wherever space would permit. It seemed like the number of pottery pieces increased every time I visited. I silently looked at all the masterpieces and thought to myself that they all resembled travelers who had wandered to this place from some place unknown. Perhaps they were all resting their weary bodies here, or maybe they were all making sighs of longing for their hometowns which they left behind. It might even be possible that they were just biding their time, humming songs while waiting for their new owner to come along. When I stood up, it seemed like all of the pieces of pottery were welcoming me with endlessly open arms and I had a special karma with the pottery, so a long time ago, I started buying the pottery one by one each time I visited the Traveler's Teahouse.

The shopkeeper always tries to wear a smile. Maybe it was because she would like to pass on some of the warmth she'd gleaned from friendly conversations she'd had with other travelers. It is said that the path to Nirvana lies in emptying oneself and giving up desire. However, because the shopkeeper can't give up even the small desire of sharing fellowship with other people, her path to enlightenment seems flawed.

Everything in existence looks in transit- we are all travelers. All things in nature are ceaselessly changing and we are all headed somewhere. Even manufactured products break down someday, just as all living things head inexorably toward death. There is nothing eternal in this life.

In spite of this fact, we all live our lives as if we have forgotten that we are just passing through. We live our lives under the false impression that we are immortal. How foolish this is! We are like mice busily running on an exercise wheel while chanting the mantra, 'busy, busy, busy'. If we live like this, how can we ever hope to escape from pain and affliction?

"If one doesn't rest soundly, the night is long, and for exhausted travelers, even a short distance is like a long way. For those who aren't enlightened, life is a constant cycle of rebirth in the haze of darkness."

This is an excerpt from the Buddhist sacred text. It is Buddha's admonition to those of us who live like slaves to desire. Buddha exhorts us to give up all attachments.

Today the sunlight is warm. The mountains and fields in late spring and early summer have ripened into a verdant fullness. The golden rays of sunlight and cool autumn breeze dance and ripple on a wavy sea of emerald leaves. An idle and tranquil world spreads out before us.

Outside, next to the field, there are empty cans dangling by strings from an oak tree. As the wind blows, they twist to and fro in the wind. This is called 'natural art'. The Korean expression, 'empty carts are the noisiest' comes to mind.

The sound of empty cans knocking against each other in the wind and the whistling sound of the breeze make my heart feel lighter as I leave the Traveler's Teahouse. I feel like a traveler who has unloaded excess baggage. The wind blowing in through the car window couldn't be sweeter. (2001)

제주펜무크 ❷

돌과 바람의 꿈

■ 영어번역 박경란

Je
Ju

푸른사상

'제주PEN 무크' 제2집을 내며

오성찬
(제주PEN 회장)

지난해 이맘때 회원들의 작품을 영역하여 제주PEN 무크(1) 『The Winds of Jeju Island』를 내고, 이어 다시 두 번째 책을 내는 기쁨은 크다. 이 모두가 회원 여러분의 적극적인 동참에 의해서 이뤄지는 것으로, 격려와 고마움을 전한다.

지난해 떨리는 마음으로 번역·출판작업을 서둘렀으며, 그 결과는 일단 성공적이었다. 우리는 발간한 책을 국내는 물론 국제PEN 회원국 중 50여 개 나라 140여 분의 대표와 임원들에게 보냈다. 그 후 미국에 있는 국제PEN클럽 망명작가 센터 미국지부 IrYna Dybko Firipchak 회장을 비롯해서 런던, 샌프란시스코 등 몇 군데의 대표들로부터 뜨거운 격려의 편지를 받았다. 그들의 반응은 "우리는 제주도라는 새로운 지역의 문학과 만났다."는 반가운 내용이었다.

이것은 어쩌면 의례적인 것이라고 말할 수도 있겠지만, 그러나 이런 격려가 있었기에 우리는 두 번째 무크지를 내면서 더욱 신바람이 났던 것이다.

제주PEN 무크 두 번째 책의 제목은 '돌과 바람의 꿈'이라고 지어봤다. 잘 알려져 있는 대로 우리 고장 제주 섬은 돌 많고, 바람 많고, 여자가 많은 삼다三多의 섬이다. 그와 비교되는 개념으로 "도둑 없고, 거지

없으니 대문조차 만들어 달 필요가 없는" 삼무三無의 미풍은 오랜 동안 우리의 긍지이기도 했다. 그런 중에도 거치른 돌과 거센 바람은 이 섬에서 살아온 우리 선인들이 극복하지 않으면 안될 우선적 대상이었던 것이다. 따라서 그들의 역사, 그들의 꿈은 이것들을 극복하는 한 과정이었다고 해도 과언이 아닐 것이다. 그런 뜻에서 책의 제목을 선택했음을 밝힌다.

이 책에 실린 시, 소설, 희곡, 아동문학, 수필 등 작품들은 모두 제주 PEN클럽 회원들이 스스로 골라 낸 것들이다. 이 작품들을 제주대학교 통역대학원 부설 통역번역센터 주임교수인 박경란님이 여름내 더위와 싸우면서 번역해 주셨으며, 센터 여러분이 교정, 편집 등을 도왔다. 그 정성과 노력에 대해서도 고마운 인사를 드린다.

아울러 이 사업 역시 지난해에 이어 제주도의 지원으로 이루어졌음을 밝힌다.

수월찮은 여건 속에서도 우리의 문학작품 번역, 배포 작업은 앞으로도 계속될 것임을 다짐하며 약속드린다.

2005년 겨울

□ 차례

□ '제주PEN 무크' 제2집을 내며 • 오성찬 • 219

■ 시 · 시조

- 양중해 227
  가장 아름다운 별은 • 228   유적지에서 • 230
- 강통원 232
  제주도 Ⅱ • 233   제주도 Ⅲ • 235
- 김승립 237
  등외품等外品 • 238   이파리 • 239
- 김양수 240
  면벽面壁 • 241   커피를 마시며 • 243
- 김용길 245
  하류下流에서 • 246   가을 숲에서 • 248
- 김종두 249
  대학낭 • 250   서귀포 겨울 1 • 252
- 나기철 253
  서귀포에는 내가 • 254   겨울 비자림에서 • 256

▫ 돌과 바람의 꿈

- 문태길 ··· 257
  - 마라도 등대 • 258　　매화 • 260
- 신승행 ··· 261
  - 빠스까의 4월 • 262　　제주찬가 • 266
- 양전형 ··· 267
  - 구억리 • 268　　조천리 쑥부쟁이 • 270
- 오영호 ··· 271
  - 화산도 오름에 오르다 • 272　　행원리에 가면 • 273
- 윤봉택 ··· 274
  - 그리움이 없는 곳에서 • 275　　빗물은 • 276
- 정인수 ··· 277
  - 낚시 • 278　　연가戀歌 • 280
- 한기팔 ··· 282
  - 섬 • 283　　내 오후의 인생人生 • 284

□ 차례

■ 소설

• 최현식 ··· 287
　먼 산山 • 288

• 고시홍 ··· 315
　표류하는 이어도 • 316

• 오성찬 ··· 337
　달 뜨는 내 고향 • 338

■ 아동문학

• 강순복 ··· 363
　장롱 속의 새 모시옷 • 364

• 박재형 ··· 372
　까마귀 오서방 • 373

ㅁ 돌과 바람의 꿈

■ 희곡

• 장일홍 385
　우리를 잠들게 하는 새들의 합창合唱 • 386

■ 수필

• 강태국 415
　줄탁동기啐啄同機 —깨달음의 순간 • 416
• 김가영 420
　내 가슴은 꽃이어라 • 421
• 조명철 424
　길섶 나그네 • 425

시 · 시조

가장 아름다운 별은 · 유적지에서
제주도Ⅱ · 제주도Ⅲ
등외품 · 이파리
면벽 · 커피를 마시며
하류에서 · 가을 숲에서
대학낭 · 서귀포 겨울 1
서귀포에는 내가 · 겨울 비자림에서
마라도 등대 · 매화
빠스까의 4월 · 제주찬가
구억리 · 조천리 쑥부쟁이
화산도 오름에 오르다 · 행원리에 가면
그리움이 없는 곳에서 · 빗물은
낚시 · 연가
섬 · 내 오후의 인생

양중해

가장 아름다운 별은
유적지에서

필자 소개
《사상계》를 통해 데뷔.
한국문협 제주도지부장과 한국예총 제주도지부장 역임. 한국문화원연합회 제주도 지부장, 국제펜클럽 한국본부 이사(현)
시집 「파도」 「한라별곡」 「수평선」

가장 아름다운 별은

양중해

넓은 우주 안에서
가장 아름다운 별은
지구라는 별이리라.

아침
동쪽 하늘에서 솟아오르는 해보다도
깊은 밤
높은 산을 넘는 달보다도
밤 하늘
은하수로 흐르는 어느 별보다도
가장 아름다운 별은
지구.

하늘에는 별도 많지만
우리가 살고 있는
오직 하나의 별,
산이 있고 바다가 있고,
산과 바다에는 비가 내리고 바람이 불고,
풀과 나무들이 꽃을 피우고 열매를 맺고,
새와 짐승

버러지들까지도 사랑을 하고……

이 넓은 우주 공간의
수 많은 별들 가운데
이렇게 아름다운 별이
지구 말고 다시 있으랴?

사람들아!
별을 사랑하자.
우리를 사랑하고
우리가 사랑할 수 있는 별,
별 가운데서도 가장 아름다운 별,
지구를 사랑하자.

풀과 나무들이
새와 짐승들이
지구를 사랑하듯
우리도 가장 아름다운 별
지구를 사랑하자.

유적지에서

여기는
더 떠밀려날 수도 없는
하늘 가
극악의 유적지.
한양에서 맺힌 한이
섬 끝까지 흘러와
물결 소리로 울던 곳.

종일을 기다리고
다시 기다려도
사람은 없고,
그리움의 수평선
망망한 바다만,
바다가 울부짖는
물결 소리만,

사람들아 잊지를 말아!
이 섬 끝에서
바다하고 울다가 떠난
한이 있었음을,

그 한이
오늘도
물결 소리로 울고있는 내력을.

* 조선왕조 궁중비극의 한 여주인공 인목대비의 친모인 광산부부인 노(盧)씨가 제주 섬에서 6년 동안 유배되었다가 풀려 돌아갔다. 지난 3월 27일 그 슬픈 사연을 오래 간직하고자 제주 섬 동쪽 산자락에 <대비공원>이 마련되고, 기적비가 세워지고 있다.

강통원

제주도 Ⅱ
제주도 Ⅲ

필자 소개
제주대학교 영어영문학과 졸업, 명예문학박사. 1977년 《시문학》으로 등단.
한국예총 제주도지부장과 한국문협 제주도지부장 역임. 한국현대시협 중앙위원. 한국시문학회 지도위원., 제주대학교 명예교수(현)
시집 『무적 霧笛』 『상류와 하류』 『Cheju island Eulalia Flower』

제주도 Ⅱ

강통원

제주도濟州道는 하나의 창窓
하늘을 향하여
빛을 향하여
무시무종 열어 놓은
지상地上의 창
자연의 창으로 여기에 있다.
사시 장철 열려 있는
창을 통하여 빛나는
빛의 세계.
천지 개벽의 여명에
어느 신神이 바라보았던
원초의 빛
생명의 빛이
하늘의 은총으로
하염없이 쏟아져 내린다.
영원히 닫히지 않는
제주도의 창窓
제주濟州의 빛.
한정없는 되풀이의
탄생과 사멸

죽음과 부활復活이
제주濟州의 창과 더불어
빛과 더불어 무시무종하다.

제주도 Ⅲ

사람과 사람들 사이에
살아가는 일로 하여
가슴 쓰릴 때
제주濟州여
하루에도 몇 번이고
지척에 두고서도
山이 그립고
바다가 그리워
山이여 바다여 라고 부르면
제주에서는
그것이 그냥 한라산漢拏山이 되고
제주바다가 되므로
내 이 지상地上
어느 산굽이 물굽이에서도
고향 그립고
고향의 산과 바다가 그리워
아아 山이여 바다여 라고 다시 부르면
그것은 그냥 제주도濟州島가 되고
한라산이 되고
제주바다가 되어

깨어 있거나
감은 눈 속에도
선연한 모습
눈 시리도록 새파란
빛으로 다가오는
한라산이여 제주바다여
사랑하는 제주濟州여.

김승립

**등외품
이파리**

필자 소개
제주시 이도2동 402-11, 064)753-3185, 019-9101-3185
시집 『등외품等外品』

등외품等外品

김승립

한일소주 경품시절이었습니다.

가겟집 아저씨는 이십오도二十五度짜리 한일 소주를 썩 잘 즐겼습니다. 창밖에는 이십오도二十五度의 취기로 반짝이는 눈〔雪〕이 몇 개씩 쌓였고 아저씨는 조금쯤은 우리나라 기침소리를 흘렸습니다. 멀리 아저씨가 비운 두홉들이 깡소주 딱지는 그러나 아저씨의 퀭한 얼굴처럼 동그라미가 멋적게 앉아 있었습니다.

그후로 아저씨는 등외품等外品이었고 우리나라 기침소리를 한층 잘했고 그 겨울 아저씨는 아저씨가 사랑하는 아저씨의 이십오도二十五度짜리 두홉들이 한일소주를 끊었습니다. 가겟집 지붕도 어깨가 몰래 내려앉았고 등외품等外品 눈만 비인 소주병에 자꾸만 쌓였습니다.

이파리

1

못생긴 산山
내 사랑 맑은 눈동자에는
깊은 가을 맨 나중 떨어지는
참 바보 같은 나뭇잎 하나
흐르고 있다.

2

우리나라 어느 귀퉁이에는
팍팍한 가슴 안에 없는 듯
앉아 있던 한숨들이
사랑소리 잦아지며 잦아지며
쌓이고 있는 줄이야.

김양수

면벽
커피를 마시며

필자 소개
1990년 5월 심상지 신인상으로 등단.
시집 『바람도 휴식이 그리울 것이다』 외 4권 상재.
산문집 『추억은 초콜릿처럼 달콤하고』 외
제주문인협회, 한국시인협회, 심상시인회 회원

면벽面壁

김양수

내 산다는 것이
화롯불에 드는 한 점 눈꽃일지라도
내 살아 있다는 것이
잠시 눈을 감았다 뜨는 흔적일지라도
수면을 흔드는
일순의 파장만으로 뜨거워라
말문을 닫아걸고
마음마저 얼려 놓고
되돌릴 수 없는 먼길을 가듯
유년을 접고 나면
어둠은 역사로 새겨지고
밝음은 신화로 남는 것에 가슴저려라
본디
세상을 흔드는 것은 사람과 사람의 일이라지만
허공을 가두는 것은 바람이고
시공을 넘나드는 것은
목숨을 떨구는 한 잎 꽃이파리인 걸
잡히는 것이 다
내 것이 아님으로 한숨보다 가벼워라

나를 버리고
오늘을 버리고
관계만으로 버거웠던 이름이거나
얼굴들을 버리고 나서야
홀연한
적광寂光을 만날 수 있음이라

나는 때때로 너를 마주하고
나를 지워 내는 연습만으로도
당산堂山보다 높은

준령을 가벼이 날아 오르는
호접胡蝶 마침내
푸른 바다에 이르러 온 몸이 풀려라.

커피를 마시며

일회용 종이컵에
인스턴트 봉지를 뜯고
물을 받는다.

불꺼진 창처럼 은근한 향내가
당신의 속내같이 아늑하다.

한 모금에
그리움이 데워지고
또 한 모금에
안타까움이 삭아지고
다시 한 모금에
당신과 내가 녹아드는 걸 안다.
급하지 않게
또는 너무 한적하지 않게
체액과도 같은 안부를 삼키면서
손안에 남는
온기를 오래, 되도록 깊이
간직하는 것은
얼마나 큰 기쁨인가
그러나

비어진 종이컵이
버림받은 가슴이 되어
소슬해지는 때,
그 아픔이 빈 하늘처럼
커가기만 할 때,
카페인에 감염된
내 사랑도 버려지는가 글썽여신다.

김용길

**하류에서
가을 숲에서**

필자 소개
제주도문화상(예술부문)과 서귀포시문화상 수상.
한국문협 서귀포지부장 역임.
시집 『바다와 섬의 이중주』 외
대한민국 제주도 서귀포시 서귀동 118 정방빌라 206
064)762-4943, 011-694-9229

하류下流에서

김용길

깜깜한 어둠 속
풀잎은 고개를 꺾고
바람으로 넘어서는
강울음 소리 들었다

이제 풀잎은 안다
강의 흐름이
끝난 데가 온 것을

하류下流의 언덕에 누워
떨어지는 별들의 이름을 외운다
사유思惟의 시간에
지워질 이름들

수천 리 지맥地脈을 짚고 돌아
침전되어오던 역사의 흐름
신음처럼 일어섰다 쓰러지던 물살

깊은 어둠을 뚫고
바다에 닿으면

강은 알리라
그어놓을 선線 하나 없는
외로운 방황의 시작인 것을.

가을 숲에서

신록의 무성한 시절이 있었다고
자랑하지 말라
부정사不定詞처럼
그대 마른 입술

아, 가을이다 말하기 전에
숲을 떠나지 말라
빈 계절의 산 그늘
발목 적시는 어둠

갈대처럼 몸을 꺾고
버려진 숲 속
이 몸 뉘인들
그대 나를 어쩌겠느냐

김종두

**대학낭
서귀포 겨울 1**

필자 소개
1976년 《소년》 지에 동시 추천. 전남아동문학가협회,
제주아동문학가협회 회장 역임. 한국문협 제주도지회장 역임.
한국아동문학상, 소청문학상, 전남아동문학가상 수상.
시집 『사는 게 뭣산디』 외, 동시집 『햇님이 사는 꽃밭』 외.

대학낭

김종두

어느 한 시절
밀감 나무를
대학낭이라 불렀지.

텃밭
밀감 나무 몇 그루로
자식들 대학공부 시켰다고 해서
대학낭이라 애지중지 했었지.

보리밥도 가리던 시절
노릇노릇 밀감 익어 가는 가을이 되면
밀감나무를 키우는 집
아방 어멍네들은 배가 불렀지.
황금 열매 바라보면서 빙긋이 웃었지.

밀감 팔아서 학자금 빚 갚고
아들 딸 시집 장가 보낼
혼수감 마련하면서도
힘이 났지.

지금이야
제주 천지 어딜 가나 밀감낭
그 흔한 나무가 되어
베어내고 뽑아버리는 나무가 되었지마는
어느 한 시절 밀감낭은
황금열매 여는 돈낭이라 했지.
대학낭이라 하며 대접받았지.

서귀포 겨울 I

밤새 내린 눈도
한낮 반짝 햇살이면
그냥 녹아 버리는
서귀포 물겨울

한라산정은
흰감티*를 눌러쓴 채
눌러앉아
상록常綠 포구 바라만 보네.

기력 잃은
남진 설풍
빙벽氷壁 타고 내려와
서귀포 앞바다에서
자맥질하고 있네.
벌써 봄을 건져내고 있네.

*감티 - 짐승 가죽으로 만든 모자.

나기철

서귀포에는 내가
겨울 비자림에서

필자 소개
1953년 서울 출생. 제주대 국문학과 졸업.
1987년 《시문학》으로 등단. 〈깨어있음의 시〉 동인
시집 『섬들의 오랜 꿈』 『남양여인숙』 『뭉게구름을 뭉개고』

서귀포에는 내가

나기철

서귀포에는 내가
달맞이꽃이라고 부르는 여자가 있다
바다 남빛 물결에
피는 꽃
수백 송이 흩으려 놓고
자지러지다가도
정작은 수줍은 달맞이꽃이
되고 싶은,

서귀포에는 내가
휘파람새라고 부르는 여자가 있다
이젠 반쪽의 자리가 비어도
슬프지 않고
아침 식탁에 수저가 한 벌이어도
외롭지 않다고
잠시 휘파람새가 되어 보는,

서귀포에는 내가
삼매봉이라고 부르는 여자가 있다.
어느 날 찾아가

시와 그림을 보고
한 바퀴 돌아 내려와
새섬 앞 통통배 소리처럼
떠내려가는 나를
잡아 주던
그 봉우리 같은,

겨울 비자림에서

하늘 향해
고갤 쳐들고 있는
오래된 비자나무 바라보면
씽, 씽, 씽,
바람 견디는

비자나무 숲에 와
고갤 쳐들고 있는
오래된 비자나무 바라보면

나도 천 년 만 년
죽지 않고 살 것 같다

문태길

마라도 등대
매화

필자 소개
한국문협 제주지회장 역임. 제주시민상 수상.
시집 『마라도 등대』 외

마라도 등대

문 태 길

그 누가
버렸는가
복숭아 씨알 하나

바위 틈에
싹이 돋아
별과 함께 살아간다.

친정집
그리울 때면
눈동자만 굴린다.

배 한척만
떠 있어도
섬은 외롭지 않다.

둥그런
수평선 끝
돛폭마저 잠기고 나면

뭍으로
뭍으로 향해
또 한 겹 갈기를 세운다.

안다. 그는 누군가에
기대고픈
사람들을

막내둥이 등대지기
마라도 등대지기를

북극성
차디찬 마음도
밤새 앓고 있었다.

매화

한라산 골골마다
잔설로 핀 이월인데

점잖은 촌 샌님도
아, 얼굴을 붉히십니까

움트던
수양버들도
다시 눈을 감는다.

한평생 살아봐도
못 다한 꿈이 있어

구천을 맴돌던 넋
등걸에 다시 돋아

증손댁
제사상 위에
피어오른 향이여.

신승행

빠스까의 4월
제주찬가

필자 소개
호 : 구산(龜山)
시인, 문학평론가
한국문인협회 회원, 한국문학비평가협회 부회장, 국제PEN클럽 제주지회 감사
저서 『언어와 문학의 만남』 『시가문학의 정체성』 『문학과 사랑』
시집 『섬바다 숨비소리』 『문풍지』

빠스까의 4월
- 4·3을 추도하며

신 승 행

<1>
4월은
지친 목소리가 있었습니다.

마음이 아프도록
숨이 차도록……
불기둥에는 가녀린 원혼들이 꽂혀 아스라이 있고
바다에는 톱상어 떼가
산에는 빨간 깃발들이
4월은
제주섬을 포식하고 있었습니다.

당신의
숨골은 온통
빈 아침을 맞았습니다.

<2>
4월은
지쳐, 삭풍에 몸살을 앓던 날

채찍당하던 우마는 쇠살쭈의 흥을 돋구고
세월은 흘렀어도

영 떠나질 않는
지친 목소리 그 4월이
낮에는 형제였고
밤에는 검붉은 벽에 앉아

당신은
골고타의 산길
또 긴 밤을 맞았습니다.

<3>
이 4월의 제주섬은
조각난 난파선처럼

팽나무 가지에는 아기 울음이 걸려 있고
포구에는 할퀸 파도가
다랑쉬 굴에도
가시나무에도

어찌하여 4월은
떠날 수 없는
지친 목소리가 되었습니까?

당신은
형틀로 묶인
다람쥐가 되었습니까?

<4>
이제, 4월은
한을 푸는 바라춤이 되었어라.

어둠은 빛으로
억압은 자유와 해방으로
이 4월은 빠스까*의 생명이 되었습니다.
대양에서 이어지는
젖줄 따며
시름 달래며……

들머리
제주의 4월은
민주 목소리가 되었습니다.

*빠스까(Pascha) : "부활"의 의미로 쓰이는 의식의 명칭.(過越祭)
*골고타(Golgotha) : "해골산"이라 함.

제주찬가

백두야 가슴을 펴라 한라는 춤을 추어라
여기는 세계가 살고 있는, 사랑이 움트는 곳
늘푸른 산과 바다 이어도라 구성진 노래
제주는 환상의 섬 내일을 심는 예술의 고장
아……
파도여
춤을 추어라
돛을 올려 함께 추어라.

태평양 푸른 꿈을 돛을 올려 함께 저어라
여기는 대양을 누비는, 젊음이 숨쉬는 곳
우리는 하늘을 품고 미래는 영원한 것을
제주는 모두의 쉼터 세계를 여는 평화의 고장
아……
파도여
춤을 추어라
돛을 올려 함께 추어라.

양전형

구억리
조천리 쑥부쟁이

필자 소개
한라산 문학동인. 열린문학상, 한국자유시인상 수상.
시집『나는 둘이다』『길에 사는 민들레』『사랑은 소리가 나지 않는다』 등.
(064)725-3960, 010-6685-3960
E-mail : yjh3960@hanmail.net

구억리*

양전형

얼마나 멀었으면
남제주 대정 구억리
오십 년 달려 마침내
풍진 세월을 겹겹이 누벼 입은
내 작은 이모의 옷자락을 봤다

무자년* 불길에 화 데일 즈음
생각이 서로 수억 리 먼 두 사람
생사를 가늠 못할 길 구억 리 달려와 담판하던
옛 학교터는 말이 없고
망동산* 까마귀의 목 잠긴 곡소리 아파라
지방틀 할망당*에 든 바람이
무시로 액막이 푸닥거리를 하지만
묵은 상처의 알갱이쯤은 묻어 둔다
파닥이는 텃새들의 도약
애당초 구억리의 꿈은 별이었다

구억리!
이보다 아득한 그리움이 어디 있으랴
효자비*에 한 절 하고

옹기파편을 줍는 길손이여
누구든 오래 걸은 자가 구억리에 닿는 것
구억리 하늘 아래 있으면 누구든
총총히 뜬 별 하나이지

*구억리(九億里) : 남제주군 대정읍에 있는 산간마을
*무자년 : 제주 4·3 사건이 난 해
*망동산 : 구억리에 있으며 옛날 망을 보던 동산
*지방틀 할망당 : 구억리에 있는 당으로 마을의 본향신
*효자비 : 구억리에 있는 박창진의 효자비

조천리 쑥부쟁이

조천리의 가을은 쑥부쟁이가 이고 온다
북망 가신 어머니들 모두 돌아와
마음을 활짝 열어 보이는 듯
신선한 갯바람 속 은은한 향 피우면서
마을 가득 가을을 드리운다

높은 하늘을 한층 더 밀어올리고
낮은 하늘에서 불꽃놀이를 벌인다
가지런한 얼굴 꽃잎은
언젠가 불을 쏘아 올리고 싶었던
불쟁이 딸의 전설처럼 아리땁다

길섶마다 몇 송이씩 더 피어오르면
가을 장만에 손 바빠지는 사람들
가슴이 차츰 부풀어 오르는 사람들
소식 없던 누가 행여 돌아오시려나
만세동산에 올라 먼 바다를 손짓하기도 한다

조천리의 설레임은 가을을 기다리는 일
조천리의 가을은 쑥부쟁이가 이고 온다

오영호

화산도 오름에 오르다
행원리에 가면

필자 소개
제주시조문학회 회장 역임.
한국시조시인협회 이사, 제주펜클럽 부지부장(현)
시집 『풀잎 만한 이유』 『화산도, 오름에 오르다』
한국시조비평문학상 수상

화산도 오름에 오르다

오영호

한라산자락 심줄들이 봉긋봉긋 솟아오른
너의 야윈 등을 다시 밟으며 오른다
내 발길 이끄는 대로
참회하며
가는 죄인.

반백년 삭힌 생각 툭툭 털고 피어 있는
제비꽃 춤사위를 그저 보고만 있다.
화산석 구멍 속으로 넘나드는 4월 바람.

이제는 탓할 언어 마저 멍들고 지쳐버린
어머님 젖무덤이 저리 고운 것은
오늘도 신원을 꿈꾸는
꽃이 핀다
꽃이 진다.

행원리에 가면

행원리 풍차들은 365일 깨어 있다

실바람만 다가와도 네덜란드 풍으로

날개 짓 에너질 모아 낯선 길도 밝힌다.

욕망도 부려놓고 슬픔도 부려놓은

바닷가 양어장 살 오른 넙치들도

팔려 갈 악몽을 꾸며 눈을 뜨고 자고 있다.

반좌욕을 하고 있는 집체만한 갯바위엔

파도에 머릴 감고 있는 풋풋한 톳나물을

망사리 가득가득 채워 끌고 오는 해녀들.

숨비소리 물속으로 천만 번 꺾어 들어

늙은 해녀의 집 기둥 하나 세울 때

바다는 또 하나의 섬을 가슴팍에 낳는다.

윤봉택

그리움이 없는 곳에서
빗물은

필자 소개
서귀포시 출생.
월간 《문예사조》 신인상 시 「바람 부는 섬」 외 당선.
시집 『농부에게도 그리움이 있다』 『이름 없는 풀꽃이 어디 있으랴』

그리움이 없는 곳에서

윤봉택

배를 타고 스르시 떠나면
갓밝이에는
그 섬에 닿을 수 있으리
그리움은 뱃길 끊겨도
자꾸만 흘러가는데,
느꺼운 불빛 타고 밀려오는
머언 섬의 아픈 너울들
그대 그 곳에 있어
그리움이 남아 있는
가난한 포구에 기대어
기다리는 난파된 영혼의 그림자
돌아누워도 감기지 않은
그리움 가득 안고
하늬바람 불면
어느 곳을 향해
그대 돛을 올리리

빗물은

스미는 것
흐르다, 겨울강 하구로 머물다
그대 만나면 닻 내리고
지나가면
강물 아래로 기다리다
꺾이고 돌아와 굽이쳐 가는 것
빗물이여
오! 빈貧물이여
물物밖으로 흐르다
그대 다시 만나면, 되넘어
울어 삭히고
칭원허게 빚어 가다
빈貧물로 옷 벗어
돌아가야 하는 것을
......

정인수

낚시
연가

필자 소개
1974년 《한국문학》 신인상 당선. 제주도문화상 수상.
시집 『삼다도』

낚시

정인수

우도*가 보이는 바다에 서면
홀로라도 외롭지 않다.
낚싯줄을 던지나 마나
심심찮아서 좋다.

바다 하나 가득 넙죽이 엎드린 우두봉*이
느긋하게 쓰다듬어 내려온 품속에
섬마을이 아슴푸레 잠들었고,
산호사* 해안에 밀리는
파도가 눈부시다.

낚싯대 끝으로 하늘을 재고
답답한 세상 후려치듯
하늘을 치면
휘파람 불며 날아가는 포물선….

살아온 세월
아무리 헛살았어도
포물선은 제대로 그어야 한다.

소라 속 뒤틀린 세상 빠져나와
우도가 보이는 바다에 서서
우도까지 포물선을 던지자.

*牛島: 제주도 구좌읍 종달리에서 약 2.8km 떨어져 있는 섬. 엎드린 소 같다하여 우도
 라 함.
*牛頭峰: 우도의 머리부분의 봉우리. 등대가 있음.
*珊瑚砂: 우도남쪽 해안에 길게 펼쳐진, 희귀한 산호사 백사장

연가 戀歌

여름 땡볕 내려 쬐는 대낮엔
비자림*에서 만나요.
그리운 사람끼리 둘이서.
웃통은 벗지 말아요.
아름드리 비자나무가 내뿜는 태고의 바람이
겨드랑이까지 간질여줄 터이니
코를 풀지 말아요.
풍란을 품어 기르는 가지마다 여물어가는 비자향기….

만장굴*에서 만나요.
사시사철 언제나,
외로운 사람끼리 둘이서.
끌어안지 말아요.
만장을 가다보면 업고 가는 일도 있을 터이니.
소리 지르지 말아요.
천년 잠든 용암들이 용틀임으로 깨어나는 소리….

한 여름 밤에는
토끼섬*에서 만나요.
이별을 앞둔 사람끼리 둘이서.
투정부리지 말아요.

달빛내린 문주란꽃밭 속에만 파묻혀 있으면
꽃잎들이 다 알아서
빛바랜 사랑을 쓰다듬어 줄 터이니.
손뼉 치지 말아요.
파도가 물장구치며 들려주는 축복의 노래….

*비자림 : 제주도 구좌읍 평대리 지경에 자생하고 있는 비자나무 원시림.
*만장굴 : 제주도 구좌읍 김녕리 지경에 있는 용암동굴. 길이가 만장(萬丈)이라 하여 만장굴(萬丈窟)임
*토끼섬 : 제주도 구좌읍 하도리 바닷가에 있는 문주란 군락지의 작은 섬.

한기팔

섬
내 오후의 인생

필자 소개
1975년 《심상》으로 등단.
한국문협 제주도지부장, 한국문협 서귀포지부장 역임.
제주도문화상, 서귀포시민상, 제주문학상 수상.
시집 『말과 침묵 사이』 외 5권.

섬

한기팔

시詩를 쓰다가
망연히
달이 기우는 서쪽으로
섬 그늘 물소리 잦아지면
나도 때로는
그렇게 세상 밖으로
나앉고 싶어집니다.

밀리는 파돗소리도
바람의 해맑은 울림도
그 섬의 울음소리만 같아
잡동사니 생각 다 풀어놓고
뒤척이고 뒤척이다
잠 못 이룬 밤
불빛 하나 얻어서
내가 섬이 되면

내 오후의 인생人生

발을 씻으며
내 작은 발가락 끝의
티눈을 들여다 보며
물 한 모금 떠 마시고
남은 물을 휙 뿌려버리는
내 오후의 인생人生
삶이란 또 무엇이냐
돋보기 안경 너머
가늘게 떠는 하늘의 거울 속을
언뜻 비치다 사라지는 새들처럼
무엇인가 놓치고 마는
나의 일상日常
밤마다 쏟아지는 너무 많은 별들
난 그 별들의 이름을 모른다

소설

먼 산
표류하는 이어도
달 뜨는 내 고향

최현식

먼 산

필자 소개
1924년 11월 28일(음력) 함경남도 홍원 출생.
1957년 조선일보 신춘문예에 소설 「노루」 당선.
한국문협, 국제PEN클럽, 한국소설가협회, 한국문협 제주지회 회원(현)
소설집 『홍상紅裳』 『흑묘일기黑描日記』 『먼 산山』 등.

먼 산山

최현식

밖에 눈이 흩뿌려지고 있었다.
나는 T씨에게 탐석探石을 가자고 전화를 걸었다.
"어디로 가 볼까요?"
T씨는 쾌히 응하고 행선을 물었다.
"세천교 쪽으로 가 봤으면 싶습니다만…."
"간 밤 눈에 횡단로가 막혀 버리지 않았을까요?"
"아침 뉴스론 마이크로 버슨 다니고 있대요."
"눈은 계속 쌓이고 있을 건데요?"
"막혔으면 돌아올 셈으루…."
열한시에 버스터미널에서 만나기로 약속했다.
우수철의 큰 강설은 20년래의 일이라는 것이다. 그러나 적설은 한라산뿐이고 바닷가서는 쌓이질 않았다. 기온은 해발 100미터를 한 금으로 1도씩 내린다고 한다. 그러니까 항구에서의 0도는 해발 1천950미터의 정상에서 영하 19도가 된다는 셈인 것이다.
일요일이어서 그런지 버스는 붐비지 않았다.
차는 바닷가를 벗어나 횡단로의 눈길에 들면서 숨이 가빠지기 시작했다. 해발 500…700, 1도씩 내린다는 기온을 적설량이 나타내고 있었다. 제설은 되어 있지만 싸락눈이 안개처럼 내리고 있었다.

"싸락눈이라기보다 눈안개라고 말하는 것이 좋겠군요."

나는 T씨에게 창 밖을 가리켜 보였다.

"이런 설무는 한라산이 아니면 볼 수가 없지요. 안개의 저 습기 때문에 조난을 당하게 된다고 합니다. 몸에 붙으면 잘 털어지질 않는다는군요."

"정말 신기하군요."

감탄해 보이는데,

"아바이네 함경도 눈은 어떱니까?"

T씨는 농조일 때의 아바이를 꺼내고 눈웃음을 짓는다.

"꽃송이 같은 함박눈이죠. 밤새 소리없이 내리군 하는…."

"많이 쌓이겠군요?"

"그렇죠, 녹을 것 같다가는 다시 쌓이군 하면서 3월 중순까지 가지요."

"올해도 서울의 화가들이 설경을 잡으려고 많이들 내려온 모양입니다만, 제주의 설경은 그리기가 매우 힘이 드는 소재라고 합니다."

"왤까요? 같은 설경일 텐데요."

"언어들은 지식입니다만, 한라산의 관성은 편광이어서 풍경 전체가 완전한 백색이거나, 역광일 때는 완전한 회색이 되고 말기 때문에 포인트를 어디에다 둬야 할지 당황하게 된다는군요."

"완전한 회색이라구요?…."

혼잣말을 중얼거리는데,

"그런 잡을 수 없는 포인트로 해서 캔버스를 회색의 범벅으로 망쳐놓게 된다는군요."

T씨는 덧붙였다.
"네…."
나는 조금 멍해지는 기분으로 담배를 붙여 물었다.
윈도 브러시가 쉼없이 설무로 흐르는 시야를 닦아내고 있었다.
"겨울의 제주도는 회색의 범벅이라는 표현이 맞겠군요. 그리고 보니 제가 잃어버린 먼 산도 회색에 속하는 돌이었군요."
나는 말하고 줄곧 창 밖에만 눈을 주고 있는 T씨의 얼굴을 살폈다.
"그 돌, 제주 먹돌의 산수경석으론 일품이었지요. 누구의 심술인지는 몰라도 정말 아까운 것을 잃었어요."
T씨는 눈을 밖에 준 채 말했다.
"아깝기야, T형의 목자석이죠."
"애정은 마찬가지가 아닐까요."
"잊어버리기로 했습니다만…."
…'먼 산'은 먹돌에 가까운 암회색의 경석景石이었다. 수석으로 가장 알맞다는 좌우 30센티미터의 크기였다. 진흑석이라기엔 석질이 좀 약하다는 평이 되겠지만, 그렇다고 배(梨) 살갗도 아니었다. 먹사오기(산벚꽃나무) 맏침에 앉혀 놓으니, 그 단순과 한적의 운치는 한결 더 유달라지는 것이었다.

'먼 산'은 내가 수석이라는 것을 배우기 시작하여 얼마 안된 때의 수확이었다. 6년 전 상석회賞石會에 어울리게 되면서 거의 매 일요일을 돌 찾으러 다녔었다. 혼자일 적도 있었지만 대개는 회원들하고의 동행이 되었다. 외도천外都川, 성산포城山浦, 비양도飛揚島, 가파도加波島로 돌들의 체온을 더듬어 다녔었다.

입문 1년여, 어느 쾌청한 늦가을 날이었다. 세천교를 찾아 혼자서 억새꽃의 한라산 횡단로를 넘게 되었다. 서귀포에서 동으로 반 시간을 더 버스를 타야 하는 먼 길이었다. 아침 여섯시에 집을 나섰다. 마침 택시 합승을 잡게 되어 횡단로로 서귀포까지 한 시간, 버스를 갈아타고 세천교 어귀의 S마을에 닿은 것은 여덟시가 좀 지나서였다.

마을은 고구마 수확이 한창이었다. 귤나무들과 해묵은 동백나무들의 푸르름 때문인지 풍요하다는 첫인상이었다.

버스를 내린 나는 주춤 걸음을 멈추었다. 직선으로 나 있는 길 저편 동쪽 끝에서 상여가 오고 있었다.

버스는 길을 피하듯 머뭇머뭇 멀어져 가고, 그 빈 자리에 백지만으로 새로 장식한 상여가 천천히 이쪽으로 다가오고 있었다. 아침 햇빛 속에 상여는 깨끗했고, 장렬은 아주 길었다.

"큰 집에 상 난 거군요…."

나는 눈웃음으로 내 바로 곁에 있는 사나이의 시선을 사로잡았다.

"아니우다."

예순일여덟 살 가량 나 뵈는 사나이는 고개를 저어 보이고는,

"해녀장이우다."

했다.

아흔한 살의 원로 해녀가 세상을 떠나, 마을의 모든 해녀들이 모여서 장사를 치른다는 것이었다.

  요 세상 살단 사름
  무신 일로 죽었는고
  에형어야 어화로세
  이제 가믄 어느제 오코
  한 번 가믄 못 올 질가
  어헹어야 어화로세…

먹이며 받으며 출렁이는 노랫소리는 무척 낭랑하고, 장렬은 어느 한

구석도 드티질 않는 정연함이었다.
 나는 가슴께에 손을 모아 쥐는 뿌듯함으로 멍하니 서 있었다.
 장렬은 마을을 벗어나서 산길로 드는 모퉁이께로 멀어져 갔다.
 비탈길로 들어서게 되었는지 노랫소리가 멎었다.
 …그렇구나, 해녀들만으로 상여를 지고 해녀들만으로 무덤을 만들어서, 아흔 한 살의 긴 바다생활을 회향回向한 한 노인의 마지막을 완성하였다.
 나는 속으로 이런 말을 뇌까리며 그곳을 떠났다. 마을 동쪽이라는 세천교를 향해 발걸음을 옮겨 갔다.
 두어 참이 되는 길이었다. 제주 특유의 쓸쓸한 마른내에 이르렀다. 아득히, 동지나해의 수평선. 바다는 유난히 잔잔하다
 나는 다리 아래켠의 개펄을 택했다. 석질이 좋아뵈는 먹돌이 깔려 있었다.
 인기척에 숨어 버리는 간조선干潮線의 게들과 해조음뿐으로 사위는 죽은 듯한 고요였다.
 …전석불생태轉石不生苔… 구르는 돌에 이끼가 나지 않는다. 이것이 암석미의 제일장이라고 누군가가 가르쳤었지….
 나는 뜨적뜨적 쉼없이 움직였다.
 이렇듯 세 시간여, 나는 문득 허리를 일으켜서 사위를 두리벙벙 살펴보았다. …나 혼자였구나… 종일을… 이런 쾌청인데… 이 적막은?….
 나는 해녀들의 상여가 올라갔을 산을 헤아려 보았다. 짙푸른 하늘과 검붉게 물들어 있는 단풍뿐으로 전혀 잡히는 것이 없었다. 비이이 비이이. 바다 쪽에서 새의 울음소리 같은 소리가 설핏 귓전을 스쳐 갔다. 시선을 들어 소리의 모습을 찾는다. 그러나 수평선과 범섬뿐, 고깃배 하나 떠 있지 않는 망망한 해면이었다.

…이 허허막막은 웬일일까? 아흔 한 살 해녀의 명복을 비는 날이어서….

나는 한동안 해조음 속에 스스로를 잊고 있다가 다시 탐석을 시작했다.

그러할 무렵에 나는 '먼 산'을 만난 것이다. 그리고 이 하나만으로 서둘러서 세천교를 떠난 것이었다.

그로부터 일주일 후에 '먼 산'에게는 먹사오기의 받침이 주어졌고, 책상 위에서 나하고의 대화가 시작된 것이다.

나의 '먼 산'. 왼편으로 주봉을 놓고 능선 하나로 밋밋하니 흘러내린 산, 우리 나라 어느 산하 어디서나 흔케 접할 수 있는 평범한 야산, 그런 단순함인 것이다.

그런데 어느 날 밤, 밖에서 술이 거나해져 집에 돌아온 나는 책상을 마주하게 되자 부지중 이런 노래를 응얼거리게 된 것이었다.

> 옛날의 금잔디 동산에
> 매기 같이 앉아서 놀던 곳
> 물레방아소리 들린다.
> 매기 내 사랑하는 매기야.

…나이 오십에 이 무슨 얄팍스러움이냐! 나는 눈에 물기를 담을 뻔한 스스로를 아프게 뉘우쳤다. 그러나 뇌리에 휘돌다 멈추면서 마침내는 노래를 응얼거리게까지 한 그것은 떠나 주질 않고, 머릿속은 더욱 맑아지기만 하는 것이었다.

나는 눈에 힘을 주어 '먼 산'을 다시 지켜보기 시작했다.

그것은 40년 전의 우리 마을의 뒷동산이었다. 남녘 기슭의 소나무밭을 제외하면 잔디 일색의 벌거숭이였다. 꼭대기에서 여남은 살의 소년들이 종이비행기를 날리고 있었다. 명태와 털게의 겨울은 한정없이 길기만 하다. 그 깊은 겨울잠에서 깨어나는 환희는 날 것만 같은 것이었으리라. 종이비행기에 싫증이 난 소년들은 전쟁놀이로 기분을 바꾼다. 편을 갈라 산꼭대기를 차지하는 공방전이 벌어진다. 겨루기를 여러 차례, 마침내 지쳐서들 쓰러진다. 모두들 잔디 위에 벌렁 나뒹군다. 후우후우, 숨결을 가라앉힌다. 이윽고 바람소리가 귀에 또렷해진다. 새 잔디의 흙 냄새도 깨닫는다. 이번엔 무슨 놀이로 신바람을 낸다? 몸을 일으킨다… "야, 꽃이야!" 목소리에 엉거주춤들 모여든다. "야, 정말 꽃이구나!" 믿어지지 않는다는 놀라움들로 오랑캐꽃은 에워싸인다. "야, 여기두…노랑꽃이다!" 목소리의 자리에는 민들레 꽃망울.

나는 그 금잔디 동산의 꽃들을 보고 있는 것이다.

그런데 이상하게도 소년들의 얼굴이며 이름은 생각해 낼 수가 없었다. 단 하나만이라도 생각해 내자고 기억을 한 곬으로 몰아세워 보았으나 끝내 안 되었고, 뇌리는 조그만 오랑캐꽃 모습만으로 더욱 맑아지기만 하는 것이었다.

그 후로 '먼 산'은 이따금 40여 년 전의 뒷동산으로 모습이 바뀌면서 여러 가지 생각에 이어지는 것이었다. …백사장에 널려진 정어리박, 고추잠자리, 썰매, 어느 노인의 철도자살, 철쭉과 구렁이, 그 헤헤의 이름은 운돌이었든가… 유걸이들, 연싸움의 가을 하늘.

아무튼 나는 '먼 산'으로 해서 봄이면 봄, 가을이면 가을의 고향을 생각하게 된다는 일이 적어 흡족스러웠다. 그리고 그럴 적마다 그날 세천교에서 아흔 한 살의 해녀가 바다를 떠나면서 남겨준 전복, 그런 베푸심인지도 모른다고 은근한 미소를 잊지 않아 오는 터이기도 했다.

어느 크리스마스 무렵이었다. 우리 상석회(회원 12명)는 전시의 모임을 갖게 되었다. 각자 3점 한도의 출품으로 D다방을 빌리게 되었다.

나는 '먼 산' 한 점만을 출품했다.

그런데 일주일간의 전시를 마치기 전날밤, 전시품 중의 두 점을 도둑맞은 것이었다. T씨의 '목자석'과 나의 '먼 산'이었다.

참으로 놀라운 도난사건이었다. 이내 경찰에 신고되었고, 다방의 종업원 등 여러 모로 수사가 퍼졌으나 전혀 실마리가 잡히질 않았다. 분명히 수석을 아는 자의 소행일 것이다. 밤(통금이 없는), 늦게까지 자리를 지키고 있다가 외투 속에 숨겨서… 이런 분석으로 초점이 좁혀지는 것이었으나 수사는 쉽사리 풀리질 않았다.

…세천교쯤에서 비슷한 것으로 또 만나지겠지. 나는 체념이 될 수 있었으나 T씨의 심정은 이렇듯 홀가분한 것일 수가 없었다. 관광을 온 일본인이 소문을 듣고 찾아와 50만원을 내겠다는 사정이었는데도 내주지 않았던 희귀석이었다.

망실 후 첫 일요일, 나는 백사百事를 제쳐 두고 세천교를 찾아갔다. '먼 산'에의 바람은 허사였고 먹돌 두 개만으로 돌아왔다.

두 번째도 헛일이었다. 그리고 얼마 전 일요일에는 숱한 돌들이 마냥 비웃고 있는 것 같은 괴로움을 당했다. …대체 무슨 마음으로 그 '먼 산'을 그렇게 허술히…유일미라는 것을 몰랐는가….

"여기가 해발 1천 100미터의 정상입니다."

차장의 '안내'와 동시에 나는 머릿속의 상념을 놔 버렸다. 밖의 설무는 조금 엷어진 것 같았다. 서귀포까지의 반길은 산남山南의 내리막 길이 된다. 차는 자주 브레이크를 걸었다.

"T형의 목자석은 가파도 산이었나요?"

나는 한참 동안의 침묵을 헐었다.

"아니예요. 외도천이었어요."

"50만 원이라면 수석 값으론 적은 돈 아니잖아요?"

"적은 돈 아니죠. 제 분수엔…하지만 수석을 놓고 돈을 내미는 사람은 진짜 수석인이 못 되지요. 물건으로 교환하는 경우라면 몰라도 돈을 놓고서의 흥정은 도에 어긋나는 일이지요."

"다시 만나질 것 같아요?"

"글쎄요…인연이 닿으면 만나지겠지요. 연분이란 정말 묘한 것이더군요."

하고 T씨는 인연에 관한 이야기라면서 이렇게 덧붙였다.

5년 전이었던가, P하고 둘이서 외도천으로 탐석을 갔다. 익혀온 버릇이라는 것이 있게 마련이어서, 탐석 요령도 열 사람이면 모두 같을 수는 없겠지만, 대개는 첫눈에 택하게 되는 경우는 드물다. 마음에 들 음직한 돌을 만나면 눈에 잘 뜨일 자리에 챙겨 두었다가 돌아오는 길에 재삼 음미해 본 연후에 취사를 결심하게 되는 것이다.

그날의 목자석은 P가 만난 것이었다. 반신을 흙 속에 묻고 있는 타원형의 돌이었다. 짙은 회색의 색깔은 살아 있었지만 질이 좀 물러 보였다. 무심히 들어보고 돌 위에 올려놨다.

예정했던 시간이 되어 돌아올 참이었다. P는 그 흙 반신의 돌을 들어 뜯어보다가 곁의 T씨에게 "마음에 들거들랑 가져갑서" 하고 내주었다.

T씨는 십분 마음에 차는 것은 아니었지만, 권하는 성의를 마다할 수 있으랴는 생각으로 덤덤하니 받아서 자기의 것 한 개와 함께 륙색에 챙겨 넣었다. 집에 돌아와서 전등 불빛 속에 반신의 흙을 닦아내고 보니 나무 목자였다. 짙은 회색바탕에 정조正調의 목木은 백색이었다. 거듭 만져 보고 다시 지켜보며 잠을 설쳤다.

"그래, P형에게는 이야길 안 해주었는가요?"

"안 해줬지요. 상심할 것도 뻔한 일이고, 또 소유권을 놓고 실랑이도 있을 것 같구 해서요."

"후에 보고두 자기가 버린 돌인 줄 모르던가요?"

"일년 가까이 캐비닛 속에 잠궈 두고…일체 내색 안 했지요."

"하하하…."

함께 웃음을 터뜨렸다.

"아마 다신 인연이 닿기는 어려울 겝니다. 너무 허술하니 생각했다가 벌 받은 거지요."

T씨는 말하고 그늘이 서리는 듯한 눈시울을 창 밖으로 돌렸다.

해발 700의 표지. 설화雪花의 숲속으로 차는 속력을 내고 있었다.

S마을서의 첫 순서는 다방에 들르는 일이었다.

우체국 곁의 '위미'爲美라는 조그만 간판이 한 길을 향해 얼굴을 내밀고 있었다. 그러나 다방 안은 그런대로 구색을 갖추고 있었다. 카운터에는 늘 화분이나 꽃병이 놓여지게 마련이었고, 낮은 음악 속에서 테이블들은 언제나 깨끗함을 잃지 않았다. 커피 맛도 괜찮은 편이었다.

버스를 내리자 막바로 다방을 향했다. 자리는 텅 비었고, 김양이 함뿍 웃음을 머금으며 맞았다.

"벌써 수선화가…"

나는 카운터의 수선(검은 질그릇 단지에 무더기로 꽂은)에 놀라 보이고, 창가의 테이블을 잡았다. T씨가 커피 두 잔을 청했다. 나는 잠시 숨결을 가다듬어 수선의 냄새를 헤아려 보았다. 잡힐 듯 말 듯한 엷은 것이었는데, 커피잔이 오면서 그만 놓치고 말았다.

"미스 김도 같이 들지."

내가 권하자,

"네, 고맙수다."

하고 김양은 얼른 자리를 떴다. 이윽고 자기가 마실 커피를 들고 테이블에 돌아왔다.
"미스 김, 이뻐졌는데…."
나는 참말이라고 정색을 해보였다.
"어머머…."
그녀는 시선을 떨구었다가,
"참, 아줌마가 왔수다."
하고 고개를 들었다.
"아줌마라니, 주인 언니?"
"네"
"언제?"
"그저께 마씸."
"안에 계셔?"
"미장원에 갔수다."
"조마담 말인가요?"
잠자코 있던 T씨가 끼어들었다.
"조마담 말구 또 주인 언니가 있수과?"
김양이 받았다. 말끝의 '과?'가 농조임을 말하고 있었다.
"내가 실수했는가…."
T씨는 허어로 얼버무리고는,
"자, 일어서 볼까요?"
자리를 뜨자고 했다.
"언니가 오면 이따 돌아오는 길에 다시 들른다고 일러 줘."
나는 김양에게 말하고 T씨를 따라 다방을 나섰다.
눈발은 걷히고 바다 위에 햇빛이 어른거리고 있었다.

…어째설까?

나는 걸음이 떠지는 자신을 생각했다.

…철 이른 수선화…돌아왔다는 '위미'의 여주인…전혀 충격일 수 없는 일에 이렇게 다리가 힘을 잃게 되다니….

나는 속으로 자신을 웃었다. 그러나 웃음은 이내 언짢은 기분으로 바뀌었고, 발걸음은 더 떠지는 것이었다.

…S마을에 다방이 있으리라고는 생각지 않았던 터에 만난 위미였다. 정말 뜻밖의 일이었다. 그런 심리적 작용 때문이었는지는 모르지만 조 마담의 첫 인상은 신선한 것으로 느껴졌다. …"어머니의 고향은 원산이예요. 아빠는 신의주고요." 같은 실향민이라는 거였다. "이런 한촌에서…." 나는 장사가 되느냐고 물었다. "그럭저럭요…." 그녀는 눈시울에 씁쓰레한 파문을 지어 보였다.

세 번째 만나던 날, 두 사람은 바닷가의 술집에서 전복을 안주로 소주를 먹었다.

그 술자리를 뜨면서 나는 조마담의 내력—다방을 차리고 들앉기까지의 15년—을 알게 되었다.

…스물한 살에 만난 첫 남자가 실패하였다. 여고를 졸업한 다음해 중매로 만났었는데, 아버지는 재산에다 그만한 물이면…였지만, 어머니가 반대했다.

남자가 남자답게 생기질 못했다는 불만이었다. 혼담은 오래 끌다가 아버지 뜻 쪽으로 기울어지고 말았다.

결혼하고 3년, 딸 하나로 헤어졌다. 머리맡에다 식칼을 놓고 자야만 마음을 놓을 수 있다는 그런 의처증이었다.

두 번째 정식은 아니었지만 머리에 기름을 바르지 않는 날이 없었기 때문이었다. 1년 만에 물러서고 말았다.

후부터 술집에 나서게 되었다. 서울은 피하고 싶었다. 부산, 마산, 대구 등 경상도 땅을 전전하다가 3년 전에 제주에 들어왔다. 다방은 약간의 재산을 이룬 보람이었다.

다음 번 세천교 때에 T씨와 동행하게 되었다.

해질녘, 세 사람은 바닷가의 술집을 찾아나섰다.

술자리의 화제는 주로 수석에 관한 것이 되었다.

"전 돌을 방 안에다 들이는 일을 반대하고 싶어요."

미소만으로 잠자코 있던 조마담이 입문을 열었다.

"반대라니요…… 어째서지요?"

T씨가 물었다.

"태어난 제 자리에다 놔두는 것이 돌을 위하는 일이 되지 않을까요?"

조마담이 되물었다.

"그렇다면 방에다 들여놓은 꽃은 어떻게 되지요?"

하고 T씨.

"씨를 뿌려서 키워내는 꽃과 만들어 낼 수 없는 돌과… 같을 수가 있을까요?

"알겠어요. 본연적인 것과 인위적인 것은 다르다, 그런 말씀이군요."

"이론이 아니구요… 느낌이 그저 그렇다는 거에요."

"조마담의 지론이 옳을 것 같아."

내 말을,

"아니지. 꽃이든 돌이든 제자리를 벗어난다는 점에선 마찬가지지. 죽여버리는 일이 된다면, 똑 같다고 말해야 옳지, 뭐가 달라요?"

T씨는 허리를 펴 보이는 멋으로 받았다.

"차라리 시들게 해서 죽여버리는 꽃, 그 편이 마음 편해서 낫지요.

그렇지만 돌은 죽이지도 않고 바보로 만들어 버리니까요. 안 그래요?"

"바보요?"

하고 T씨의 눈이 동그래졌다.

"하하하…."

나는 소리를 내어 웃고는.

"T형 생각해 봐요. 그렇게 기운 쓰지 마시구요. T형의 목자석만 하더라도 돌 그 자체의 마음은 흙 속에다 나무목자를 감추어 두고 싶었을 게 아니에요. 그 숨겨 두고자 했던 미덕이랄까 진실이랄까요, 그것이 드러나 버리고 말았기 때문에 결국은 도둑이라는 죄악을 낳고 만 게 아닙니까. 자, 토론 그만 하시구 술이나…."

뇌까렸다.

"T선생님, 미안해요."

하고 조마담은 T씨에게 고개를 숙여 보였다.

…이 여자, 보통이 아니다. 어쩌면 백전노장일는지 모른다.

나는 술기운으로 발갛게 물들어 있는 그녀의 눈시울을 훔쳐보며 이렇게 속으로 혼잣말을 중얼거렸다.

바다를 향해 창은 열려져 있었다. 만발한 넝쿨찔레의 내음새를 날라 오는 해연풍海軟風. 그런 정취 속에 세 사람은 어지간히들 거나해졌다.

"참, 바다 한복판에서 나빌 본 적이 있나요?"

바다 쪽으로 눈을 주곤 하던 조마담이 문득 생각난다는 듯 호들갑이었다.

"나비가요?"

T씨가 그녀의 눈길을 사로잡았다.

"신기한 일이지예? 작년 한 여름이었어요. 범섬으로 놀러 갔다가 돌아오는 길이었죠. 바다 한복판으로 나비가 날아 들어왔지 뭐예요. 쪼

꼬마한 노랑나비 두 마리였는데요, 우리가 탄 똑딱선을 줄곧 따라오는 게 아니겠어요. 너무너무 신기하고 황홀해서요… 서로 어울리며 범섬 쪽으로 멀리멀리 사라져 가는 나비들을 놓치지 않으려고 지켜 봤지요. 한없이요….”

그녀는 눈에 빛을 띠고 있었다.

“바다에서 나비를 만난 적은 없지만 어느 시인의 '바다와 나비'라는 시로, 나비는 꽃밭뿐이 아니고 바다에도 찾아간다는 것을 알고는 있어요.”

내가 눈웃음으로 건네었다.

“바다와 나비, 어떤 신데요?”

“가만 계세요.”

나는 턱을 쓰다듬으며 한동안 생각에 잠겨 있다가,

“공주처럼 지쳐서 돌아온다… 였던가요. 이런 구절이 있었던가요… 생각이 안 나는군요.”

했다.

“공주처럼 지쳐서요?”

그녀는 혼잣말로 중얼거리다가 바다 쪽으로 시선을 돌렸다. 무엇인가를 지그시 지켜 보는 듯 약간 굳어지는 표정이 되었다.

“집에 시집이 있을 겁니다. 적어서 편지로 부쳐 드리지요.”

하고 나는 침묵을 헐었다.

“정말예요?”

그녀의 시선이 주석으로 돌아왔다.

“숙녀에게 거짓말을…”

나는 웃어 주었다.

다시 몇 순배. T씨가 자리를 뜨자고 먼저 일어났다.

"실례도 많았고… 많은 것을 배웠어요. 참말 즐거웠습니다."

그녀는 깍듯이 인사를 했다. 조금도 흐트러지지 않은 단정함이었다.

우리들은 버스정류장에서 헤어졌다.

이튿날, 나는 '바다와 나비'가 들어있는 시집을 찾아내어 그 전문을 적어서 수첩 속에 간직했다. 편지의 약속이었으나 재회 때에 멋을 곁들여서 읽어 주자는 생각이었다.

여름 한철의 탐석은 가까운 곳이 되었고, 가을도 그럭저럭 세천교에 가보지 못하고 보냈다. 그러다가 크리스마스 무렵, 어느 날 S마을을 찾아가게 되었다.

첫 순서인 위미다방.

김양이 언제나 앳된 표정으로 맞아들이고는,

"아줌마 마씸, 서방님 얻어서…."

일러주었다. 서귀포에다 큰 밀감밭을 가지고 있는 육지 분인데, 아줌마는 밭 관리를 책임지고 있기 때문에 바쁜 모양이어서 그 동안 두 번 다방에 다녀갔을 뿐이라는 것이었다.

"그래, 미스 김이 이 큰 살림을 혼자서?…."

나는 꽃이 놓여 있지 않은 카운터며 못해 뵈는 테이블이며를 살펴보다가 입문을 열었다.

"네, 아줌마가 마담을 두자는 걸 제가 마다했어요."

"제법 서울말을…."

나는 웃어 보였다.

"듣기 싫지 예?"

"싫긴… 그래, 어떻게 혼자서 감당하지? 밥 지을 때랑, 어쩌다 비우게 될 땐 어떡하지? 손님들은…."

"다 아는 뻔한 손님들 아니우꽈. 비었으믄 전축이나 넣구 앉아서요…."
 김양은 생글거린다.
"그렇구나…."
 내가 말끝을 흐리고 멍해 있는데 "전축 넣을까 마씸?"
 김양이 물었다.
"음."
 나는 끄덕여 주었다.
 김양은 카운터로 물러가고, '라 쿰파르시타'가 방안을 울리기 시작했다.
"좀 낮추자."
"네."
 볼륨이 낮춰졌다.
 나는 수첩을 뒤적여 '바다와 나비'의 쪽지를 꺼냈다.

 …아무도 그에게 수심을 알려 준 일이 없기에/ 흰나비는 도무지 바다가 무섭지 않다/ 청무우 밭인가 해서 나려 갔다가/ 어린 날개가 물결에 젖어서/ 공주처럼 지쳐서 돌아온다/ 3월달 바다가 꽃이 되지 않아서 서글픈/ 나비 허리에 새파란 초승달이 서리다.
 쪽지를 접어서 잘게 잘게 찢어 재떨이에 버리고 나는 다방을 나섰다.
"뭘 그렇게… 빨리 갑시다!"
 T씨가 부르는 소리에 나는 걸음을 빨리 했다.
 T씨가 기다리고 있다가,
"다리 위쪽을 먼저 잡아 볼까요?"
 물었다.
 '목자' 같은 문양석은 다리 위쪽 계곡의 하상河床이어야 하고 '먼 산'

같은 먹돌은 아래켠의 바닷가가 되어야 하는 것이다. 그렇다고 자기의 목적만을 위해서 아래 위로 헤어질 수도 없는 일이었다. 속이 들여다 뵈는 야박스러움이 될 터이니까. 그래서 묻는 선후일 것이다.

"좋도록 해요."

나는 선을 우기고 싶었으나 걸음이 뒤쳐진 일을 사과하는 셈으로 양보해 주었다.

"그럼 두 시간 예정으로 위쪽부터 잡아 봅시다."

T씨가 앞을 선다. 비탈길을 내려 하상에 들어섰다.

"T형, 우리 오늘은 한번 이렇게 해보면 어떨까요, 누가 캐내든지 간에 다리 위쪽의 것은 T형 차지가 되고 아래쪽의 것은 제 차지가 된다. 어때요?"

"공동작업이란 말씀이죠? 좋습니다. 단 겉장 피우긴 없기예요."

"물론이지요."

"또 한 가지 약속할 일이 있어요. 오늘도 빈손으로 끝나게 되면 다시는 동행해 드리지 않기예요. 외도천을 놔두고 늘 따라만 다닐 수는 없는 일이니까요."

"저도 단념하고 외도천으로 같이 가드리겠어요."

"정말입니까?"

"그럼요."

"거짓말 마세요. 조마담은 어떡하구요…."

"어떡하다니요?"

"자길 속이긴 없깁니다, 우리끼린…."

T씨는 싱글거린다.

"속이다니요?"

"그만한 미모에다, 상냥하겠다, 어디 나무랄 데가…."

"한번 해보시지요."
"제가 먼저였었다면 절대로 안 놓치지요."
"하하하…."
함께 웃음을 터뜨렸다.
"자, 시작해 볼까요. 오늘이 마지막이 될지도 모르니까요…."
T씨는 손목시계의 시간을 보고는,
"한시가 좀 지났으니 세시에 바닷가로 옮기기로 합시다."
하고 앞장을 섰다.
계곡 깊숙이에까지 더듬어 올라갔으나 두 사람은 한 점의 수확도 못 본 채 발걸음을 돌리게 되었다.
"선생님!"
해조음이 가까워졌다고 느꼈을 때였다.
"선생님, 저예요오!"
소리는 계곡에 메아리치며 울려 퍼졌다.
나는 허리를 세워 소리 쪽으로 눈을 들었다. 목소리는 다리 위 난간에서였다. 작은 원을 그리고 있는 손끝이 이쪽을 부르고 있었다.
"야호!"
나는 목소리의 주인이 조마담임을 알아차리자 손을 높이 들어 대답해 주었다.
"누군데요?"
하고 등 뒤의 T씨.
"조마담 닮았군요."
"야따, 야혼 뭡니까?"
"실순가요?"
"대실수죠."

"허어참, 인정이 메말랐군요."
"인정 많으신 분, 빨리 달려가 보시죠."
T씨는 빈정거린다.
"그만 거두구 가봅시다."
"좇아갈게요. 먼저 가보세요."
T씨는 응해 보이면서도 일손을 거두자는 기색은 아니었다.
나는 발부리를 조심하며 빠른 걸음을 옮겨갔다.
"다방에 들르셨다기에요…,"
조마담은 비탈길을 내려왔다.
"오래간만입니다."
그녀의 검은 스웨터의 해맑은 얼굴이 좀 야위어 뵌다고 생각하면서 나는 악수를 청했다.
"돌아갈 때에 다시 들른다구 김양에게… 나오시지 않아도…."
내가 말 끝을 흐리는데,
"저도 수석을 배우고 싶어서요."
그녀는 밝은 눈웃음으로 받았다.
"살림은 어떡하시구요?"
"혼잔데 뭘요."
"헤어졌나요?"
나는 입 밖에 낼 뻔한 말을 삼키고는 호주머니를 뒤적거려 담배를 꺼냈다.
"돌을 방 안에 들이는 것은 바람직한 일이 못된다구…."
내 말을,
"안 잊으셨군요. 술기분으로 공연히 해본 소리예요. 이제부터 다 버리구 돌이나 찾아다니면서요…."

조마담의 의연한 미소였다.
"아이고, 오래간만입니다."
T씨가 다가왔다.
"일이 안 끝나셨겠지요?"
조마담이 묻는 말을
"네, 바다 쪽을 한차례 뒤져보고 일찌감치 넘어가야지요."
T씨가 받았다.
세 사람은 한길로 나왔다.
"돌아가실 때 저희 집에서 저녁을… 산딸기술 있어요."
그녀는 누추한 방이지만 초대를 받아 주면 싶다고 했다.
T씨는 내 표정을 언뜻 살피고는,
"고맙습니다만 산에 눈이 많이 쌓여 있을 것 같아서요…."
망설여 보였다.
"택시는 밤늦게까지 있어요. 못 가시면 내일 새벽 첫 버스로 넘어가셔도 출근시간까진…."
"어때? 호의신데… 일곱시에 일어설 약속으루…."
"일곱시 약속, 지키지겠지요?"
"돌아갈 걱정은 피차 마찬가질 텐데…."
"그럼, 기다리고 있겠어요."
하는 조마담에게 T씨는 다섯시를 약속했다.

조마담은 엷은 화장에다 옥색치마에 흰 저고리의 단장으로 기다리고 있었다.
"누추합니다만…."
다방에 이어진 네 평 가량의 방이었다. 제주 느티나무의 고담한 제주궤와 작은 책상 하나의 조촐함이었다. 궤 위에는 수선화와 문단(文旦)이 놓여졌는데, 그 내음이 방 안 전체를 꼭 휘어잡고 있어 청결한 느낌이었다.

산딸기술은 됫병으로 하나 가득하였고, 더덕무침, 도미구이, 오분자기 따위의 안주도 깔끔히 차려져 있었다.

술 도수가 높아서인지 몇 순배로 이내 취기를 느꼈다.

"어때요? 못 가믄 내일 새벽 첫 버스루⋯."

나는 여덟시 삼십분의 막버스(서귀포까지의)를 놓쳐서 난처하다는 T씨에게 건네었다.

"아따, 기분은 알고 있어요, 쇠뿔도 단김에 빼자고 들면 몸 다치기 쉬우니까, 일어섭시다."

T씨는 깔깔해진 목소리로 막버스를 고집했다.

"정말 너무하시는군요. 세천교에서, T형의 돌 찾기는 되두 좋고 안 되두 좋다는 건성일 수 있겠지만, 전 달라요. 오늘은 비슷한 것이라도 좋으니, 빈손으로 돌아가지 말자구 생각했었는데, 또 이 꼴이 됐으니 어떡합니까. 술이라두 마시고 봐야지요."

나는 혀가 드티는 것 같은 취기를 깨달았다.

"헐어논 술⋯ 다 드셔야지요."

조마담이 방실거리며, 반가량 내려가 있는 술병을 눈으로 가리켜 보였다.

"네. 좋아요. 이렇게 되고 만 것, 기분 내키는 데까지 막 가봅시다요."

T씨는 조마담이 건넨 잔을 받아 단숨에 비웠다.

"저도 이제부터 수석이나 배우며 지내볼까 해요."

그녀는 T씨가 돌린 잔을 받아 놓고 말했다.

"살림은 어떡하구요."

내가 물었다.

"거, 카지노란 게 있잖아요?…."

그녀는 말하고, 숨결을 가다듬는 듯 한동안 침묵을 지키고 있다가,

"저도 얻어들은 풍월루 조금은 알게 되었지요. 스물 한끗으루 먹는 블랙 잭, 루렛, 다이스, 바카라는 가보잡기라나요. 아무리 말려 봐도 막무가내예요. 5천 평짜리 귤밭 하날 날리구두 말입니다. 그냥 미쳐 있으니… 싫으면 헤어지잔 데야 어떡해요. 물러서기로 결심했어요. 돌 찾기도 힘들다지만요, 사람 만나기두… 정말, 다시 시집가면 사람 아니에요."

했다.

"독신주의… 그게 아무나 되는 일이 아니지요."

내가 조심스레 꺼낸 말을,

"알고 있어요. 그래서 참아 보자고 했어요… 정말, 이젠 진절머리가 나서요… 구질구질해서요. 혼자일 때가 몇 배 속 편했다는 생각이에요. 이젠 철엔 수선이나 벗삼구, 또 돌이나 찾아다니면서요… 혼자서 살겠어요."

그녀는 받았다. 그리고는 물기를 담은 듯한 시선을 수선화께에 주고 있다가,

"참, 언젠가 '바다와 나비'… 적어서 보내 주신다구…."

내게로 눈길이 돌렸다.

"적어서 수첩 속에 간직하구 다니다가 찢어 버렸지요."

"왜지요?"

"공주가 도망갔으니까…."

"어머…."

"몇 구절만 읽어 드리지요. 청무우밭인가 해서 나려갔다가는… 어린 날개가 물결에 젖어서… 공주처럼 지쳐서 돌아온다…."

"청무우밭인가 해서… 갔다가… 지쳐서 돌아온 조수진… 호호호… 저 취했지 예?"

그녀는 하들하들 웃었다.

"어린 날갠 아니지. 지쳐서 돌아올 만큼의…."

나는 따라 웃으며 뇌까렸다.

"그러니까, 청무우밭인가 속아서, 다신 나려가지 않는단 거예요."

하고 그녀는 깔깔한 목소리가 되었다.

…아, 이건 상처에 관한 이야기가 너무 길어지는군….

나는 수선화 이야기로 화제를 바꾸었다.

"제주도의 수선화를 맨 먼저 발견한 사람이 완당 김정희 선생이었대요. 그 전까진 중국에만 있는 꽃인 줄 알고 있었는데, 완당 선생이 제주에 유배되어 와서 우리나라에도 수선화가 있다는 걸 알게 되었다는군요. 『완당집』이라는 책에 제주 수선화를 예찬한 글이 있는데…."

나는 말하고 취기를 가다듬어 이런 뜻의 이야기를 덧붙였다.

…수선화의 개화는 정월 말로부터 2월 초에 비롯 3월까지 이르는데, 이때는 산야나 밭둑이 모두 이것으로 가득 차 만만함이 백설이 대지를 덮어 쌓인 것과도 같아 동문 밖이나 서문 밖이나 어디를 가든지 모두 그런 화경花景을 이루고 있어 바라보기에 눈이 부족한 형편으로, 눈만 떠도 눈 속에까지 하얀 수선화가 가득 찬 듯하다.

"완당 선생이 유배되어 와서 사신 곳이 어디지요?"

"대정大靜골 아시지? 산방산山房山 기슭의… 갇힌 몸으로 9년간 살면서 그 신필을 완성했대요. 수선화 외에도 한란을 발견해서 이것이 난초라고, 섬사람들에게 가르쳐 주었다고 전해지고 있지요."

"그 전까지는 우리나라에 야생하고 있는 줄 아무도 몰랐었나요?"

"그랬을는지도 모르지요. 제주도보다 청나라 연경이 더 가까웠던 시대였으니까요. 음력 정월이면 한양의 규수들은 중국에서 수입해 온 꽃으로, 향기를 즐겼다는군요."

"요샛말로 꽃꽂이란 건가요?"

"원래 우리나라의 꽃꽂이는 꽃단지에다 무더기로 꽂아 놓은 것에서 멋을 찾았던 것 같아요. 조마담 방의 수선화처럼 말입니다."

"제 방처럼요?…."

그녀는 놀라 보이고 다시 수선화로 눈을 주었다.

"자, 그만…."

T씨가 일어서자고 했다.

"아따…."

내가 퉁겨 놓자,

"술도 다 바닥났어요!"

T씨는 비어 있는 술병을 흘기는 듯한 눈짓으로 가리켰다.

"몇 시지요?"

"여덟시 십분이에요. 바로 나가면 막차가…."

T씨는 서둘자고 재촉이다.

"섭섭해서요…."

조마담은 아쉽다며 먼저 마루에 나섰다.

"언제, 제주시에 한번 넘어오세요. 제가 한턱 내겠어요."

T씨가 말하고, 두 사람은 빈 륙색을 챙겨들고 방을 나섰다. 한길에는 다방 안을 통해야 나오게 된다. 김양이 좇아 오며,

"잘 갑서. 또 옵서예."

방실거렸다.

조마담은 버스정류장까지 배웅하겠다고 따라나섰다.

유난히 맑은 별무리. 밤공기가 목덜미에 차갑다. 남풍인지 해조음이 무겁게 들렸다.

"별도 많군요…."

T씨가 중얼거리며 발걸음이 떠졌다.

"돌도 많구요…."

내가 먹이자,

"사람도 많지요."

조마담이 받았다.

버스는 정각에 닿았다. 대여섯 사람이 내리는 것 같았는데 오르기는 우리 두 사람 뿐이었다.

"안녕히…."

나는 가로등 가에 오래도록 서 있는 조마담을 창 밖으로 지켜보다가,

"T형은 실향의 아픔을 잘 모르실 겝니다."

입을 열고 T씨의 시선을 사로잡았다.

"왜 모르겠어요… 알지요."

"아신다면, 아마 개념이랄까, 그런 정도겠지요. 실감이 어떤 것인가는…."

"실감이라면, 얼마만큼 크고 깊은 겁니까?"

"아찔할 만큼 크구 깊은 거지요."

"말씀해 보세요."

"실향 30년… 산천이 변한다는 10년이 세개 아닙니까. 이건 전혀 과장된 얘기가 아니에요. 우리 마을 뒷동산이라구, 어릴 때 놀던 낮은 산 하나 있죠. 그 산에 한번 올라가 보구, 그 자리에서 바로 죽는다, 그래도 좋겠다, 이런 막잡은 생각일 때가 한두 번이 아니지요."

"그러니까 고향에 가보는 일과 죽음을 바꿀수 있다, 그런 말씀이 되는군요."

"나이 탓도 있겠죠. 엄벙덤벙 떠밀려 오다 보니, 아차, 이젠 요지부동으로 막혀 버렸구나, 길은 아득한데… 이제 기껏 산댔자 20년이 아닌가, 그래서 바꿀 수 있다, 그런 순간적인 충격이 되는 거겠지요. 그런데 그곳에 살고 있을 사람들은 보고 싶지 않아요. 늘 눈앞에 가물거리는 것은, 뒷동산의 할미꽃이라든가 아카시아 꽃길이라든가, 그런 따위 자연에 속하는 것들이란 말이에요."

"기억에 또렷합니까?"

"또렷할 리가 있나요. 삼삼하지요. 그런데 꿈에서 아주 생생할 때가 때가 있지요. 전혀 생각 못하던 골목길에서 공차기를 한다든가요…."

"꿈에서요?"

T씨는 혼잣말을 중얼거리고는,

"'먼 산' 찾으러 다시 세천교에 안 오시겠어요? 약속한 대루요."

"와야지요. 꼭 찾아내겠어요. 뒷동산의 고향을 찾는 일인데요, 왜 중단합니까. 더군다나 수석을 배우겠다는 여자친구도 생겼잖요."

"명심해서 동행해 드리지요."

"고맙소다만, 외도천서 찾아야 할 목자석은 어떡하구요?"

"여자친구가 생겼지앤요. 하하하…."

…아무렴, 웃어 주어야지. 20년 후면 이 남녘땅에서 자취마저 사라지고 말 아바이네 사투리가 아닌가.

나는 뇌리에 아물거리는 '먼 산' 속에 흔들거리다가,

"앤요… 가… 앤요."

입속의 말을 뇌까렸다.

어둠속을 차는 힘찬 속력으로 달리고 있었다.

(창작집 『黑日記』 중에서)

고시홍

표류하는 이어도

필자 소개
1972년 제주대학 국어국문학과 졸업. 《월간문학》 신인상 데뷔.
한국소설가협회, 제주학연구소 등 회원, 제주시교육청 장학사(현).
탐라문화상 수상.
소설집 『대통령의 손수건』 『계명의 도시』 외

표류하는 이어도

고시홍

1)

 마을이 내려다보이는 둔덕을 내려섰다. 등에 지고 있던 멱서리를 팡돌(쉼돌)에 부려놓은 억순이는 머릿수건을 벗어들었다. 땟국에 전 수건으로 얼굴이며 가슴팍의 땀방울을 찍어냈다. 끈끈한 땀내음이 코를 찔렀다. 가쁜 숨을 잠재울 때마다 쓸개물이 입 안에 고였다. 조 이삭이 담긴 멱서리를 지탱하고 있는 오금이 후들거렸다. 억순이는 가쁜 숨을 몰아쉬며 팔을 뒤로 젖혔다. 조 이삭을 헤집어 햇고구마 한 개를 꺼내 멱서리에 슥슥 문질러 겉껍질을 벗겨냈다. 조반 전에 집을 나섰던 것이다.
 희뿌연 먼지가 연기처럼 피어오르던 신작로 모퉁이로 화물차 한 대가 모습을 드러냈다. 확성기에서 울려 퍼지던 흥겨운 노래가락은 이내 먼지 속으로 사그라들었다.
 …문화와 예술을 사랑하시는 리민 여러분 안녕하십니까아! 여기는 여러분들의 사랑 속에서 무럭무럭 자라고 있는 제일 이동영화반입니다아! 오늘밤, 리민 여러분을 모시고 상영해 드릴 영화는, 김승호 황정

순 주연에 눈물 없이는 볼 수 없는……

　억새풀을 실은 화물차가 확성기에서 흘러나오는 육성을 도막내며 지나갔다. 멍석날 같은 손등으로 입술에 묻은 고구마 진을 훔쳐낸 억순이는 신작로를 가로질러 마을로 들어섰다. 이동영화반의 확성기에서 뿜어나오는 흥겨운 노래가락이 마음을 앵하게 했다. 구리동전 한 닢이 아쉬운 판이었다. 자국을 내딛을 때마다 을선이와 길수의 낯바닥이 돌부리 위로 나앉았다. 영화비를 달라고 졸라댈 걸 생각하니 절로 가슴이 저렸다. 두어 달에 한 번, 닷새장날에 찾아오는 이동영화반이건만 한 번도 영화비를 줘 보지 못했다. 언제나 다음 번엘랑 꼭…틀림없이…란 말을 수박꼭지 따내듯 하며 어르달래곤 했다.

　마당 한가운데 펴놓은 멍석에다 먹서리를 부려놓았다. 똥글똥글하게 송이진 조 이삭들이 물결치는 소리를 내며 쏟아져 나왔다. 먹서리에 달라붙어 있는 이삭을 떨어내고 났어도 바다 우는 소리는 여전했다. 아무래도 물질하러 가긴 글러먹은 것 같았다. 바다 우는 소리가 그치지 않는 것은 물살이 거세다는 징조였다.

　억순이는 장독대 쪽으로 몸을 돌렸다. 바닷가에 접한 돌담부리를 디딤돌 삼아 통나무처럼 모착한 몸뚱이를 끌어올렸다. 뒤꿈치를 세워 난 바다 쪽으로 뻗어내린 포구로 고개를 내밀었다. 파도는 많이 누그러져 있었다. 그러나 높새바람 기운은 완전히 가시지 않은 것 같았다. 물질하기에 알맞은 물때가 다 지나버린 게 안타까웠다. 해산물을 따내기에 안성마춤인 너댓 물찌 때부터 계속 높새바람이 불어닥쳤던 것이다. 연일 휘몰아치는 높새바람이 억순이의 애간장에 불을 질러 놓았다.

　남편 제사가 내일인데 아직 모두 터에 놓았다. 여차하면 숭늉만 떠놓고 제사를 지내게 됐다. 달포 안으로 다가선 시아버지의 담제일이며 비료값, 을선이 남매의 사친회비. 금년엔 해묵은 초가지붕도 갈아덮어야 한다. 이엉질하는 것은 마을 사람들이 모여들어 그냥 해주는 것이긴 하지만, 품삯 대신 하다못해 풍년초나 파랑새 한 갑씩은 내밀어야 한다. 지난번 태풍 때 무너진 돌담도 여태 그냥 있다. 돈 들어가야 할 곳이 돌담 구멍만큼이나 많았다. 말 모른 돈이 발 뻗고 앉아 숨돌릴 여유를 주지 않았다. 돈 나올 구멍이라곤 이승과 저승의 문턱, 바다 밑의 설드럭 밖에 없다. 믿고 의지할 곳이라고는, 숨통을 뒤웅박 하나에 저당 잡혀 놓고 해물을 건져 낼 수 있는 바다 속의 토지뿐이다. 겨울이 지날 때마다 초가지붕을 덮씌우는 은빛 모래가 사금파리였으면 했다. 아니, 바다를 잠재우는 수면제만 되었어도 좋겠다. 뒤웅박을 여嶼 삼아 바닷 속을 들락날락할 수 있게만 해줬어도 여한이 없겠다. 바다만 숨기척을 하지 않는다면 돈은 등짐으로 지어 나를 수 있을 것 같았다. 우뭇가사리, 미역, 소라, 전복…… 이 모두가 억순이에게 있어선 금은보화였다. 열 개의 발가락으로 하늘을 걷어차며 물 속으로 곤두박질 칠 때마다 숨통이 부어오르는 고통이 따를망정, 바다에서 거둬들이는 것들은 김을 매지 않아도 되고 비료값 걱정을 할 필요도 없기에 더욱 소중한 보물이었다.

"어쩐 일루 그리 함박주둥일 허고 서 있는 것고?"

토방으로 들어서던 억순이는 의아해하며 댓돌 밑으로 내려섰다. 마당가 돌담을 기대고 서 있는 을선이에게로 다가섰다.

"학교엔 갔다 와시냐?"

사친회비를 주지 않으면 학교에 가지 않겠다던 일이 떠올랐다.

을선이는 고무신짝을 발가락으로 도닥거릴 뿐 말이 없었다.

"누구하고 싸웠느냐?"

입을 실룩거리던 을선이가 고개를 가로저었다.

"그럼……"

"사친회비 가져 오지 않았댄 돌려보냅데다!"
선생님들이 야속했다. 한두 번 당하는 일은 아니지만 부아가 보글보글 끓었다.
"길수도 공부 못해 봔 오라시냐?"
"예."
아이들과 같이 이동영화반 와 있는 곳으로 가더라고 했다.
"잘 말헐 거 아니가. 요샌 높새바람이 불어 물질을 못해 돈이 없으니, 한 메칠만 더 기다려 줍서 하고……"
"에이구, 그런 이야긴 이제 통허지두 아니 헙네다!"
을선이는 허리에 동여매고 있던 책보자기를 방 안으로 내동댕이쳤다.
"잘 됐져. 이제부털랑 글 공부허는 거 치워 두고 나랑 같이 물질허는 법이나 배우라. 그만허민 이렛 강아지 눈 뜰만인 해여시난……"
억순이의 목소리는 떨리고 있었다. 비록 뱃물질 나갔다 돌아오다가 축항에서 낳은 딸일망정 중학교 마당까진 보내고 말겠다던 각심만큼이나 가슴이 아렸다.
을선이에게는 물질하는 법을 가르쳐 주고 싶지 않았다. 해녀의 대代를 물려줄 용기가 나지 않았다. 을선이 남매를 입학시키러 학교에 갔었을 때 봤던 여 선생님이나, 면사무소 남자 직원 틈에 끼어앉아 있던 여직원이 그렇게 부러울 수가 없었던 것이다. 칠십여 가호의 곶마을에서는 딸을 초등학교에 보내는 집이 열 손가락으로 꼽을 정도였다. 능력이 없어 그런 것만은 아니었다. 아들을 고등학교, 대학에 보내는 집에서도 딸들은 대부분 집안 살림의 밑천으로 삼으려 했다. 그래서 곶마을 사람들은 딸부자가 알부자라고들 했다. 딸이 많으면 해녀가 많게 되고, 들녘에서의 일손도 많아지는 것이다.

"죽으면 죽었지 물질은 배우지 않을 거우다. 성내市內에 나가 식모살이나 아기업개 노릇은 헐지언정……."

을선이의 앙칼진 목소리가 파도에 밀려갔다.

"너 지금 뭐라 했느냐."

"학교 그만 다녕, 돈 벌어오겠다고 했수다!"

어금니로 꼭꼭 씹으며 삭이던 울화가 치밀어 올랐다.

맷돌을 앉히려던 억순이는 빗자루를 거머쥐고 난간으로 나왔다. 기둥을 끼고 서 있던 을선이의 팔을 나꿔챘다. 개도 안 때린다는 빗자루로 을선이의 등허리를 후려쳤다.

"당장 나가거라, 이년아. 누구 때문에 내 신세가 이 모양 요꼴인 줄 아느냐."

"아이고, 잘못했수다!"

억순이의 손아귀에서 바둥거리던 을선이가 댓돌 밑으로 몸을 비틀었다.

딸그락 탁!

기둥에 걸어뒀던 뒤웅박이 그물망사리에 뒤엉켜 댓돌 위로 떨어졌다. 심장에 금이 가는 소리에 억순이는 빗자루를 내던졌다. 마당으로 나동그라진 뒤웅박을 끌어안았다. 꼭지 부분이 좁쌀방울만큼 타개져 있었다. 그러나 물질하는 데엔 전혀 지장이 없을 것 같았다.

2)

맷돌 앞에 앉아 맷돌을 휘휘 돌려대는 억순이는 이내 한숨 섞인 가락을 뽑아냈다.

이여이여 이어도, 이여돗길은 저승문이더냐. 한 번 가니 올 줄 모르는구나. 이여이여 이여도 호라. 신던 보선에 볼 받아 놓곡, 입던 옷에 풀해여 놓앙 애가 타게 기다려도, 다신 올 줄 모르더라. 이여이여 이어도 고레(맷돌)에……

가슴에 응어리졌던 온갖 시름이 메밀가루와 함께 맷돌 언저리에 소복소복 쌓여갔다. 일을 하면서 부를 노래가 있기에 들녘에서 바다로 줄달음치듯 하며 하루 해를 보내고 있는지 모른다. 일을 하며 부르는 노래는 마음의 보약이었다.

"아침엔 밭에 가서 집에 없더구나, 장 구경이나 같이 갈까 했었는데……"

"남자 같으민 불알망태라도 들고 간다, 쥔 게 없언 못 갔져."

억순이는 다시 맷돌노래 가락을 이었다. 보리쌀이나 햇좁쌀을 두어 말 지고 가봤댔자 뻔한 일이었다. 똥값 받고 팔아 봐야 장터에서 나올 땐 엉덩이춤만 늘 뿐이다.

나들이 차림으로 들어왔던 빌례도 치마를 걷어붙이고 맷돌자루를 마주 잡았다. 맷자루를 쥐고 있는 어깨가 한결 가벼웠다.

"오늘랑 물에나 들게. 내일 길수 애비 제상에 올릴 걸 하나도 준비 못해서 큰일이여."

"죽은 사람 제사지내려다 초상 날 소리 허지도 말라."

"바다 우는 소린 채 누그러들지 않았주마는, 순덱이 에미도 가기로 약속했져."

억순이는 계속 매끄럽게 돌아가는 맷돌 따라 애잔한 가락을 이었다.

"이젠 물질허는 이야기만 들어도 등살이 으스스헌다."

"팔자 좋은 소리 허지 말라."

콧물을 짜낸 손가락을 몸빼 가랑이에 문지르고 난 억순이는 맷방석에 쌓인 메밀가루를 매함지에 퍼담았다.

"해마다 돌아오는 제사 아니가. 오늘 같은 날, 물 속에 들어가 잡아온 해물 차려 놓앙 제사 지낸다고 물귀신 된 서방이 살앙 돌아오느냐."

"허기사, 빌례 말이 네 귀 반듯헌 말이여."

하긴 그렇다. 스물 두 살 적부터 십여 년 동안 지내온 남편 제사였지만, 진설해 놓은 멧밥 한 숟갈 축내고 간 적이 없다.

그러나 남편 제사만큼은 제상 다리가 휘어지게 차려놓고 싶었다. 남편의 넋을 달래는 일은 곧 바다에 대한 치성이라 생각했다. 용왕님을 위하는 일이라 믿었다. 남편의 뱃노래가 깔려 있는 뱃길을 닦는 일이었다. 그것은 곧 억순이 자신의 물길을 닦는 일이라 생각했다.

남편 제삿날마다 제관도 없는 제사상 앞에서 두 손 모아 비는 것도 그런 때문이었다. 동東의 바다 서西의 바다로 물고개를 넘을 때랑, 미역이며 생복, 소라가 많다는 이어도로 데려다 줍서……남편의 뱃길이 바로 해저의 보물섬인 이어도로 통하는 길처럼 여겨졌다.

"아야 허리여. 억순이년 고레(맷돌) 갈아주는 거 도와주단 허리만 빼었져."

맷손을 놓고 일어선 빌례가 숨 넘어 가는 소리를 지르며 허리를 도닥거렸다.

"미친 년. 엊저녁에도 왔다가는 거 닮안게 서방과 밤일허다 다친허리지, 나 때문이냐."

억순이는 맷돌 구멍에 박힌 메밀가루를 쓸어내던 빗자루로 빌례의 엉덩짝을 달싹 후려치며 눈을 흘겼다.

"말이 났으니 말이주마는, 이제 대국놈이 오지 않은 날은 잠을 못 잔 큰일이여."

"애간장에 붙은 불을 한숨으로 끄며 사는 사람 생각도 허라."

"그건 그렇고, 이따 물질허래 갈 때랑 나도 같이 불렁 가라."

"대국놈 밥상에 오를 찬거리가 신통치 않은 모양이로구나. 그 사이 맘이 변한 걸 보니."
 "네 서방 제상에 올릴 제숙거리나 도와줄까 해서 허는 소린 줄이나 알라."
 억순이는 메밀가루가 담긴 매함지를 차앉은 채 빌례의 얼굴을 더듬었다.
 "고맙긴 허다마는 홑몸도 아니고 헌데……"
 콧등이 찡하게 아려 더 이상 말을 잇지 못했다. 바다 우는 소리가 돌담구멍으로 서랑서랑 밀려 들었다. 곳마을에서 함께 뼈대가 굵었고, 지금도 돌담 줄기를 사이에 두어, 윗아랫녘에 살고 있지만 오늘처럼 빌례에 대한 고마움을 느껴보긴 처음이었다.

3)

 둘은 줄곧 치마저고리마냥 한데 어울려다니며 자랐다. 여남은 살부터는 물질하는 법도 함께 익혔다. 여름이면 수심이 얕은 포구 안에서 자맥질 연습을 했다. 물안경을 끼고 물 속에 들어가 전각이며 우뭇가사리를 캐며 하루를 보내곤 했다.
 예닐곱 살이 되자 둘은 물질하는 데 필요한 용구를 고루 갖췄다. 바다로 나가 어른들과 해녀가 된 것이었다. 바다에 들어갈 때 머리에 쓰는 물수건이며, 잠수할 때 입는 물적삼과 소중이, 물안경과 작살, 소라며 전복을 따는 비창, 미역을 캐는 데 소용되는 정게호미, 그리고 물 속에서 캔 해산물을 담는 그물망사리에 매다는 뒤웅박이 부모에게서 물려받은 유일한 재산이었다.
 감포, 구룡포, 외연도 등지로 해녀벌이를 다닐 때도 둘은 뒤웅박과

망사리마냥 늘 붙어 다녔다. 해풍에 그을린 구리빛 살결을 맞대고 한 방에서 잠을 자면서. 가을, 겨울 동안 대엿 명씩 모여 야학을 할 때도 마찬가지였다. 같은 곳에서 구구법과 자기 이름 자를 터득했다. 시집도 이웃사촌 남정네한테 갔다.

그런데 누가 누구의 운명을 본받고 태어났는지 모르나, 스무남은 살에 모두 청상과부가 됐다. 그것도 약속이나 한 듯이 같은 해에 남편을 잃었다. 빌례 남편은 봄에, 억순이 남편은 가을에 세상을 등졌다.

"나도 군칠이처럼 땅에서 죽을 생각은 않고 사는 놈이여."

빌례 남편의 시체가 이웃마을 해안가에 떠올랐던 날부터 억순이 남편은 술만 마셨다 하면 이런 말을 입버릇처럼 곱씹었다.

입살이 보살이라 하던가. 바다에 쳐 놓은 그물을 걷어오지 못해 안달을 하던 남편은 폭풍우가 멎자 주낙 상자를 둘러메고 어둠 속으로 사라졌다. 그날 밤에는 밤새껏 초가지붕이 날려가는 바람이 불었다. 억순이는 바닷가에서 뜬눈으로 밤을 새웠다. 그러나 남편 일행이 타고 출어했던 배는 끝내 돌아오지 않았다. 아낙네들의 통곡소리가 포구를 메웠다. 남편의 시체는 고사하고 머리카락 한 올도 건져내지 못했다. 물귀신이 돼 버린 것으로 단념할 수밖에 없었다.

억순이는 물귀신이 된 남편과 을선이 남매만을 위해 살기로 마음을 다잡았다. 하루 해가 어떻게 뜨고 지는지 모르게 일에 미쳐 지냈다. 신들린 사람처럼 나날을 보냈다. 길수 녀석이 한창 재롱을 피울 때까지만 해도 단잠을 잘 수 있었다.

억순이 마음에 틈이 생기기 시작한 것은 빌례가 대국놈(키가 크다 하여)의 첩이 되고 나면서부터였다.

빌례가 4대 독자인 대국놈의 첩인지 씨받이가 되기로 작정했다는 말을 귀넘겨 듣던 날 밤에도, 억순이는 거듭 문고리가 제대로 잠궈졌는지를 확인하고서야 잠자리에 들었다.
"명일이 하나 믿엉 곱게 늙을 생각허라, 자손 귀한 집안에 아들 낳아줘서 팔자 고칠 궁리 말앙……"
"아들 하나 믿고 5년 동안 홀로 산 것두 억울허고 칭원하다, 야."
"그래두 시앗싸움 본전 만드느니, 차라리 본서방의 아들 하나 믿엉 사는 게 젊어서는 고생이 될지언정 말년에 편안헐 거여…시앗싸움엔 돌부처도 등 돌아앉는다고 한 옛어른의 말도 되씹어 봐서 결정허라."
"그것사 하느님밖에 모를 일이주마는, 터진 보선 볼 같은 마음을 꿰맬 자신이 없는 걸 어떵 허느냐. 젊은 시절이 계절마다 돌아오는 것도 아니고…… 억순이, 너도 한번 잘 생각해서 미리 마음의 준빌 허는 게 좋을 거여."
"내 걱정은 안 해도 좋으매, 느(네) 앞길이나 잘 닦으라!"
억순이는 을선이와 길수가 잠든 옆으로 몸을 눕혔다. 억순이는 굳게 입을 다물었다. 어떤 배신감 같은 걸 느꼈다. 저런 화냥년과 여태껏 벗해 왔다는 게 부끄러웠다.
그게 빌례와의 마지막 상종이었다. 그 전처럼 대면할 기회도 별로 없었다.
대국놈의 첩이 된 이후, 빌례는 거의 일을 하지 않았다. 물질하는 것도 거의 중단했다. 어쩌다 길거리에서 마주쳤을 땐 억순이가 먼저 얼굴을 모로 돌리곤 했다. 골목길을 가로지르는 구렁이를 목격했을 때마냥 침을 뱉고 돌아섰다.
그러나 억순이네 집 울타리에 접해 있는 밭을 집터로 팔아 달라는 청까지 거절하진 못했다.
"아들인지 딸인지 확인허지 않아도 새 집 지어 주겠다고 해냐."
억순이는 뒤웅박만한 배를 안고 나타난 빌례에게 짐짓 불퉁스럽게 쏘아붙였다.
"집터를 팔아 줄 것가, 말 것가?"
"너네 서방 하룻밤만 빌려주켄 허민 팔아 주켜."
"아예 데려서 살아 불라."
두 사람의 웃음소리에 을선 남매가 눈을 떴다. 억순이는 못된 짓을 하다 들킨 사람마냥 얼굴을 붉혔다.
"새 달 안에 집짓는 일 착수헐 걸루 알라, 이."
빌례는 재차 다짐을 받고서야 마당을 나섰다.
"집턴 팔아 주키여마는 홀어미 옆에 살면서 이것저것 허드렛일 거 들어주잰 허민 귀찮을 거여."
"우리 서방과 눈만 맞추지 않으민 좋다."
서슴없이 우리 서방이란 말을 꺼낼 수 있는 빌례가 부러웠다.
"난 용왕님의 첩으로나 살다 죽을 몸이여. 이 세상 남자들은 이제 화물차루 실어다 줘도 싫다, 야."
그런데 이상한 일이었다.
빌례와 담줄기 하나로 금을 긋고 지내면서부터 억순이는 잠을 설치는 버릇이 생겼다. 댕기머리처럼 곱게 땋아져 있던 마음이 헤실바실 헝클어져 갔다. 해거름녘이 돼 가면 심신이 나른해 일찌감치 일손을 멈추곤 했다. 끈 떨어진 망태기마냥 아무데나 퍼질러앉아 한숨을 내쉬기 일쑤였다. 이유없는 증오와 배신감을 품었던 것만큼이나 빌례를 선망의 눈초리로 지켜봤다. 생채기난 옷가지나 구멍 뚫린 양말짝을 깁다가도 등피불에 시선을 꽂고 앉아있을 때가 많았다. 이리 살다 죽으나 저리 살다 죽으나 북망산 차지밖에 더 되느냐. 빌례의 목소리가 파도를 이루며 억순이 귓가에 부딪쳤다. 그럴 때마다 억순이는 바느질 대신 자신의 허벅지를 침질하듯 톡톡 쏘아댔다. 차라리 밤이 없었으면 했다. 일 년 내내 바다와 들녘으로 헤갈아다닐 수 있는 낮이 아닌 게 한스러웠다. 문고리를 안으로 걸어잠그지 않은 채 자고 일어나선, 괜히 을선이 남매에게 신경질을 부리는 것도 전에 없던 일이었다. 뜯어진 문짝을 고치거나, 실어다 놓은 낟가리를 쌓는 것 같은 잡일은 대국놈이 도맡아 할 만큼 빌례를 닮아 버렸다. 언젠가는 일부러 울담을 무너뜨리고 나서 대국놈을 데려다 부려먹기도 했다.

4)

하늘은 여전히 우중충한 상태 그대로였다.
억순이는 물질 용구를 담은 대구덕을 짊어졌다.
"오늘은 영화비 줘야 헐 거라, 예!?"
부엌에서 점심을 먹던 길수 녀석이 숟갈을 손에 든 채 마당으로 나왔다.
"사친회비 못내 공부도 못하고 되돌아온 주제에 무슨 영화 구경이냐!"
을선이가 숟가락 자루로 길수 뒤통수를 도닥거렸다.
"너가 먼저 영화비 달라는 말 하라고 시키지 않았냐!"
"너, 이따 죽을 줄 알아."
을선이는 눈을 흘깃거리며 부엌으로 몸을 숨겼다.
"어디 가서 네 에미 사갈 사람 데려오라. 글 공부도 하고 영화 구경을 가고 싶거들랑……"
"에이구. 우리한텐 거짓말하면 나쁜 사람 된다면서 약속을 안 지키면 됩니까."
"알았져. 남의 닭들 와서 쪼아먹지 않게 조 이삭 널어 놓은 거나 잘

지켬시라."

"와아, 신난다. 우리 엄마 최고다!"

억순이는 길수의 환호성을 뒤로 하고 바닷가로 향했다. 오늘은 단 몇 분이라도 더 물 속에서 살다 나오리라고 다짐했다.

괫마을 몽땅 뒤져도 라디오 있는 집이 여남은 가호밖에 되지 않아서 그런지 이동영화반이 들어오는 날은 명절날과도 같았다. 아이들은 가을 운동회 날만큼이나 즐거워했다. 영화비가 있거나 말거나, 불배를 따르는 멸치떼마냥 정거장 근처에 자리잡은 가설극장으로 몰려가는 것이었다. 입장을 못한 아이들도 대부분 장막 바깥에서 기다렸다. 저절로 시야를 가리고 있는 장막이 걷히길 고대했다. 영화의 마지막 장면이나마 눈요기할 수 있다는 기대감 하나로 버티었다.

어른들도 마찬가지였다. 흥겨운 노래가락이나마 들어 볼 수 있는 것은 이동여화반이 찾아오는 날뿐이었다. 그러나 억순이에게는 이동영화반이 찾아온 날일수록 마음이 심란했다. 혼잣몸이 된 후에는 더욱 그랬다. 처녀 시절, 처음으로 입맞춤하는 법을 가르쳐 주고 달아난 어느 이동영화반 녀석의 잔영을 지워 내기 위한 것 때문만은 아니었다.

지난번만 하더라도 길수 녀석이 아니었으면 가설극장까지 홰걸음을 치지 않았을 것이다. 길수 혼자서 일 주일 동안 변소 청소를 하게 됐다는 이야기를 들은 바로 뒷날이었다.

설거지를 끝내고 났어도 길수는 계속 끙끙 배앓는 소리를 했다. 부엌문을 닫았다 열었다 하며 영화비 타령을 했다.

"똥구르마나 끌고 다닐 주제에 영화는 무슨 영화냐."

억순이 딴에는 녀석의 입을 봉해 버리려고 한 말이었다.

"모르는 건 언제든지 선생님께 물어봐야 공불 잘헐 수 있다고 하니까 그랬던 거우다."

"내가 그런 것까지 물어보랜 해시냐."

"일학년 때 물어보지 못했던 거난 알아보잰 기영 했수다!"

여자 선생님은 무엇을 먹고 살까 하는 궁금증 때문에 그랬다는 것이다. 여자 선생님이 변소 안으로 들어가는 것을 목격한 것은 그날이 처음이라 했다. 선생님도 우리 엄마처럼 밥을 먹고 사느냐고 여쭤보기 위해 기다리다, 자기도 모르게 여자 선생님이 들어가 있는 변소 문고리 틈으로 눈이 갔다는 것이다.

길수는 징징거리며 을선이와 함께 어둠 속을 사라졌다. 가설극장이 세워진 정거장 쪽에서 날아드는 노래가락이 이슬처럼 내리깔렸다. 억순이는 남매를 불러세울까 하다가 이내 입을 오무렸다. 해묵은 쌀독 속에 구겨놓은 지전마냥 눅진한 마음을 접어둔 채 자리에 누웠다. 그런데 확성기에서 흘러나오던 노래가락이 멎고 얼마 없어서 길수 놈의 목소리가 창문을 흔들었다.

"엄마, 내 신발 찾아다 줍서."

억순이는 성냥을 찾아 등피에 불을 켰다.

"빨리 가서 내 신발 찾아다 줍서게."

길수는 깨끔질을 하듯 발을 동동거렸다. 맨발이었다.

"어디 가서 신을 찾아오라는 것고?"

"영화허는 데 갔다가 뺏겼수다."

옷을 주워입은 억순이는 부리나케 한길로 나섰다.

"어른이 그래냐, 아이가 그래냐?"

"영화비 받는 사람이 그랬수다."

"그 날강도 종내기들하곤."

"구멍치기 허단 그랬수다."

영화비는 없고, 영화는 보고 싶고 해서 출입구에 앉아있는 사람이 한눈파는 새에 장막밑으로 숨어들어가다 들켰다는 것이다.
"다음부턴 영화비 주크매 그런 나쁜짓거리 허지 말라."
"자, 약속……"
녀석이 억순이 손을 끌어당기며 새끼손가락을 걸었다.
"꼭야!?"
"으응, 꼭 주마."
다음에 꼭 편지할게…하는 말 한 마디를 남긴 채 어둠 속으로 자취를 감추던 그 녀석의 얼굴이 안개처럼 시야를 덮었다.
그 날도 하늘에는 별이 총총 박혀 있었다.

5)

수평선 위에 떠 있던 이어도는 다시 구름 속에 잠겨버렸다. 바다로 뛰어들기 위해 물옷으로 갈아입고 있던 해녀들은 다시 한담으로 시간을 끌었다. 좀더 바다가 누그러지기를 기다렸다. 이어도가 자취를 감춘 날은 십중팔구 물살이 거세거나 바닷 속이 어두침침했다.
"오랫만에 몸(멱)이나 감고 가려 했주마는 그냥 가야 헐 것 닮다."
억순이 옆에 앉아 있던 빌례가 몸을 일으키며 수평선 쪽으로 몸을 돌렸다.
"어떤 날에 난 사람은 가을철에도 해수욕허래 댕기는고?"
"아직두 하룻밤을 자고 나면 깻말이나 쏟아지는 모양이로구나, 오늘 같은 날에도 더위를 타는 거 보난……"
"밭 좋고 씨 좋으니 그럴만도 헐 테주."
"대국 놈 얻은 지 두 해짼가, 삼 년짼가."
남의 집에 콩죽 팥죽 쒀 먹어난 잡담에 끼어들었던 사람들 모두 한

마디씩 말곁을 놓았다.

"빌례야, 키가 크난 그 물건도 커냐."

"크다 말다, 이만큼한 말좆만이 헙데다."

귀 죽은 듯 딴청을 부리고 있던 빌례가 좌중을 향해 양 손을 벌려 보였다.

"기영허민 동지섣달에두 바다에서 해수욕을 해도 되엄직허다."

웃음소리가 된하늬에 실려 날아갔다. 어린애를 둔 해녀들은 땅을 치며 깔깔거렸고, 처녀들은 손으로 얼굴을 가려가며 킥킥거렸다.

"등 때 밀어줄 대국놈이나 데리고 와서 그런 소릴 헐 거 아니냐. 남의 웃음 본전 만들지 말고……"

"너년까지 날 놀리기냐."

빌례가 보조개를 지으며 억순이의 어깻죽지를 꼬집었다.

억순이는 고개를 숙였다. 얼굴이 따가웠다. 그러나 다른 사람들은 머쓱한 낯색으로 둘을 쳐다볼 뿐 별다른 반응이 없었다. 여간 다행한 일이 아니었다. 빌례에게도 그날 낮에 있었던 일은 아직 입 밖에 내지 않았던 것이다.

조 파종을 하러 갔던 날이었다.

밭갈이를 끝낸 대국놈은 망태기를 둘러메고 좁씨까지 뿌려 줬다. 씨뿌리기만은 나대로 하겠다고 말하려다 입을 다물었다. 조밭 밟기를 할 말들 쉬남은 마리가 몰려들었다. 조 밭은 학교운동장처럼 딴딴하게 밟을 수록 씨앗이 튼튼하게 자라고, 이삭이 여물었다.

막걸리 사발이 두어 순배 돌자, 말몰이꾼 한 사람이 입을 열었다.

"천생연분이라더니, 궁합이 똑 들어맞겠는걸."

"어허허, 암톨쩌귀와 수톨쩌귀의 짝은 짝도 아니겠어."

"서방은 하늘 높은 줄 알고, 각시는 세상 넓은 줄 아니 만사형통이

겠구먼."

"아주머니, 요리 이렇게 한번 서봅서."

제일 앳돼 보이는 말몰이꾼이 억순이의 뚱뚱한 몸집을 굴리듯 하며 대국놈 옆으로 끌어다 세웠다. 거기다 대국놈까지 덩달아 억순이의 팔목을 잡아끌었다.

"남들 보는 앞에서 이러지 맙서!"

억순이는 흠칫 몸을 도사렸다. 그러나 좁은 입으로 꺼내 넓은 치맛자락으로 거둬 담지 못하는 게 사람의 말이라 어쩔 도리가 없었다. 무의식 중에 내뱉은 말이기에 더욱 얼굴이 화끈거렸다. 오뉴월 땡볕에 그을리고, 땀과 흙먼지로 뒤범벅돼 있었던 것이 다행이었다.

밭에서 돌아오자 대국놈은 막걸리만 한 주전자 비우고 일어섰다.

"저녁 다 됐수다, 먹엉 갑서."

대국놈은 갑자기 귀가 먹었는지 그대로 울담을 넘어 자기 집으로 들어갔다.

억순이는 난간 기둥에 머리를 기댔다.

열엿새달이 초가지붕 너머로 동긋이 떠올랐다. 초가지붕을 덮고 있는 하얀 박꽃과 풀벌레 소리가 더욱 마음을 어지럽게 했다.

달이 중천에 이르러서야 억순이는 옷가지를 챙겨들고 바닷가로 향했다. 먹을 감기 위해 선창가 옆으로 걸음을 옮겼다.

"꼭 물질만 해서 먹고 살란 법이 어디 있어."

"그래도……"

맨살에 샘물 부딪치는 소리가 들렸다.

"잔소리 말고 아들이나 하나 더 낳으라구."

"아이구, 간지럽수다."

대국놈이 빌례의 등때 밀어주는 광경을 떨치고 돌아선 억순이는 귀신들린 사람마냥 중얼거리며 자국을 옮겼다.
─먹돌(차돌)이라면 돌담이나 쌓나, 쇠牛 멍청한 건 잡아나 먹나, 허리 굽은 낭은(나무는)장작이나 한다, 멍텅 볼락은 구어나 먹지. 사람 멍청한 걸 무엇에 쓸꼬……

6)

 선창에 매어져 있던 고깃배 두 척이 포구를 빠져나왔다.
 억순이는 남아 있던 동료들과 함께 물가로 내려섰다. 아홉 사람을 제외하곤 헤실바실 모두 집으로 돌아갔다. 이어도가 수평선 위로 나앉을 때까지 기다리던 사람들만 남아 있었다.
 이어도는 해맑은 날에만 하늘과 수평선이 마주붙은 사이에 모습을 드러냈다. 한파가 몰아치는 겨울 석 달은 좀처럼 구경하기가 힘들었다.
 해녀들의 생명선을 끌고 다니는 뒤웅박 같은 섬이었다. 바람부는 대로 떠다니다가 영등할망이 찾아와서 온갖 해산물의 씨앗을 제주 바다에 뿌리고 간 뒤에는, 어느 마을에서나 볼 수 있는 신비의 섬이었다.
 미역이며 소라, 전복이 많은 보물섬이라 했다. 그러나 아직 아무도 가 본 사람은 없다. 이어도를 찾아나섰던 사람은 수없이 많으나, 되돌아온 사람은 단 한 명도 없다. 배를 타고 가면 갈수록 수평선 너머로 뒤물러 앉는 섬이라는 이야기가 남아 있을 뿐이다.
 바다가 거칠기로 이름난 곳이라기에 더욱 가보고 싶은 섬으로 해녀들의 마음속에 자리잡고 있는지 모른다. 아무도 범접할 수 없는 곳에 위치한 섬이기에 전복과 소라를 동산을 이루고 미역으로 숲을 이루고 있다는 것일까. 먼 발치에서 지켜보며 한숨이나 쉬게 하는 이어도. 꿈결에나 가 닿을 수 있는 섬이기에, 맷돌 앞에 앉았을 때나 방아채를 쥐고 있으면서도, 밭이랑에 앉아 김을 매거나 마당질을 하면서도 이어도를 불러대는 것이라 생각했다.

억순이는 메주덩이만한 돌멩이를 주워 망사리에 달린 끈에 매달았다. 물살이 거셀 때는 닻돌이 있어야 했다. 그렇지 않으면, 자맥질을 하고 나왔을 때마다 뒤웅박에 끌려 천방지축 달아나 버리는 것이었다.

뒤웅박을 가슴에 안고 미끄러지듯 바다로 몸을 던진 억순이는 이내 구슬픈 노래가락을 뽑아냈다.

―우리 어멍(엄마) 날 나을 적엔, 해도 달도 없는 날에 낳아신가, 이어도사나 이어도사나……

억순이는 계속 가락에 맞춰 헤엄을 쳐 나갔다. 바닷가에서 멀찌기 떨어져 있는 여嶼에 앉아 있던 갈매기들이 깃을 치며 날아올랐다. 물오리들은 억순이와 나란히 헤엄을 쳐 나갔다.

호오이―

호오이―

여기저기에서 가쁜 숨을 토해내는 숨비질(자맥질) 소리가 바다 위로 널브러졌다.

억순이는 동료들의 허우젯소리를 뒤로 하고 한참 난바다 쪽으로 나간 후에야 작업을 시작했다.

호오잇!

수면 위로 몸을 끌어올린 억순이는 휘파람을 불듯 틀어막았던 숨통을 터뜨렸다. 하얀 포말이 수면 위로 흩어졌다. 다시 하늘을 향해 발길질을 했다. 물구나무를 서듯 하고 물 속으로 들어갔다. 들녘길을 줄달음치듯 바다 밑바닥을 더듬어 나갔다. 숨통이 저려오기 시작했다. 용왕님은 바다 속 어딘가에 산다 했으니, 물 속에도 숨돌릴 곳이 있을 법한데 해초의 숲과 물고기뿐이었다.

―생복도 큼도 크다. 암천복인지 수천복인진 모르주마는… 껍질이 넓둥글진 걸로 봐서 암컷인 듯했다. 수천복은 껍질이 움패어져 있다. 억순이는 전복 하나를 따내기 위해 거듭해서 수면 위와 바다 밑을 오르내렸다. 거친 숨을 몰아쉬며 곤두박질쳐댔다. 설드럭 틈에 박혀 있어서 힘이 들었다.

비창을 거머쥐고 대엿 차례 자맥질을 하고 나서야 전복 하나를 따냈다.

7)

한기가 전신에 퍼지는 것으로 봐 두어 시간 이상 흐른 것 같았다. 바다에 남아 있는 사람은 억순이 혼자뿐이었다. 바닷가 화덕에서 불을 쬐고 있는 모습이 가물거렸다.

해물이 담겨 있는 그물망사리가 묵직했다. 전복만도 세 개였다. 전복은 남편 제사상에 올릴 적을 하고, 소라와 우뭇가사리 같은 잡동사니는 팔아서 사친회비를 마련하기로 작정했다. 갱거리할 물고기는 한 마리도 쏘지 못했다. 소라는 적을 하고, 값이 많이 나갈 전복은 팔아야겠다고 마음을 고쳐먹은 억순이는 발놀림을 빨리 했다. 그런데 이상한 일이었다. 다리는 계속 놀리고 있는데 몸은 점점 바다 밑으로 가라앉는 것이었다. 억순이는 물안경을 이마로 밀어올리고 뒤웅박을 뒤척였다.

"아이고, 이 내 원수야!"

머릿속은 온통 딸그락 탁! 하고 숨통에 금이 가던 소리로 꽉 찼다. 좁쌀방울만큼 타개져 있던 뒤웅박 꼭지 부위에 팥알맹이만큼 상채기가 나 있었다.

동료들이 불을 쬐고 있는 화덕 쪽을 향하여 소리를 지르기엔 너무 멀었다.

행여나 하고 사위를 두리번거렸다. 물오리들이 한가롭게 노는 모습 밖에 눈에 띄는 게 없었다.

머리에 쓰고 있던 하얀 물수건을 벗어 소살 끝에 걸쳤다.

"사람 살려!"

"………"

"사람 살려!"

소살을 허공으로 추켜올리며 외쳐대는 억순이의 육성은 메아리도 없이 사그라졌다. 땅 위라면 담배 두어 대 피울 시간이면 닿을 수 있는 거리였다. 구명 신호를 보내던 물수건마저 바람에 날려 갔다. 소라, 전복이 담긴 망사리는 점점 바다 밑으로 가라앉았다. 그러나 숨통이 닳게 거둬들인 것들이기에 어느것 하나도 내던져 버릴 수가 없었다. 뒤웅박에 물이 차서, 몸뚱이가 물 속으로 가라앉는 한이 있어도 그냥 헤엄쳐 가기로 마음을 굳혔다. 모든 걸 용왕님께 맡기기로 했다. 해풍에 밀려오는 시커먼 매지구름이 더욱 숨통을 조였다. ……속상한 일도 하도 많으니 놀기도 하면서 살아 보세. 니나노 닐니리야 닐니리야 니나노 얼싸 좋아…… 이동영화반이 와 있는 신작로 가에서 날아드는 구성진 노래가락이 억순이의 구멍 난 뒤웅박 속으로 콸콸 스며들었다. 이어도에서 밀려오는 구름은 액운을 막아준다. 이어도의 물살은 한숨을 씻어내린다. 이어도에서 불어오는 바람은 이내 간장에 붙은 불을 꺼준다.

억순이는 혼백魂魄 상자와도 같은 뒤웅박을 껴안은 채 쉬지 않고 다리를 놀려댔다.

이어도사나 이어도사나. 바다에도 쉼돌이 있나, 산전山田에도 의지할 돌담이 있나. 이어도사나……

오성찬

달 뜨는 내 고향

필자 소개
제주도 서귀포 출생. 1969년 〈신아일보〉 신춘문예 소설 당선.
신문기자와 박물관 큐레이터 역임. 도서출판 반석 대표(현)
소설집 『한라산』 『어두운 시대의 초상화』 『나비로의 환생』 등.
요산문학상, 한국소설문학상, 한국문학상 등 수상.

달 뜨는 내 고향

오성찬

1

 이제 환갑도 넘긴 나 같은 사람에게 도대체 고향의 의미는 무엇일까. 나는 버스 창에 기대어 잠을 자다가 깨어서 문득 그 생각을 했다. 마침 긴 다리가 나타났고, 그 다리를 건너자 갈랫길이었다. 왼손 편으로는 포구로 내려가는 길이며, 오른 쪽으로 가면 우리 고향, 월출리月出里 마을이었다. 마을 뒷편으로 월출산이 언제나 그랬듯이 의젓한 모습으로 앉아 있었다. 나는 그 산을 바라보며 정거장에서 버스를 내렸다. 이것은 언제나 내가 고향으로 내려올 때마다 되풀이하는 과정이었고, 이쯤에서부터 나는 어머니를 만났을 때처럼 가슴이 설레었다. 그런데 나는 버스에서 내려 마을로 들어가면서도 이상케 아무런 감동도 받을 수가 없었다. 그것은 마을에 여기저기 들어선 고층건물들이 왠지 낯설어 보였기 때문이다.
 나는 다리 밑을 흘러와 오른손 편에 펼쳐진 호수같은 바다를 바라보았다. 그런데 거기 언제나 떼로 와 앉아 있곤 하던 갈매기, 고니, 두루

미 같은 철새들은 보이지 않았다. 저쪽 산과 구름 그림자가 드리워져 있는 텅 빈 잿빛 호수가 냉담하게 가라앉아 있었다. 나는 천천히 호숫가를 에둘러 뻗어있는 아스팔트길을 걷기 시작했다.

'아아, 이것이었구나!'

나는 그만 호수의 수면을 살피다가 속으로 적잖이 놀라버렸다. 우리가 어린 시절에 물수제비를 띄우며 놀고, 자갈도 모래마저도 셀 수 있을 것처럼 맑았던 그때의 물이 아니었다. 뜨물 같이 흐릿한 수심에 아직까지 한번도 봐보지 않았던 푸른빛의 수초가 돋아나 물결이 일 때마다 흐늘흐늘 흐늘거리고 있었다. 그 수초들 사이로 옛날에는 본 적 없었던 송사리처럼 보이는 작은 고기들이 천천히 헤엄쳐 다니고 있었다. 그러나 어린 시절에 뛰던 숭어는 어디로야 갔는지 한 마리도 보이지 않았다. 물은 차라리 죽어 있다고 하는 표현이 옳았다.

우리 마을은 언제 설촌設村 했는지는 모르나 처음에는 어부들이나 몰려 사는 갯촌이었을 것이다. 그러던 것이 일제 식민지 시대가 되면서 그들은 근해에 많이 나는 어류와 패류, 해산물들에 눈독을 들이게 되었다. 그래서 그 방면의 사람들을 식민植民하고, 이 마을을 수산기지水産基地로 발전시키기 시작했다. 그리 크지 않은 포구 마을에 색시들까지 둔 술집이 세 집이나 있었던 것이 그것을 증명하고 있었다. 그러나 내가 철이 들 무렵에는 이미 해방이 되어 있어서 성시를 보냈던 그 집들도 시들해지고, 다만 그들이 만들어 놓은 적산 소라통조림 공장만이 남아 있었다. 어머니의 말씀에 따르면 우리 가족이 여기로 오게 된 것은 아버지가 이 공장의 공장장이 되어서 여기 근무하기 시작하면서부터였다. 그러나 그 공장이 결국 망하게 되자 아버지는 할아버지 고향에서 땅을 팔아와 인연이 있는 이 마을에 여관을 지은 것이었다. 그래서 나는 어렸을 때 '여관집 아들'로 통했었다.

아버지는 그때만 해도 이 마을에 여관이 없어 포구를 통해 염소섬, 토끼섬 등 가까운 섬으로 가는 사람들이 폭풍을 만나거나 무슨 일이 있을 때 어려움을 당하는 것을 여러 차례 보아왔기 때문이었다. 마음이 여린 아버지는 여관을 하기 전에 실지로 그런 사람들을 우리 집으로 데리고 와서 잠을 재워주고, 밥을 지어 먹이고 하던 일을 나도 어렸을 때 봤었다. 그러나 내가 고향에 있을 때만 해도 여관업이 잘 되질 않아서 그저 근근히 먹고 살 정도였다. 그 무렵 아버지는 자기 일을 찾아서 한동안 잠수부들과 함께 '머구리 배'의 기관장이 된 적도 있었으나 어머니가 극구 말려서 그만 두었다.

정미소를 지나면 키 작은 할머니가 쪄서 팔던 찐빵집이었다. 기어 들어가야 할 정도로 납작한 초가집, 그러나 빵집도 정미소도 이젠 다 사라지고 그 두 집을 아우른 자리에 낯선 새 건물이 들어서 있었다. 나로서는 추억 어린 장소였는데, 아쉬웠다. 심난해서 마을 중심으로 들어서는데 나는 옛날 가끔 친구들과 함께 와서 밥도 먹던 납작한 기와집 <월출식당> 옆에 <달맞이 레스토랑>이라는 전혀 어울리지 않는 삼층 건물이 들어서 있는 것을 보았다. 월출식당은 그때도 그랬지만 삼층 레스토랑의 그늘에 가려져 버린 이제 더욱 초라하게 보였다. 그런데 나는 우리 <월출여관>이 앉아있는 곳까지 와서 진짜 놀라운 장면과 부딪쳤다. 일층 기와집의 우리 여관 바로 옆에 대충 짐작으로 십 층은 실히 돼 보이는 거대한 관광호텔이 들어서 있었기 때문이었다. 거기 간판에 <달맞이호텔>이라는 금빛 찬란한 글씨가 반짝이며 나를 놀리는 듯했다. 나는 그만 어안이 벙벙했다. 큰 것과 작은 것, 높은 것과 낮은 것은 이렇게도 안 어울리는구나. 상대적 빈곤이란 이제 도시에만 있는 것이 아니었다.

나는 비로소 아무 것도 들고 있지 않은 나의 빈손을 내려다봤다. 내가 쓰고 있는 등산모, 아무렇게나 꿰어 신은 헌 등산화도 떠올렸다. 가슴이 을큰하게 아프며 이제 더 늙으셨을 부모님 얼굴이 떠올랐다. 가진 것 모두를 이 잘난 아들을 위해 쓰고도 오히려 그것을 자랑스러워 하셨던 어머니, 아버지. 그런데 이제 나는 도대체 이게 무어란 말인가.

게다가 나는 얼마 없어 퇴출을 당할 것이다. 사실 그것이 명퇴라고 하지만 어느 세상에 거의 반생 몸담아 온 직장을 밀어내듯 내보내는 처사가 있단 말인가. 옛날부터 고향은 금의환향하는 곳이라고 했다. 나에게도 그런 세월은 없지 않았다. 내가 세상이 다 알아주는 일류대학을 졸업하자마자 대기업에 입사를 하고 처음으로 고향에 왔을 때 부모님은 물론 친척들이나 고향 사람들 모두가 나를 그렇게 부러워했었다.

―누구 누구해도 너가 젤 출세했다.

―나도 서울 간 때 차 타고 지나가며 그 건물을 보았는디 느가 그런 델 들어가다니 참 잘했저.

만나는 사람마다 내 어깨를 두드리며 내게 찬사를 보냈다. 그러나 솔직히 그 높은 건물에서 근무했던 시절 그렇게 자랑스럽고 긍지를 가질만 했는가 누가 묻는다면 나는 난처했을 것이다. 돈 가진 사람들은 언제나 더 많은 것을 갖고 싶어했고, 그러다 보니까 언제나 불안하고, 뒷감당하기 힘들어 했다.

나는 한창 시절에 한동안 우리 왕회장의 비서로 지낸 적이 있었다. 그리고 그와 함께 유럽과 미국 등지를 돌아다닌 적이 있었는데, 그때 거대한 회사의 회장 자리, 그 허상이 어떤 것인가를 처절하게 알아버렸다.

그는 가는 곳마다 목적지 호텔에 도착하면 샤워도 하기 전에 본사로 전화를 거는 게 일이었다.

—야, 정 사장! 내가 말한 백억 원 어떻게 했어?

그리고 한참 저쪽의 보고를 듣고 있다가는 다시 버럭 역정을 내었다.

—아직까지 그걸 못 막으면 어떻게 돼? 어떻게 해서라도 오늘 안에 꼭 막으란 말이야!

자고 나서 이튿날도 새벽부터 전화질이었다. 이번에는 다른 자회사의 사장이 불려 나왔다.

—야, 한 사장. 내가 그때 말했잖아. 그 이 백 오십 억 어떻게 했냐구?

늘 이런 식이었다. 나는 그와 함께 여행을 하면서 부자도 별 게 아니구나 속으로 치부를 해버렸다. 부자에 대한 환멸을 뼈 속 깊이 느낀 것이었다. 그 등골에 땀이 나는 여행 이후로부터 나는 매사에 시들해지고, 기회만 있으면 한직을 찾게 되었다. 그리고 나는 마침내 밀리고 밀려 이제 벼랑으로 떨어지게 되었지만……

부모님은 텅 빈 여관 넓은 마루에서 둘이 맞잡으며 이불깃을 바꾸고 있다가 내가 들어서자 화들짝 놀라서 내달았다.

"어쩐 일이냐? 아무 기별도 없이……"

긴 실을 꿴 바늘을 들고 일어서는 어머니의 주름진 얼굴에 구름이 끼는 걸 나는 보았다.

"전화라도 걸고 오지."

아버지의 얼굴도 그 동안 많이 늙으셨다. 어쩌면 그들은 자기들의 경험에 의하여 내 귀향 이유를 짐작하고 있을지도 모른다.

"저어, 부산까지 출장을 왔다가 갑자기 고향엘 와 보고 싶어서마씀."

나는 말끝을 흐리며 궁여지책으로 둘러대었다. 그런데 내 입이 어느새 고향 말을 되찾은 것은 다행스런 일이었다. 그것은 얼마나 정겨운

톤이던가.

"잘했다. 잘했구말구. 그런데 점심은?"

"오는 길에 읍내에서 친구들과 먹고 왔수다."

"그럼 커피라도 한잔 타오마."

어머니께서 부엌으로 가는데 "커피는 매날 마시는 거, 타 올 테면 다른 차를 타오지." 하고 아버지께서 등뒤에다 대고 말씀하셨다. 어차피 아무거나 마셔야 할 판이니 나는 아무 말도 하지 않았다. 나는 신발을 벗기 전에 집의 뒤뜰이랑 사방을 휘휘 둘러보았다. 옛날 식구들이 살던 사가는 뜯어 고쳐 별채로 쓰고 있고, 보이는 것마다 너무 낡았다. 아무거나 만지면 파삭 부서져 버릴 것만 같다. 세월 뿐 아니라 태풍의 계절이면 몰아오는 짠물이 낡아지는 것을 도왔을 것이다. 이제 이런 것은 도시에 익숙해져버린 나로서는 너무 낯설었다.

우리는 응접 탁자에 둘러앉아 어머니께서 타온 차를 마신다. 아버지와 어머니는 커피, 나는 꿀에 재운 인삼차다. 그런데 그 날리던 어머니의 손맛도 낡아졌는가. 옛날 그 개운한 맛이 아니다.

"옆에 큰 호텔이 들어서 버려서 손님이 많이 줄었겠네요?"

나는 고개를 돌려 호텔 쪽을 바라보며 조심스럽게 말을 꺼냈다.

"옛날이나 이제나 언제 그렇게 큰돈 벌었던 시절 있냐? 그래도 호텔 못 가는 사람이 아직은 더러 있다. 느 아부지야 언제는 욕심이 있는 사람이냐?"

아버지는 차만 마시고 어머니께서 응대하신다.

"맞수다. 부자, 그거 별 거 아니라 마씀."

나는 짧게 대답한다. 그 짧은 대답 속에서도 나는 이미 내 속의 말을 하고 있다. 더 길게 얘기하다가는 자칫하면 내 처지를 발설하게 될지도 모른다.

"더러는 돈 있는 사람들도 우리 같은 여관이나 민박을 찾더라."
마침내 아버지께서 입을 여셨다. 나는 부모님의 이런 긍정적인 면이 고맙다.
"당연히 그래야 하는 거 아니우꽈."
나는 그만한 것도 다행이라고 생각한다.

2

성게와 소라를 사다가 저녁을 지으마 하고 밖으로 나가시는 어머니를 뒤따라 나도 밖으로 나왔다. 언제 넓힌 것인지 길 양쪽이 내가 자랄 때보다 배는 넓게 넓혀졌다. 그때는 차 두 대가 양쪽에서 지나가기가 빠듯했는데 지금은 네 대가 지나가고도 남게 사차선으로 그려졌다. 우리 여관에서 한 오 분 걸으면 네거리가 나오고, 거기 옛날엔 수산물 전진기지가 있었는데 지금은 수협으로 바뀌어 있다. 수협 앞에 농협, 그 옆에 지서, 그리고 그 맞은쪽엔 우리들이 노상 들락거리며 빙과를 사 먹던 가게가 있었는데 지금 그 가게는 온데 간데 없고 그 자리에 극장 같은 패밀리 마트가 들어서 있다. 나는 그 안으로 들어가 볼까 하다가 그만 둔다. 소비의 시대라고 하더니 이 작은 마을에 저런 큰 마트라니 어울리지가 않다. 이런 시골까지 저런 것들이 들어서 소비심리를 부추기고 있으니 전 국토가 상대적 빈곤감을 느낄 것은 두말할 필요도 없겠다.

거기서 좀 떨어져서 빨간 우체통이 서있는 뒤에 우체국이 들어서 있다. 저 자리는 내가 고등학생 시절에도 우체통이 서있던 자리다. 나는 그때 달걀처럼 얼굴이 갸름한 한 반 여자친구를 좋아하고 있었는데 2학년 겨울방학 때 가슴 조이며 쓴 편지를 눈이 사선을 그으며 내리는 날에 오버를 뒤집어쓰고 나와서 통 속에 집어넣던 기억이 떠올랐다. 그렇다. 그리고 또 한 아이, J라는 아이가 있었다. 여자가 조숙하다는 얘기를 흔히들 하지만 이제 생각하니까 그 아이는 나보다 훨씬 조숙했던 것이 분명하다. 여관집 아들인데다 공부도 잘했던 나는 친구들뿐 아니라 여자아이들로부터도 분명 선망의 대상이었다.

그때도 지금처럼 이른봄이었을까. 아니 가을이었는지도 모르겠다. 다만 바닷가에서도 그리 춥지 않은 계절이었던 것만은 분명하다. 그 무렵 나는 외삼촌이 일본에서 올 때 사다 준 하모니카를 한동안 연습해서 잘 불 수 있었다. 그 계절의 어느 날 저녁. 그녀는 나에게 하모니카를 불어달라면서 월출봉 벼랑 밑의 달뜨는 아래 모래판으로 나를 끌고 갔었다.

내 발길은 무엇에 끌린 듯 그날 저녁처럼 자연스럽게 마을 안 길을 걸어 그 달뜨는 아래 바닷가로 나가고 있었다. 그때 그녀네 집이 아마 바다로 나가는 어귀 이 근처 어디쯤이었을 것이다. 그러나 그 주변도 옛날 집들은 다 사라지고 새 건물들이 들어서고 길도 새로 나서 어디가 어딘지 분명히 알 수가 없다. 그러나 일제 시대 원양 어부들이 자주 드나들던 색시집이 늘어섰던 그 골목만은 변하지 않아서 오랜 세월과 먼지를 뒤집어쓴 건물들이 퇴기처럼 낡아가고 있었다. 그런데 나는 그 골목을 지나쳐 달뜨는 아래 모래판으로 나가다가 밀물이 들어와 그 모래판이 아주 사라져있는 것을 보았다. 그때도 밀물이면 파도가 여기까지 밀려 왔던 것일까? 그것을 기억할 수가 없다. 나는 거기서도 낯선 것을 경험했다.

그런데다 거기 바다는 옛날 바다가 아니었다. 파도가 이는 가까운 해변에는 스티로폴과 골판지, 배가 부서진 낡은 조각널 같은 것들이 무수히 떠다니고, 그 푸르던 바다는 수면마저 시커멨다. 무수히 떠다니던 갈매기, 수면 위를 떠다니다가 고기를 잡으러 수심 깊이 자맥질해 들어가던 오리들도 하나 보이지 않았다.

그때 우리가 앉았던 모래판이 어디쯤일까. 그때 그 아이는 자기 손수건을 꺼내 내가 앉을 자리에 깔아 주었다. 내가 극구 사양을 했지만 그녀는 먼저 맨바닥에 자기 엉덩이를 내려놔 버렸다.

─그 대신 하모니카를 불어주면 되잖아.

그녀는 이런 말로 미안해하는 나를 달랬다. 나는 그때 '고향의 봄'과 '내 고향 남쪽 바다'같은 어른스런 곡을 하모니카로 불었을 것이다. 그것은 그 무렵 내가 잘 불었던 노래였으니까. 그러고 나서 그녀는 내게 바짝 다가앉으며 속삭이는 말로 물었다.

─나를 좋아하긴 좋아하는 거야?

그녀는 그 무렵 학교에서 공부도 잘하고 예쁘고, 어쨌든 잘 나가는 축에 들었기 때문에 나는 차마 아니라고 대답할 수가 없었다. 그러나 나는 자꾸 그녀와 함께 있어도 달걀처럼 갸름한 그녀, 다른 얼굴이 가끔 떠올랐다. 그러나 나는 대답했다.

─응.

─그런 대답이 어디 있어? 혁이가 나를 좋아한다면 솔직히 손이라도 잡아줘야 하는 거 아니야?

나는 덜덜덜 떨리는 손으로 그녀의 손을 잡았다. 그러자 그녀가 다시 물었다.

─내 손 따뜻하지?

바닷가에 오래 나와 있었는데 손이 따뜻할 리가 있는가. 오히려 섬뜩하다는 편이 옳을 것이다. 그러나 나는 사실대로 말할 수가 도저히 없었다.

─응.

그래서 나는 또 마음에도 없는 대답을 하고 말았다. 그 순간 그녀는 몸을 돌려 와락 나를 안아버렸다. 나도 얼떨김에 그녀에게 안겼다. 나로서는 처음 여자였다.

그러나 이제 비로소 고백하거니와 그 눈이 사선을 그으며 내리던 날 오버를 쓰고 나와서 우체통에 편지를 넣은 여자는 그 아이가 아니었다. 그 무렵부터 내 마음을 사로잡은 아이는 따로 있었던 것이다. 어린 마음에 J의 저돌적임이 부담이 되었던 것일까. 그때 나는 한 여자로부터 사랑을 받았고, 다른 한 여자를 사랑했다. 그러나 나는 그 두 여자에게 아무 말도 못하고 서울로 올라가서 한동안 공부에 파묻혀 버렸다. 그 여자들과 나를 떼어놓은 것을 거리였을까. 아니 세월일 수도 있겠다. 이제 그것들은 밀물이 밀려와 모래 위에 쓴 글씨를 지우듯 모두를 덮어 버렸다. 초로의 그녀들은 지금쯤 어디서 무엇을 하고 있을까? 갑자기 그녀들이 보고 싶었다.

3

나는 추억이 서린 모래판을 돌아 나와 바로 월출봉을 올라가는 코스 쪽으로 돌았다. 어린시절 저 우뚝한 봉우리는 우리의 희망이요 표상이었다. 더구나 음력 팔월, 추석이 돌아오면 그날 밤에는 너도나도 저 꼭대기까지 기어올라가 떠오르는 달을 바라보고자 했다. 꼭대기까지 올라가는 코스에는 지난 태풍에 무너져 내려 올라가기 어려운 고비가 한두 군데 있었으나 서로 위에서 당기고, 뒤에서 엉덩이를 바치고 하면서 올라갔다. 그러나 우리가 숨이 턱에 닿아서 올라가 보면 달은 벌써 어둡기도 전에 하얀 달로 떠올라서 우리를 내려다보고 있곤 했다. 그때의 실망감이라니⋯ 그러나 우리는 이듬해에도 또 그 꼭대기에를 올랐다. 그 봉우리에 올라 그 달을 보아야만 그해 소원을 이룰 수 있다고 내려오는 속설 때문이었다.

그러나 몇 년 전에 회사의 상사를 모시고 관광을 온 적이 있었는데 그때 걱정을 하면서 올라간 등반 코스는 돌과 시멘트로 계단을 만들어 놔서 어린아이라도 올라갈 수가 있게 되어 있었다. 그리고 나는 거기서 실지로 하이힐을 신고 올라간 아주머니 한 분을 만났다. 산이란 올라가기 힘든 맛도 있어야 하는 법인데, 이제 사람들은 지나치게 편한 것만을 좇고 있는 것 같았다.

고향에서 고등학교까지를 마치고 서울의 대학에 합격했을 때 마을 사람들은 내가 열심히 월출봉에 올라가 달을 본 덕분이라고들 했다. 월출봉의 정기가 너를 낳은 것이라고 모두들 좋아하며 마을발전협의회에서 이 코스의 입구에 플래카드를 내걸었던 일을 나는 지금도 기억하고 있다. 그러나 이제 마을 사람들은 아무도 저 봉우리에 올라가지 않는다고 했다. 대신 잘 닦아놓은 길을 관광객들이 몰려다니고 있었다. 혹 마을 사람들이 올라가는 경우가 있다해도 그들을 안내해야 할 경우가 있을 때뿐이었다. 일제 때 포구와 바다가 그들에게 넘어갔듯이 이제 월출봉도 주인이 바뀌어 있었다.

나도 등반 코스를 버리고 여길 찾아오는 관광객들을 위해 일기 좋은 때만 서는 해산물 벼룩시장 쪽으로 발길을 돌리고 있었다. 거기 바닷가로 내려가면 날 소라나 해삼도 먹을 수 있을지 몰랐다.

"야, 너 창혁이 아니가?"

걸걸한 목청이 어귀에서부터 내 발길을 걸었다. 부러 등산모를 눌러 쓰고 색안경까지 끼었는데 그는 어떻게 나를 알아보았을까.

"맞지. 너 창혁이지? 나 태부다!"

그는 날씬했던 몸이 몰라보게 뚱뚱해졌으나 분명 변태부였다. 이 아이는 학생 때 달리기 선수였고, 운동이라면 못하는 게 없었다. 그는 우리학교에서 면단위 대회, 도 단위 대회 때도 대표선수로 나가서 무조건 상을 휩쓸어오던 장래가 촉망되던 운동선수였다. 그리고 태권도를 배워서 고등학생 때는 전체 학생이 발발 떠는 기율부장이었다. 이놈은 그때 심지어 나에게도 담배 값 하겠다면서 돈 천 원을 뜯은 적이 있었다. 그러나 고등학교 졸업을 하고 가정 사정으로 진학을 할 수가 없었던 그는 고향 중학교에서 체육 코치를 한다는 소문이더니 이제 그는 날씬하던 몸매가 씨름선수처럼 비대해져서 날지 못하는 새가 되어 있었다.

"훈이 어멍, 어이, 훈이 어멍. 내 동창 친군데 말이야. 인사드려."

여자는 엎드린 채 발이 굉장히 큰 오징어들을 뒤척이고 있으면서 시선만 쳐들어 나를 보았다. 그러나 영락없는 시장 아줌마 모습의 그녀는 분명 내가 달갑지 않은 눈치였다. 척 봐서 내가 아무 것도 사지 않으리라는 것을 때려잡아 아는 눈치였다. 거기다 놈은 이 자리에서 아내에게 노상 친구들을 팔아온 게 틀림없었다.

"이 친구는 말이야 대기업의 상무야! 시시한 다른 친구들과는 다르다구."

나는 엎드려 이것저것 뒤져봤으나 내가 살만한 물건을 고를 수가 없었다.

"야, 그러지 말고 저 아래로 내려가서 소주나 한잔 빨자. 야 이거 정말 얼마 만이냐?"

내가 그 뚱뚱한 몸을 좇아 비탈을 내려가는데 새된 여자의 목소리가 뒷덜미를 쳤다.

"족족 먹엉 재기 옵서 예!"

"내가 친구가 어디 한 둘이냐? 그러니 매일 찾아오는 친구들과 한두 잔씩 하게 되거든. 그래서 그런 것이니 상관 말아."

　비탈 아래서는 잠수들이 소라와 문어, 멍게 등속을 안주로 소주를 팔고 있었는데, 그것 한 접시를 청해놓고 소주를 따랐을 때 태부가 내게 둘러댔다. 나는 대답 대신 푸시시 웃었다. 그리고 소라 한 점을 집어 입에 넣었다. 바로 이 맛이었다. 나에게 있어 고향과 소라의 이미지는 동일한 것이었다. 나는 그것을 오독오독 씹으며 한마디했다.

　"우리 동창 친구들은 다 잘 있는 거냐?"

　"응. 그런데 아마 반은 죽었을 거야. 두만이, 만호, 창식이, 그 자식들 다 가버렸어. 야, 솔직히 우리도 이제 좋은 날은 다 간 것 아니냐?"

　나는 술잔을 들고 그 투명한 속에 그 아이들의 얼굴을 떠올려 보려고 애썼다. 그러나 그 애들 얼굴을 떠올리려 해도 잘되지 않고 희미했다. 대신 떠오르는 한 얼굴. 형만이의 둥글넓적한 얼굴이었다. 그러나 나는 이내 그 얼굴을 털어 버렸다. 그 아이는 나와 초등학교서부터 고등학교까지를 같이 다녔다. 그리고 계속 나와 일·이등을 다투던 놈이었다. 어쩌면 나는 그 시절 내내 그 친구를 이기려고 기를 쓰고 공부를 했는 지도 모른다.

　"형만이는 어떻게 지내니?"

　술 몇 잔이 속으로 들어가자 나는 더욱 그에 대한 궁금증을 털어버릴 수가 없었다.

　"그 친구 학교 때도 그랬지만 요새도 유람선과 유채밭 해서 재미가 꽤 쏠쏠하다. 우리 한잔하고 그 놈 만나볼까?"

　"그러지 뭐."

　우리는 의기투합했다. 소라와 해삼 안주에 소주 두 병이 금세 바닥이 났다.

　"아, 저기 봐라. 저기! 저것이 형만이네 유람선이다."

마침 벼랑 아래를 물살을 가르며 돌아가는 작은 배를 가리키며 태부가 말했다.
"형만이 다음에 군의원 나온다고 지금부터 대단하다."
그래. 사람은 누구나 돈 다음엔 명리를 좇게 되어 있지. 나는 속으로만 중얼거렸다.
"아 참, 너 J 좋아했었지? 그 여자 생각 안나니?"
나는 또 푸시시 웃고 말았다.
"그 여자 너희 여관 옆 호텔에서 청소한다."
"남편은 어떻게 되구?"
술을 마시는 동안에 나는 다급하게 물었다.
"자식이 원래 바람둥이였잖아. 어디 갔는지 몰라."
나는 더 묻지 않았다. 나는 술잔을 들고 그 맑은 내면을 들여다보았다. 거기 세일러복의 J가 떠서 나를 향해 웃고 있었다. 나는 그 잔을 들어 단숨에 마셔버렸다. 나는 갑자기 비감해졌다. 내가 그 여자와 계속 연애를 해서 지금까지 이어졌으면 행복했을까. 그와 반대일까. 밀물 때여서 파도가 어느새 우리가 앉아있는 발 밑까지 밀려오고 있었다. 그것이 밀려오며 그때마다 내게 속삭이는 것 같았다. 허무하다. 허무하다. 모든 게 허무하다고.

4

낮술 두 병을 비우고 태부네 가게를 피하여 주차장으로 나오자 거기 차들이 빼곡이 들어찬 한쪽에 먼지투성이 지프 한 대가 외따로 세워져 있었다. 나도 얼굴이 타는 듯하고, 그놈도 얼굴이 붉었다. 그러나 놈은 나를 억지로 밀어 차에 태우더니 자기도 운전석에 올랐다.

"야, 너 술 먹고 운전해도 괜찮니?"

나는 솔직히 걱정이 됐다.

"내불라. 내 면허장은 음주면허장 아니가? 그래도 나가 아직까지는 죽지 않았다 이."

"알았다. 알았어. 핸들이나 꽉 잡아라."

형만이네 밭은 마을에서 벗어나 오 분도 안 걸리는 지척지간이었다. 길가를 따라 길쭉하게 뻗은 그 밭은 마침 학교를 가고 오는 길가에 있어서 우리는 무를 가는 철이면 밑동이 미끈한 무를 발길로 툭 차서 꺾어 죽죽 껍질을 벗기며 먹고, 고구마 철이면 이제 막 들기 시작한 애고구마를 캐서 잔디에 쓱쓱 문질러 흙을 털고 먹었다. 형만이는 자기 밭의 이런 것들을 친구를 사귀는 수단으로 삼았기 때문에 나도 몇 번 같이 무와 고구마 서리를 한 적이 있었다. 그러나 극성스런 그 아버지에게는 아이들의 그런 짓이 영 못마땅한가 보았다. 그래서 엔젠가는 산에서 가시를 캐다가 철조망처럼 쳐놓은 적도 있었는데 그렇다고 극성스런 애들의 장난을 막아질까. 고구마가 여물 무렵이면 그 가시들을 차곡차곡 재워 놓고 그 위에 시뻘건 고구마들을 캐다가 올려놓은 다음 묵은 잔디 불쏘시개에 불을 붙이고 바닥에서 불을 붙여서 구워 먹었다. 그래 맞다. 봄철에는 그 밭에 유채나물도 심어서 노랗게 꽃을 피운 적이 있었다.

그런데 나는 그리로 가면서 자꾸 이상한 생각이 들었다. 지금이 삼월인데 어떻게 오뉴월에 피는 유채꽃이 앞당겨 피었단 말인가. 나는 그 궁금증을 태부에게 물어보았다.

"태부야, 지금이 삼월인데 어떻게 유채꽃이 피나?"

"가보면 안다. 세상이 하 수상한데 철 그른 꽃이 언젠 못 피겠냐?"

태부는 취한 시선으로 앞만 보며 냅다 달리고 있었다. 그런데 과연 형만이네 그 밭에는 유채꽃이 노랗게 피어 있었다. 그 꽃은 제때 피는 유채꽃처럼 노랗기보다는 더러 푸른 색깔을 띄고 유채나물보다 키도 작았지마는 분명 꽃은 꽃이었다. 그리고 나는 그 유채밭의 양쪽가에 옛날 원두막처럼 보초막을 지어놓은 것을 보았다.

"이게 형만이 차다. 걔 돈 벌었다구."

등때기가 번득이는 시커먼 고급 승용차 뒤에서 급하게 차를 세우며 태부가 말했다.

밭은 몇 군데 자유롭게 들어갈 수 있는 입구를 만들어 놓았으나 그 입구마다 다음과 같은 작은 팻말이 말뚝에 박혀 있었다.

― 1회 촬영에 1천 원

나는 그제야 모든 것을 알 수가 있었다. 그러나 나는 세차게 고개를 가로젓고 있었다. 아니었다. 이건 아니었다.

"결혼 시즌 같은 때는 하루에 오 천 쌍도 들어온다고 하잖냐?"

앞서 걸어가는 태부가 부러운 듯이 말했다. 그러나 나는 그 유채밭을 휘둘러보며 달뜨는 아래에서 더럽혀진 해변을 보았을 때와 마찬가지로 우울했다. 그래. 맞다. 형만이 그놈은 머리가 영리해서 학생 때도 정석으로 공부를 하기보다는 언제나 '간추린 것'들로 공부를 하지 않았던가. 그것으로 나와 승부를 해서 나를 누를 때도 있었던 것이었다.

"형만아! 나와 봐라. 창혁이가 와버렸다."

보초막 앞에서 태부가 소리질렀으나 안에서는 아무 대답도 없었다. 그가 허리를 숙이고 보초막 안으로 쓱 상체를 들이밀었다. 나는 막상 거기까지 가놓고 난처해져 버렸다. 사실 나는 제 계절도 아닌 철에 씨를 뿌려놓고 추운 계절에 피어나 주인의 돈벌이를 도와주는 그 꽃들을 보면서 서울의 요정에서 무시로 만났던 어디서 왔는지도 모르는 꽃다운 아가씨들을 연상하고 있었다.

'아 참으로 잔인한 세월이다!'

나는 허니문 아가씨들이 각양 자세로 꽃과 더불어 사진을 찍고 있는 유채꽃밭을 바라보며 속으로 탄식했다. 이런 것쯤 옛날에야 어찌 돈 받을 생각을 했을 것인가. 형만이 머리니까 이런 것을 구상해냈을 것이다. 그러니 관광이란 결국 현지의 인심을 각박하게 만드는 것밖에 다름 아니었다.

"야 들어와라. 어쩐 일이냐? 대기업 상무님께서 이런델 다 오시구?"

나는 오두막 안으로 들어가 낯설게 살이 찐 형만의 손을 잡았다. 그런데 나는 그 보초막같은 건물의 안엘 들어가 보고 또 한차례 놀라 버렸다. 대개는 바깥을 치장하고 안이 허술한 법인데 여기는 완전히 그 반대였다. 분명 어느 외국에서 구해온 카펫 위에 외국산 원목고급 탁자가 놓여있고 자기가 앉은 의자의 등 바침에는 호랑이 가죽이 깔려 있었다. 그런 의자 위에 떡 버티고 앉아서 그는 여유 있는 시선으로 나를 바라보고 있었다.

"너 아주 돈 많이 벌었구나."

나는 겨우 이 한마디를 했다.

"돈 벌어봤자 대기업에 비하면 새 발의 피지 뭐."

형만이는 코웃음치듯 말했다. 이놈은 어느새 졸부들의 행동거지를 영락없이 익히고 있었다. 그가 핸드폰으로 어딘가에 전화를 걸자 여직원 하나가 불이 낳게 달려왔다.

"정 양아, 서울에서 높으신 손님이 내려오셨으니 좋은 차로 한 번 타 봐라."

"예."

처녀는 고분고분 옆에 놓인 진열장에서 찻잔들을 꺼내 차를 타기 시작했다.

"쟤가 우리 동창 성두 딸인 거라. 맡아달라고 졸라서 내가 맡아 있다만…"
"그래, 성두는 뭘 하니?"
나는 성두의 얼굴을 떠올릴 수 없었으나 그렇게 물었다.
"뭐하긴, 배나 타지."
이번에는 태부가 대답했다.
"창혁이도 왔으니 태부야, 네가 아이들을 좀 모아라. 오늘 저녁은 내가 쏘지."
"야, 참말이가?"
"야는 내가 거짓말만 하고 산 것처럼 말하네."
형만이가 태부에게 눈을 흘겼다. 그러자 술 한잔해서 기세등등하던 태부도 찍소리 못했다.
"누구들을 부를까?"
태부는 사전 결재까지 받는 것까지 잊지 않았다.
"경식이하고, 일만이, 또 대호도 불러라. 여섯 시, 장소는 월출정으로 하고… 솔직히 창혁이가 이리 출세해서 내려온 게 우리 모두에게 경사 아니가?"
나는 분위기에 휩쓸려서 아무 말도 못하고, 얼굴을 들 수도 없었다.

5

회식은 예정대로 여섯 시에 월출정에서 베풀어졌다. 경식이, 일만이, 대호와 태부도 나왔다. 그들은 나와 형식적인 인사를 나눴는데, 나에게보다 형만이를 더 어려워한다는 것을 나는 대번에 느낄 수 있었다. 누가 예약을 한 듯 앉은배기 큰 상 두 개 위에 백지를 덮어놓고 손님

숫자대로 물컵과 물수건이 놓여 있었다. 시렁 쪽에 나와 형만이, 태부가 앉고 나중 불려온 친구들은 맞은쪽에 앉았다. 형만이는 여기가 단골인 듯 인사차 들어온 마담에게 한마디로 지시했다.

"아이들은 여럿 필요 없으니까 셋만 들여보내고, 술과 안주는 늘 그랬던 것처럼 가져와요."

"예에."

술과 안주가 들어오고 아가씨들도 들어왔다. 형만이는 잔마다 술을 따르게 한 다음 잔을 들고는 한마디 건배사를 하는 걸 잊지 않았다.

"우리들은 다 같은 학교 동기들이다마는 오늘은 알다시피 대단히 경사스러운 날이다. 우리 친구 창혁이는 서울로 가서 공부를 하고 까마득한 대기업의 상무까지 출세를 하지 않았냐? 아마 다음에는 틀림없이 사장을 할 것이니 자 이보다 더 경사스러운 일이 어디 또 있겠냐? 자 그를 환영하는 뜻에게 내가 '지화자' 하거든 '좋구나'로 건배를 하자. 자, 지화자!"

"좋구나!"

그들은 이미 이런 구호를 한두 번 아니게 해본 듯 했다. 처음 불려온 친구들은 처음엔 예비군 동원령에 불려 나온 것처럼 서먹서먹해 보이더니 술이 들어가기 시작하자 제 표정들을 찾아갔다.

"자, 술도 먹을 때는 실컷 먹고, 일할 때는 일도 열심히 하는 거다. 그렇지 않냐?"

"왜 아니냐? 형만이 말이 똑 맞다."

앞장서 발라맞추는 건 태부였다.

"그 맥주잔 이리 다고."

형만이는 맥주잔에 맥주를 거의 가득 따르더니 또 작은 잔에는 양주를 따라서 큰잔 속에 담가 폭탄주를 만들고 있었다. 그 한 시대 욕심

많은 군인들에 의해 번지기 시작한 나쁜 술버릇이 이 변방까지 유행해 있는 것에 대해 놀라지 않을 수 없었다. 내가 초대된 손님이니까 첫잔은 의례 나에게로 돌아왔다.

"나 정말 술 못해."

말로는 그렇게 하면서도 나는 옛날 동기들과의 모처럼의 술자리, 처음으로 돌아온 잔을 거절할 수가 없었다. 이 친구들 앞에서 주정을 하거나 창피를 당해서는 안 된다. 그러려면 이 자리를 무난히 모면해야 한다. 이런 자리란 사실 거래를 위하여 손님을 만났을 때는 무슨 방법으로든 치러내야 했다. 어쩌면 나는 대기업에 있는 동안 그 기술만을 배워왔다고 해도 과언이 아니었다. 그러나 나는 첫잔부터 속일 수는 없었다. 그리고 나는 내 속에서 강하게 술을 당기는 것을 어쩔수가 없었다. 나는 그 잔을 건네 받아 얌전하게 바닥을 비웠다. 방안의 아가씨들이 짝짝짝 박수를 쳤다. 동기들도 손뼉을 쳤다.

"자, 다들 봤지? 술이라는 건 저렇게 마시는 거라구."

형만이는 다시 빈 잔을 받아 크고 작은 잔에 두 가지 술을 따르고 있었다. 이렇게 두 차례를 돌았다. 그리고 나선 노래방 기계가 들여오고, 돌아가며 노래를 부르는 순서였다. 노래도 내가 초청된 손님이니까 맨 먼저 불러야 했다. 나는 무슨 노래를 부를까 궁리하다가 얼른 '기다리는 마음'을 패러디해서 부르기로 했다.

> 월출봉에 달뜨거든 날 불러주오.
> 일출봉에 해뜨거든 날 불러주오.

나는 간신히 낙점을 받았다. 옛날에는 노래를 부르라면 서로들 뒤로 뺏는데 지금은 저마다 먼저 부르려고 난리들이었다. 그리고 어느 누구도 노래에 서툴거나 어려워하지 않았다. 어느 시대에 일어났던 '전국토의 노래방화, 전국민의 가수화'는 대체로 성공을 거둔 셈이었다. 나는 변소엘 가는 척 일어나 밖으로 나왔다. 바깥은 이미 어두워 있었다. 문득 소라와 성게를 사러 해변으로 나가시던 어머니 모습이 떠올랐다. 화장실에 들러서 소변을 누고 도로 방으로 들어갈까 그만 집으로 가버릴까 망설이고 있는 참인데 다른 방 설거지를 하고 그릇들을 잔뜩 안고 나오던 여인이 나를 힐끗 돌아보고는 몸을 사리고 달아나려 했다. 그 여인의 뒷모습이 눈에 익었다.

"여보시오."

내가 소리를 죽여 그 여자를 불러 세웠다. 아니, 그것은 술이 한 짓인지도 몰랐다. 아아, 그 여자는 나를 알아보고 있음이 분명했다. 그녀가 숙이고 있던 얼굴을 들었다. 마침 월출봉을 비낀 보름 가까운 달이 희미한 빛을 내려 비춰고 있었으므로 나는 그 여자의 옆모습을 알아볼 수 있었다. 육십대 초반에 접어든 초라한 모습의 J. 나는 차마 그녀의 이름을 부를 수는 없었다. 그러나 그녀는 멈칫해 서더니 내가 묻기라도 한 듯이 서둘러 뇌었다.

"예. 나 J맞아요. 낮엔 호텔 청소를 하고, 밤엔 여기 나와서 허드렛일을 합니다. 돈을 벌어서 아이들 학교를 보내려구요."

그녀는 그 말만을 하고는 도망치듯 달아나 버렸다. 형만이 저 놈은 어쩌면 계획적으로 나를 골탕먹이려고 이 집으로 끌고 왔는지도 모른다. 저 놈은 충분히 그럴 수 있는 놈이다. 아아! 이 일을 도대체 어쩌면 좋은가. 오늘 하루 고향에서 겪은 일들이 악몽만 같았다. 나는 머리를 돌려 다시 월출봉 능선을 벗어난 찬 달을 쳐다보았다. 안개가 끼었는지 별들은 보이지 않았다. 나는 그 달을 바라보며 어린 시절에 그랬듯이 엉망진창의 이 고향을 위해 이제 뭔가를 하리라고 다짐하고 있었다. 달도 구름 속에서 빠져 나와 내게 삐쭉 인사를 하는데, 나는 어느새 노랫소리 방만한 술집 마당을 빠져나가고 있었다.

아동문학

장롱 속의 새 모시옷
까마귀 오서방

강순복

장롱 속의 새 모시옷

필자 소개
한국문인협회, 국제펜클럽, 한국아동문학회 회원(현)
한국피부관리사협회 제주지회장(현)
동화집 『종이피아노』 『키 크는 요술안경』 『네 발로 걷는 아이』 등
E-mail : ksb1234@hanmail.net

장롱 속의 새 모시옷

강순복

　요즘 들어 민서 엄마는 마음이 편치 않습니다. 엊그제까지만 해도 지칠 줄 모르고 펄펄 날아다니시던 민서 할아버지께서 기력이 많이 쇠약해졌는지 그렇게 좋아하시던 술도 잘 드시지 않고 외출했다가도 해가 지기 전 들어오시는 것이 영 딴 사람 같습니다.
　"여보, 아버님이 좀 이상해진 것 같지 않아요?"
　"뭐가 이상해요? 연세가 있으시니까 좀 자중하시는 거겠지……."
　"좋아하시던 술도 잘 안 드시는 것 같고… 노인정엘 갔다가도 일찍 들어오시고……."
　매일같이 술을 드시고 술주정을 하시는 할아버지 때문에 마음고생 심하신 엄마는 별게 다 걱정입니다. 평소에는 법 없이 살 어른이라고 말을 듣다가도 술만 드시면 어디서 생기는지 왕고집이라서 아무도 못 말리기 때문입니다.
　"아빠! 자중이 뭐예요?"
　엄마 옆에 앉아 듣고 있던 민서가 끼어들었다.
　"몸조심한다는 뜻이다. 사전을 찾아 봐라 툭하면 질문하지 말고."
　민서 할아버지가 술에 취해서 들어오시는 날은 온 집안이 비상이 걸리는 날입니다. 민서야 이리 와라. 민서야 할아버지가 술을 좀 마셨다. 민서야. 공부 열심히 해라. 민서야. 민서야……술에 취하면 잠도 오지 않는 모양인지 할아버지는 밤새도록 불러 대십니다. 그런 날이면 식구들은 일찌감치 전등을 끄고 할아버지가 주무실 때까지 죽은 듯이 지내야 합니다. 숙제가 밀려도 전등을 켤 수가 없어서 어떤 날은 숙제를 못해갈 때도 있습니다. 그래서 민서는 할아버지 때문에 짜증날 때도 있지만 솔직히 할아버지만큼 민서에게 관심을 가져 주는 사람도 없다는 생각입니다.

엄마와 아빠가 일터로 가신다고 새벽같이 나가시면 할아버지가 민서에게 우유를 먹이고 민서가 크면서는 유치원까지 데려다 주시고, 그리고 끝나서는 집에 데려와서 생선을 구워 밥을 먹여 주시던 정말 고마운 할아버지십니다.

그래서 할아버지가 술에 취해서 민서야, 민서야 잠이 드실 때까지 불러도 불평할 수가 없습니다.

"민서야, 할아버지를 이해해라. 할머니 돌아가시고 혼자 남아서 외로우셔서 술을 드시는 거니까. 알았지?"

어느 날인가 숙제를 못한 민서가 할아버지 때문에 속상해 죽겠어 하며 짜증을 부렸을 때 아빠가 하신 말씀입니다. 아빠가 그렇게 말씀하지 않으셨다 해도 민서는 할아버지가 좋습니다. 술만 조금 덜 마시면 세상에 나무랄 게 없이 좋은 할아버지입니다. 술만 마시면 힘이 펄펄 넘치던 할아버지가 요즘은 외출도 잘 하지 않으시고 민서를 잘 부르지도 않는 것이 이상합니다.

"여보 아버님이 늙어 가시나 봐요."

엄마가 아무나 들으라는 듯이 혼잣말처럼 중얼거릴 때 민서는 문득 늙어가는 것이 무엇인지 생각하게 되었습니다. 늙어간다는 것, 나이를 먹어간다는 것은 과연 무엇을 뜻하는 것일까 궁금했고, 그건 술을 덜 마시고 외출을 조금만 하는 것이라는 생각을 하게 되었습니다.

시간이 흐를수록 할아버지는 무엇을 금방 잊어버리곤 하셨는데 엄마는 그럴 때마다 긴 한숨을 내쉬며 어쩌지? 안 되는데……라고 넋두리를 하셨고 민서가 뭐가요? 하고 물으면 할아버지가 늙어서 몸과 마음이 점점 메말라져 움츠러드는 것이 걱정이라고 대답했습니다. 엄마가 할아버지를 걱정하는 것이 건망증이 아니라 치매라는, 기억을 잊어버리는 병이라는 것도 민서는 알게 되었습니다. 늙어 가는 것이 염려가 아니라 잊어버리는 것이 가장 염려된다는 것도 알았습니다.

"아버님! 외출하실 때 그 옷 좀 벗으세요. 이렇게 옷이 많은데 왜 낡은 옷만 입고 다니셔요? 아버님이 이렇게 차려 입고 다니시면 사람들은 저를 욕합니다. 맘에 드는 옷이 없으시면 하나 새로 사 드릴까요?"

하늘이 맑고 푸른 날 아침 외출하시려는 할아버지 등에다 대고 엄마는 애원하듯이 말했습니다.

"필요 없다. 이 옷이 어떻다고 그러냐? 자기가 편하면 그만이지. 아직 한참을 더 입을 수 있는데…… 그리고 장롱 속에 한번도 입어 보지 않은 옷도 있다. 지난번 민서 고모가 사다 준 옷도 있고."

할아버지는 엄마의 말에 벌컥 화를 내시며 휭 하니 집을 나갔습니다. 집을 나가신다고 해도 노인정 밖에 갈 곳은 특별히 없습니다.

아침저녁으로 길가에 떨어져 뒹구는 낙엽을 보는 민서의 마음도 왠지 우울해지고 괜스레 눈물이 날 때도 있습니다. 그런 날 저녁이면 학교에서 돌아오는 길로 할아버지 방에 들렸습니다. 할아버지도 민서처럼 낙엽을 보고 외로워서 말이 없어지고 힘이 없어지는 건 아닌가 하는 생각이 들었기 때문입니다. 그러면 할아버지는 민서에게 낮 동안 있었던 얘기를 마치 놀이터에 다녀온 어린아이처럼 신나게 말하곤 했습니다. 그럴 때 보면 할아버지라는 신분도 잊어버리시는 모양입니다. 잊어버림이 때로는 좋을 수도 있다는 생각이 문득 드는 것은 민서도 어른이 다 되었다는 증거입니다.

아빠와 엄마도 할아버지를 걱정하는 시간이 많아졌습니다.

"민서야, 학교가 끝나서 오면 할아버지 방에 가 보아라. 나이 드신 분들은 외로움도 많이 타고……"

"엄마가 말씀하지 않아도 그러고 있어요."

민서는 엄마 대신 아침에 학교에 갈 때, 저녁에 집에 돌아와서도 제일 먼저 할아버지 방문을 열어 봅니다. 학교에서 오던 길에 할아버지가 좋아하시는 과자도 사고 홍시도 삽니다.

할아버지는 민서가 사다드리는 군것질들을 받고 너무 좋아하십니다.

"할아버지, 이런 건 내다 버리세요. 이건 너무 낡았고, 그리고 좋은 거 많은데 왜 이런걸 아껴 두세요?"

"놔 둬라. 다 쓸데가 생긴다."

민서 말이라면 무어든지 오냐, 오냐, 하시는 할아버지가 오늘은 화를 내었습니다. 어쩌면 할아버지는 늙어가고 있는 것을 스스로 알면서도 애써 외면하는 것인지도 모른다는 생각이 들어 갑자기 할아버지가 가엾어졌습니다. 나이가 들어가시면서 늙어가는 것 중에서 특이한 것은 무엇이든 안으로만 움켜쥔다는 말을 들은 적이 있는 민서는 와락 겁이 났습니다. 죽음을 앞두고 세상을 향한 욕심, 미련, 아쉬움 같은 것을 이렇게 잊어 가는 것인지도 모른다는 생각이 들자 민서는 소름이 오싹 돋았습니다.

지난 여름, 겨울 양복을 입으시고 외출하신 할아버지를 어쩌다 이모님이 보시고는 민서 고모에게 호되게 야단 하신 적이 있습니다.

"어머님 일찍 보내고 홀로 계신 아버님께 참 효도 잘한다, 한 여름에 겨울 양복이라니? 형부가 겨울 양복 입고 다니더라. 창피해서 혼났다. 모시옷 한 벌해봐야 이삼십 만원 밖에 안 하는데……."

휴일에 수화기를 통해 들려오는 이모의 목소리에 민서 고모는 참 난감해했습니다.

"이모님! 아버님 옷 많으세요. 아껴서 장롱 속에 묻어 두시고는 자식들 창피 주는 거 연세 드신 분들의 특기잖아요."

민서 고모는 이모로부터 호되게 야단을 맞고 궁색한 변명을 늘어놓았습니다.

"올케, 아버님 옷 좀 갈아입고 다니게 하세요. 얼마 전에도 옷 한 벌을 사다 드렸는데, 그 옷 다 어디다 두고 맨날 헌 옷이래요? 겨울 양복을 입고 다니시는 걸 이모님이 지나다 우연히 보시고 기가 막히더라고 전화 왔는데, 저 혼났어요."

할아버지가 옷이 없는 게 아닙니다. 할아버지의 낡은 장롱 속에는 아직 한번도 입어 보지 않은 옷이 분명히 몇 벌인가 있을 것입니다.

바쁘다는 핑계로 고모는 여름이 거의 끝나 갈 무렵에야 할아버지께 옥색 빛이 나는 질 좋은 모시옷을 해드렸습니다. 나중에 안 일이지만 할아버지는 그 옷을 끝내 입으시질 않았습니다.

"아버님! 새 옷도 많은데 허구한 날 그 낡은 옷을 입으십니까?"

어쩌다 며느리가 한마디라도 하는 날에는 시끄럽다며 낡은 옷을 고집스럽게 껴안곤 하시는 것이었습니다. 아무도 할아버지의 그런 습관이나 고집을 바꾸지 못했습니다.

"할아버지! 창피하게 낡은 옷만 입지 마시고 새 옷 입으세요. 그렇게 장롱 속에 모셔 놓고 언제 입으실래요? 옷 오래 놔두면 좀 먹고 천이 삭아서 못 입게 되잖아요."

민서도 할아버지가 고집을 부리는 것으로 생각 되었습니다. 하지만 할아버지는 결코 고집을 부리는 것이 아닙니다. 지금 입는 옷이 아직도 한참이나 입을 수 있는데 굳이 새 옷을 입는 것은 낭비라는 생각이 들기 때문입니다.

할아버지는 딸이 새로 해 드린 모시옷을 몇 번을 꺼내어 만져 보았는지 아무도 모릅니다. 이따금 민서 앞에서 이거 봐라 할아버지가 옷이 얼마나 많으냐 하시며 자랑처럼 말씀하시기도 했습니다.

"그러니까 이것저것 다 입으세요. 그리고 할머니도 안 계신데 옷이라도 잘 입고 다니셔야 남들이 할아버지를 얕보지 않아요."

민서는 제법 어른처럼 할아버지에게 핀잔을 주기도 했습니다.

민서는 할아버지가 술을 조금만 마시고 제발 낡은 옷을 벗어 주었으면 하는 마음뿐이었지만 할아버지는 새 옷은 불편하다는 이유로 입었던 옷만 고집했습니다.

"민서야, 놔 둬라. 할아버지 고집을 누가 말리니? 아버님! 고모가 해 주신 모시옷도 입지 않고 모셔 두실거지요?"

엄마가 빙그레 웃으시며 물었지만 할아버지는 못 들은 척 했습니다.

그래도 민서에게는 여전히 고맙고 따뜻한 할아버지입니다. 그런데 민서에게 너무나 엄청난 일이 일어나고 말았습니다. 고모가 큰마음을 먹고 해 드린 모시옷도 할아버지에게 마지막 선물이 되고 말았습니다.

엄마가 늘 불안해하고 초조해하며 걱정하던 일이 실제로 일어난 것은 마을 어느 집에 잔치가 있은 후였습니다. 할아버지는 잔칫집에서 노인정으로 내온 음식을 먹은 후 심한 설사로 병원에 입원하셨는데 이틀 만에 돌아가시고 말았습니다. 민서는 할아버지의 갑작스러운 죽음이 도무지 믿어지지 않았습니다. 그렇게 건강하시던 할아버지가 그까짓 설사 때문에 돌아가셨다는 것이 기가 막힐 일이었습니다.

"그렇게 건강하시던 분이……."

민서네만 아니고 친척들도 갑작스런 할아버지의 죽음이 이해가 되지 않는다고 한 마디씩 했습니다.

할아버지가 돌아가시자 할아버지의 유품을 정리하시던 친척들이 민서 고모에게 야단치듯 말했습니다.

"어쩌면 입을 만한 옷 한 벌 없니? 민서 고모는 뭐 했니? 아버지께 옷이라도 좀 장만해 드리지. 그나마 이 모시옷은 새 것이라 다행이다."

이상한 일이었습니다. 민서가 알기로는 얼마 전 엄마도 옷을 새로 사 드렸고 고모도 툭하면 새 옷을 사다 드렸는데, 그리고 그 옷은 할아버지의 장롱 속 깊숙이 잠을 자고 있다고 생각했는데 입을 만한 옷이 한 벌도 없다는 것입니다.

할아버지를 보내고 시간이 흐르면서 마을에 민서 할아버지에 대한 소문이 퍼지기 시작했습니다. 노인정 할아버지들 중에 민서 할아버지에게 도움 안 받아 본 분이 없다는 소문도 들렸습니다. 더욱이 할아버지는 돌아가시기 며칠 전까지도 입을 만한 옷을 모두 노인정으로 날랐다는 것도 알았습니다.

"살았을 때 줘야 입지 나 죽은 다음에 주면 입겠는가?"

할아버지가 돌아가신 후, 민서는 삶과 죽음에 대하여, 늙어간다는 것에 대하여 다시 한번 생각하게 되었습니다. 어떻게 사느냐도 중요하지만 어떻게 살다 갔느냐도 중요하다는 걸 알았습니다.

할아버지는 삶과 죽음이란 놓아 버리는 것! 없애버리는 것이라는 걸 미리 알고 있었던 것입니다.

"인간은 어떻게 사느냐도 중요하지만 어떻게 살다 가느냐도 중요하단다. 산다는 건 말이다 민서야, 음……놓아 버리는 거란다. 비우는 것, 다 비우고 가는 거지. 우리 예쁜 민서만 두고 다 나누는 거지."

언젠가 술에 취해서 뜻 모를 말을 몇 번씩이나 반복하셨던 할아버지의 마음을 이제야 알 것 같습니다.

겨울이 오고 있었습니다.

고모가 할아버지께 사 드린 모시옷이 마지막 선물이 되었다고 생각하면 가슴이 아려왔습니다.

"할아버지가 새 모시옷 한 번 입어 보시지 못하셔서 마지막 선물이 되었구나……"

고모의 눈가에 눈물이 맺히는 걸 보는 민서의 눈가에도 이슬이 맺혔습니다.

천국에 계신 할아버지, 아직도 그 낡은 옷을 껴입고 계실까? 그런 생각을 하는데 어디선가 민서야 하시는 할아버지의 음성이 들리는 듯 했습니다.

박재형

까마귀 오서방

필자 소개
제주아동문학회 회장, 제주문인협회 부지회장 역임.
계몽아동문학상 수상.
동화집 『검둥이를 찾아서』 『내 친구 삼례』 『다랑쉬오름의 슬픈 노래』 등.

까마귀 오서방

박재형

지난 봄이었다. 아이들이랑 골목에서 고무줄 놀이를 하고 있는데, 집배원 아저씨가 자전거를 타고 다가오셨다.

"얘들아, 오지수씨가 어디 사는지 아니? 번지가 안 적혀 있어 어딘지 모르겠네."

낯선 집배원 아저씨는 가방에서 편지를 꺼내 겉봉을 들여다 보며 물으셨다.

"오지수씨요?"

집배원 아저씨의 말씀에 우리는 고개를 갸웃거렸다. 아무리 생각해도 오지수씨가 누군지 알 수 없었다.

"제주도 북제주군 구좌읍 세화리 전항동 오지수 귀하"

겉봉의 주소는 분명히 우리 동네가 맞는데 오지수씨라는 이름은 처음 듣는 이름이었다.

"우리 동네에는 그런 분이 안 사시는데요."

미희가 자신있게 대답했다.

그때 마침 주희네 아빠가 지나가시자 집배원 아저씨는 주희아빠에게 물으셨다.

"저, 오지수씨가 누구신지 아십니까?"
"오지수씨요? 누구더라? 아, 까마귀 오서방이구나, 저 집이에요."
주희네 아빠는 동네의 맨 끝인 바닷가에 있는 집을 가리켰다.
까마귀 오서방이 오지수씨라니, 나는 놀란 것까지는 아니지만, 이상한 기분이 들었다. 까마귀 오서방이 그런 멋진 이름을 가지고 있을 줄은 꿈에도 생각을 못했다. 까마귀 오서방이라고 멋진 이름을 가지지 말라는 법은 없는 일이지만, 까마귀 오서방에게는 만복이나 달용이 같은 흔한 이름이 어울릴 것 같았다. 늘 까마귀 오서방이라는 이름으로 불려서 그런지 가장 잘 어울리는 이름처럼 생각해 왔던 것이다. 그런데 까마귀 오서방이 오지수라는 멋진 이름을 가지고 있었다니.
우리는 신기한 것을 발견이라도 한 것처럼 흥을 보았다.
"까마귀 오서방이 오지수라니, 안 어울린다야."
"맞아, 개미 발에 구두 신은 꼴이야."
우리들은 코미디라도 본 듯이 웃어넘겼다. 한참 웃다가 나는 궁금한 생각이 들어 입을 열었다.
"왜 좋은 이름을 놔두고 까마귀 오서방이라고 하지?"
"글쎄 얼굴이 검어서 놀리는 말이 아닐까?"
"아냐, 발을 씻지 않아서 그런 걸 거야. 우리 어머니도 내가 발을 잘 씻지 않으면 까마귀발이라고 놀린단 말이야."
"그건 아닌 것 같다. 오서방은 늘 깨끗하잖아."
"잘 잊어 먹어서 그런가? 시간 돌아짱이라고도 불리잖아."
우리들은 까마귀 오서방이라는 별명에 대해 얘기하느라 고무줄도 멈추고 시간가는 줄 모르게 얘기꽃을 피웠다. 그러다가 다시 고무줄 놀이에 정신이 팔려 오서방은 까맣게 잊어버렸다.
그런데 방학을 며칠 앞둔 날, 헤엄을 치고 돌아오는데 오서방이 돌담 위로 고개를 내밀더니 우리를 불렀다.

"애들아, 놀다 가라. 봉숭아가 곱게 피었어."

나는 봉숭아꽃을 구경하고 싶기는 했지만, 오서방네 집으로 들어가는 게 싫었다. 오서방이 살고 있는 집은 서울 사람이 별장을 짓는다고 사서 돌보지 않는 집으로, 지붕이 다 무너져가는 낡은 초가집이었다. 그런 은정이가 가 보자고 하는 바람에 오서방네 집 정낭을 넘어갔다. 할머니(오서방의 어머니)가 돌아가신 후 혼자 살고 있는 오서방네 집은, 햇살이 가득차서 그런지 전혀 이상하지 않았다. 낡은 초가집이라 귀신이 나올 것처럼 무서운 집이라고 생각했었는데, 마당에 핀 꽃을 보는 순간 얼었던 마음이 모두 풀리고, 입이 다물어지지가 않았다. 언제 심었는지 마당에 있는 넓은 꽃밭에는 가지가지 꽃들이 피어 있었다. 봉숭아, 백일홍, 사루비아, 코스모스가 아름다운 얼굴을 뽐내고, 해바라기도 그 큰 키로 해님에게 웃음을 보내고 있었고, 이름 모를 들꽃도 꽃밭 한 귀퉁이를 차지하여 웃고 있었다.

"애들아, 봉숭아 꽃잎 따 가라. 손톱에 물들이면 아주 예뻐."

까마귀 오서방은 어눌한 말투로 봉숭아 꽃잎을 뚝뚝 따면서 말했다. 오서방도 손톱에 물을 들였는지 새끼 손톱이 붉었다.

"남자 어른이 손톱에 물을 들였어. 여자같이."

"그러니까 시간돌아짱이지."

우리는 오서방의 손톱을 보면서 쿡쿡 웃었다. 그런데 오서방은 좋아서 웃는 줄 알았는지 새끼 손톱을 우리에게 내밀며 자랑까지 했다.

"첫눈이 올 때까지 봉숭아 꽃물이 지워지지 않으면 소원이 이루어진대."

까마귀 오서방은 어린 아이처럼 싱글벙글 웃으며 자랑을 했다. 그 모습이 어찌나 천진스러운지 '시간돌아짱'이라는 말보다는 '어른아이'

라는 말이 더 어울리겠다는 생각이 들었다.
　그런데 오서방이 갑자기 목소리를 높였다.
　"꽃은 밟지 마! 조심해야지."
　"내가 밟은 건 풀이에요."
　주희가 봉숭아꽃을 따려고 꽃밭에 들어갔다가 오서방의 말에 변명을 했다.
　"그건 풀이 아니야. 얼마나 예쁜 꽃이 피는지 너 알기나 해. 그건 애기향유 꽃이야. 늦가을이 되면 아주 예쁘게 펴."
　"이런 건 들에 지천으로 깔린 건데."
　주희는 화를 내는 오서방이 못마땅한지 애기향유라는 작은 풀꽃을 짓궂게 밟아 버렸다.
　그러자 까마귀 오서방은 얼굴을 붉히며 소리쳤다.
　"풀이라도 함부로 밟는게 아니야!"
　오서방은 아주 화가 난 모양이었다.
　"왜요? 금덩이라도 되나요? 이까짓 풀."
　주희는 오서방을 업신 여기는지 풀을 더 밟으며 오서방에게 대들었다.
　나는 주희가 왜 그런 짓을 하는지 어리벙벙하였다. 마을에서는 오서방은 천덕꾸러기로 여기니까 주희도 업신여기는 것 같았다.
　그러자 오서방은 씩씩거리며 주희를 노려보다가 주희를 밀쳤다. 그 바람에 주희가 넘어져 장미 가시에 손등이 조금 긁혀 피가 배어 나왔다.
　"왜 밀려? 너 나쁜 놈이야."
　주희는 손등에 피가 나자 눈물을 흘리며 오서방에게 대들었다.
　"어서 가! 어서 가!"

오서방은 화가 났는지 손을 내저으며 우리를 내쫓았다.

우리들은 오서방이 화를 내는 바람에 겁이 나서 얼른 밖으로 나오고 말았다.

"미친 모양이야. 그까짓 풀을 좀 밟았다고 화를 내다니, 구경간 우리가 바보지. 어이구 까마귀 오서방."

우리는 주희 때문에 일어난 일이지만, 오서방만 욕하면서 집으로 돌아갔다.

"오늘 낮에 무슨 일이 있었니? 주희네 엄마가 오서방네 집에 가서 난리를 치더라."

그 날 저녁 주희네 엄마가 오서방네 집에 가서 큰 소리로 욕을 했다는 얘기를 엄마가 해주셨다. 아무리 손등이 벗겨졌기로 그까짓 일로 오서방네 집까지 가다니. 나는 마음이 언짢았지만, 모른 척하기로 했다. 주희는 내 친구니까. 그런데 엉뚱하게도 오서방이 주희를 마구 때려 상처가 났다는 소문이 나돌고, 마을 사람들은 오서방에게 욕을 했다.

며칠 후, 오서방이 우리 집에 찾아왔다.

"아주머니, 농약칠 일이 없습니까?"

"우린 다시 오서방에게 농약을 쳐 달라고 부탁드리지 않겠어요."

"왜 그러세요? 내가 농약을 잘 못 쳤습니까?"

"여러 말 할 필요가 없어요. 동네 아이를 때리다니 그게 어디 있을 법한 일입니까?"

어머니는 전 같으면 담배를 사 드리고, 점심도 정성껏 대접하면서 오서방에게 부탁하여 농약을 쳤을테지만, 완강하게 거절하는 것이었다.

"때리다니요? 전 아이를 때린 일이 없어요. 조금 밀친 것뿐인데."

오서방은 억울하다는 듯이 변명을 했다.
"그게 그거지요. 은혜를 원수로 갚는다더니."
어머니는 마음을 풀지 않으시고 끝내 거절하셨다.
오서방은 어머니에게 청을 드리다가 거절하자 힘없이 발걸음을 돌렸다.
나는 오서방이 불쌍하다는 생각이 들었지만, 오서방을 위해 변명해 주고 싶은 마음은 없었다.
그 일이 있은 후, 오서방은 동네에서 완전히 따돌림을 당했다. 사람들은 오서방에게 일도 시키지 않았다. 외양간에 거름을 치거나 과수원에 농약을 치는 일을 맡기던 동네 사람들은 일을 열심히 하지 않는다고 흉을 보던 김서방에게 일을 맡겼다.
그 후, 오서방은 집밖으로 나다니는 일이 줄어들었다. 바닷가로 내려가다 보면 마당에 우두커니 서서 꽃을 보고 있거나 먼 산을 보는 오서방의 어깨가 아주 좁아 보여 애처롭기까지 했다.
그런데 방학이 끝나 갈 무렵 주희네 집엘 갔더니 주희가 눈이 퉁퉁 붓게 울고 있었다.
"주희야, 무슨 일이 있었니? 왜 어디 아프니?"
"아니, 아무 일도 아니야."
주희는 아주 슬픈 표정으로 말을 하곤 집 안으로 들어가 버렸다.
나는 주희네 집에 무슨 일이 있나보다 하고 생각하면서 주희네 집을 나왔다.
그런데 내가 집으로 들어가자 아버지와 어머니가 마당에 서서 '병원'이라는 말이 담긴 얘기를 나누고 있었다.
"누가 아팠어요?"
"넌 알 거 없다. 들어가 공부나 해라. 아무튼 큰일이다. 이제 살 만하니까 덜컥 병에 걸리고."

어머니는 아주 걱정스런 얼굴로 말씀하시며 부엌으로 가셨다.

나는 궁금해서 견딜 수가 없었다. 그래서 아버지께 여쭈었다.

"아빠, 병원에 갔다 오셨어요? 어디 아프데요?"

"내가 아니고, 주희네 아빠가 신장에 이상이 있다는구나. 빨리 수술을 안하면 목숨을 잃을지도 모른대."

"그렇게 큰 병인 가요?"

"그럼, 누가 신장 하나를 떼어 주면 살아날 수 있다는데 누가 선뜻 신장을 나누어주겠니?"

아버지도 아주 근심스런 표정으로 말씀하셨다.

주희네 아빠는 오래도록 병원에서 돌아오지 못했다. 가족 중에서 신장을 나누어주면 좋겠다는데, 가족 중에는 같은 혈액형을 가진 사람이 없어 누군가가 신장을 기증해 주기를 기다리는 수밖에 없다는 것이었다. 반상회가 열리고 문병을 다녀오곤 했지만, 신장을 나누어주겠다는 사람은 쉬이 나오지 않았다.

아빠의 병으로 주희는 늘 우울한 얼굴로 지냈다.

나는 주희가 빨리 예전처럼 밝은 얼굴로 지내는 날이 왔으면 좋겠다고 생각하며 지냈다.

"얘, 너 꽃 꺾어 가지 않을래?"

가을 햇살이 따사로운 날, 내가 어머니의 심부름으로 호박을 따고 돌아오는데 오서방이 돌담 너머로 고개를 내밀고 말을 걸어왔다.

"무슨 꽃요?"

나는 오서방이 말을 걸어온 게 쑥스러웠지만, 꽃을 주겠다는 말이 그리 싫지 않았다. 그리고 오서방이 나쁜 사람이 아닌 걸 알기 때문에 겁을 내지 않고 마당으로 들어갔다. 그러자 오서방은 아주 기쁜 듯이 환한 얼굴로 꽃밭에서 자라는 꽃을 가리켰다.

"네 마음에 드는 꽃을 꺾어 줄게."

"정말이에요?"

나는 오서방의 말을 믿을 수가 없어 재차 물었다.

"그럼 정말이지. 내가 많이 꺾어줄게. 네 방에 꽂아 놓으렴."

오서방은 진정 가위를 들고 나와 꽃을 잘라 주었다. 사르비아, 페츄니아, 코스모스, 맨드라미 그리고 이름 모를 꽃들까지. 애지중지 가꾼 꽃을 아낌없이 잘라 준다는 게 이상했지만, 나는 예쁜 꽃을 얻을 수 있다는 게 좋아 연달아 예쁘게 핀 꽃을 가리켰다.

꽃을 다 자르고 나자 오서방은 조용히 말문을 열었다.

"너 이 꽃밭 나대신 돌봐 주지 않겠니? 네가 꽃을 좋아하는 줄 아는데."

"그럴 게요. 물만 주면 되지요?"

나는 꽃을 좋아했고, 오서방이 일거리를 찾아 잠시 나들이를 간다고 생각했기 때문에 주저하지 않고 동의했다. 그러자 오서방은 아주 기쁜 듯이 얼굴 가득 웃음을 담았다.

"그럼, 물만 주면 되지."

"풀도 뽑아줄까요? 잡풀이 많은데."

나는 꽃밭 한 귀퉁이에서 자라는 잡초를 보며 말했다. 잡초들도 당당하게 어깨를 펴고 있었다.

"아냐, 여기 있는 건 다 꽃이야. 아주 예쁜 꽃들이니까 뽑지 마라."

"아니 이건 분명히 풀인데요. 틀림없어요."

나는 씀바귀와 토끼풀을 보며 말했다.

"네 말이 맞을 거야. 그렇지만 풀이라고 생각하면 풀이지만, 꽃이라고 생각하면 꽃이 되는 거란다."

나는 오서방의 말을 얼른 이해할 수가 없었다. 그렇지만 오서방의 말에는 말로 얘기할 수 없는 무언가가 담겨 있는 것 같았다. 나는 가만히 오서방의 얼굴을 바라보았다. 좀 모자라는 것 같은 얼굴. 광대뼈가 튀어나올 만큼 마르고 볼품없는 얼굴이었지만, 눈은 아주 빛난다고 생각했다. 그러자 지금까지 까마귀 오서방이라고 업신여긴 것이 너무 부끄러웠다. 시간돌아짱이라고 거리낌없이 말해 왔던 것도. 나는 오서방에게 꽃밭을 잘 돌보겠다는 약속을 하고 집으로 돌아왔다.

그러나 나는 오서방과 약속한 것을 까마득히 잊어버렸다. 가을 운동회에 들떠 오서방과의 약속은 생각할 겨를이 없었던 것이다. 며칠 후, 일찍 일어나 저녁에 쓰지 못한 일기를 쓰고 있는데, 마당에서 어머니와 옆집 영숙이 어머니가 주고받는 말이 들려 왔다.

"주희네 아빠 수술 받게 됐다는 말 들었어?"

"응 들었어. 오서방 참 고맙네, 쉬운 일이 아닌데."

"그러게 말이지요."

"참 고마운 사람이야. 난 그런 착한 사람인 줄도 모르고 섭섭한 소리를 했지."

"나도 그래요."

나는 마당에서 들려오는 소리를 들으며 가슴이 두근거렸다. 오서방이 그런 큰 일을 하다니, 그것도 자신을 괴롭힌 사람을 도와주려고 신장까지 나눠주려고 하다니. 주희가 좋아하겠다는 생각과 오서방이 참 고마운 사람이라는 생각이 들었다. 그리고 꽃밭을 부탁한다던 오서방의 얼굴이 떠올랐다.

'아 참, 꽃밭을 부탁했었지.'

나는 꽃밭을 돌봐 달라는 오서방과의 약속을 지키지 못한 게 생각나 얼른 일어나 옷을 입고 집을 나섰다.

"어디 가니? 마당이라도 쓸던지."
어머니의 목소리가 뒤쫓아왔지만, 나는 얼른 정낭을 빠져 나와 오서방네 집으로 달려갔다.

희곡

우리를 잠들게 하는 새들의 합창

장일홍

우리를 잠들게 하는 새들의 합창

필자 소개
1950년 제주시 출생. 1985년 『현대문학』 추천으로 데뷔.
『한국일보』 신춘문예 당선. 문화관광부 창작희곡 공모 최우수상 수상.
대한민국문학상, 한국희곡문학상, 『월간문학』 동리상 수상.

우리를 잠들게 하는 새들의 합창습唱

장일홍

<나오는 사람들>

천돌 불로국의 농부
총통 기로국의 독재자
비서 총통의 측근
마담 고급 요정의 접대부
기관원 정보기관의 접대부
수사관 군 수사기관 간부
기자 1,2 신문·방송사 기자
초병 1,2 국경수비대 소속 병사

<무 대>

무대는 텅 빌수록 좋다. 보조 의자 두 개와 간이침대 하나만 있으면 족하다. 이 극에서 중요한 장치는 호리존트다. 배경막 전체가 대형 스크린으로 극의 진행과 관련된 장면들이 여기에 투영된다. 막이 오르면 거대한 기로국 국기가 분위기를 압도하는 총통의 집무실, 파이프를 문 총통이 깊은 상념에 잠겨 있다. 비서 등장.

비서 : (화색이 만면하여) 각하!

　　　　(총통, 일별 후 고개를 돌려버린다)

비서 : 각하, 기쁜 소식입니다.

총통 : (멀거니 바라기만)……

비서 : 방금 국경수비대장으로부터 핫라인으로 긴급보고가 들어왔습니다. 불로국의 농부 하나가 국경을 넘어 귀순해 왔답니다.

총통 : (파이프를 입에서 떼고) 귀순? 첩자가 아니고……?

비서 : 그렇습니다. 우리 나라가 불로국의 식민지라는 오욕과 압제의 사슬에서 벗어나 해방된 이후, 처음 맞는 쾌거가 아닐 수 없습니다.

총통 : 음, 그동안 우리 쪽에서 불로국으로 넘어간 숫자는?

비서 : 네, 재작년에 5천명이 월경했고, 작년엔 1만여 명이 도주했습니다. 국경수비대 병력을 증강해서 경비에 만전을 기하고 있습니다. 불법탈출자가 해마다 증가일로에…… (머리를 조아리며) 죄송합니다.

총통 : 자네가 죄송할 거야 없지. 모두 내가 부덕한 탓일세.

비서 : (손을 내저으며) 천부당 만부당 하신 말씀입니다. 각하께서는 이 나라의 국부이시며 이 땅에 사는 백성들은 그저 각하의 하해와 같은 은혜에 감읍할 따름입니다.

총통 : 국민들이 진정 나를 따른단 말인가?

비서 : (황송한 듯 허리를 굽혀) 백골난망이옵니다. 기로국의 독립을 위해 평생을 바쳐 싸워오신 각하가 아니었던들 이 나라는 여태껏 불로국 원수들의 밑씻개로 남아 있을 겁니다.

총통 : (끄덕이며) 나의 애국·애족심은 일월성신이 알지. 하지만, 작금의 이 불길한 사태는 무얼 뜻하지? 끊임없는 학생들의 시위

와 노동자들의 파업과 정치꾼들의 나에 대한 비방·폄하·용훼를……

비서 : 그 점에 관해선 너무 심려하지 마십시오. 사악한 사상에 물든 극소수 학생들과 노동자들의 준동을 싸그리 분쇄해버릴 작정입니다. 반체제 정치인들은 도청·검열·연금 등으로 철통같이 감시하고 있습니다. (냉소를 흘리며) 감옥은 넓고 교수대의 밧줄은 여전히 튼튼합니다.

총통 : 내무상과 국방상이 수도권 전역에 계엄령 선포를 건의하던데……

비서 : (강한 어조로) 각하! 계엄령은 정권의 마지막 카듭니다. 그것은 도저히 회생 불가능한 환자에게 극약을 투여하는 이치와 같습니다. 제가 판단하기에 현재의 정국은 그토록 절망적인 상황이 아닙니다. 만일 우리가 이 위기를 슬기롭게 극복하기만 한다면 이 나라의 안보는 만세반석처럼 확고해질 것입니다.

총통 : 자넨……어떤 대안을 갖고 있나?

비서 : (자신있게) 네!

총통 : 뭔가, 그게?

비서 : 때마침 귀순해 온 적국의 한 농부는 우리에겐 대단한 정치적 의미가 있습니다.

총통 : ……?

비서 : 아시다시피 지금 대학생들과 야당이 아우성치는 이유는 각하의 종신집권을 위한 헌법 개정에 있습니다. 그들은 개헌이 부당하다고 주장하는데 우리가 시급히 해야 할 일은 개헌의 정당성을 입증해 보이는 겁니다.

총통 : 어떻게?

비서 : 종신 집권의 불가피성을……말하자면 이 시점에서 강력한 영도력을 가진 각하께서 계속 통치해야 사회혼란과 적의 침략을 막을 수 있다고 국민들을 설득하는 겁니다. 귀순자를 이용해서……

총통 : (어이없다는 투로) 그는 농부가 아닌가? 어리숙한 촌무지렁이가 뭘 할 수 있겠나?

비서 : (단호히) 그는 농부가 아닙니다.

총통 : 아니라구? (물끄러미 보다가) 자넨 뭔가 음모를 꾸미려 하고 있군.

비서 : 우린 그 농부를 불로국 야전군 사령관으로 만들어야 합니다.

총통 : 뭐야, 사령관? 하하핫……(웃다가 기침하다 웃는다) 하하핫……자네 돌았군, 돌았어!

비서 : (정색을 하며) 각하! 제 충정을 헤아려주시기 바랍니다. 우리가 난국을 뚫고 나가는 방법은 이 길 뿐입니다. 적국 사령관의 입으로 불로국이 기로국을 침공하기 위해 만반의 준비태세를 갖추고 있다고 폭로하면……분명히 엄청난 파문이 일 것으로 확신합니다.

총통 : (무거운 신음) 흐음……전쟁을 볼모로 해서 백성들을 협박하자는 얘기이구만. 농부의 말을 믿을까?

비서 : (날카롭게) 농부가 아니라고 했잖습니까? 기필코. 귀순자를 군인정신에 투철한 장군으로 개조하고야 말겠습니다. (사이) 젊었을 적에 전 어느 지방극단의 인형극 연출가였습니다. 인형조종술에는 남다른 조예가 있다고 자부합니다. 허락해주십시오.

총통 : (파이프를 문 채 서성이다가) 자네의 인형조종술에 학생들은

속지 않을 거야. 그들에겐 순수한 정열이 있거든. 그건 진실을 꿰뚫어 보는 힘이지.

비서: 제게 묘책이 있습니다. 학생들 사이에 내분이 일어나도록 와해공작을 펼 계획입니다.

총통: 난, 때때로 자네가 고통스럽게 느껴져.

비서: (자기 말에 열중해서) 이미 종교단체협의회 소속의 온건한 학생들을 포섭해놨습니다.

총통: 순진한 청년들을 이용한다는 게 마음에 걸리는군.

비서: (입가에 조소를 띠며) 각하, 정치가는 필요하다면 예수와 마르크스를 동시에 이용할 줄 알아야 합니다.

총통: 만약에 공작이 실패했을 땐?

비서: (비장한 얼굴로) 어쩌면 이번 일은 각하의 정치적 생명을 건 모험인지도 모릅니다. 성공할 확률은 이분의 일입니다. 그러나 우리가 독립전쟁을 일으킬 때에도 가능성은 반반이었습니다. 용기 있는 사람은 결코 오십 퍼센트의 불가능을 두려워하지 않는 법입니다.

총통: (질끈 눈을 감았다 뜨면서) 내게도 불가능이 두렵지 않던 시절이 있었지. 난 너무 늙었어……

비서: (두 주먹 불끈 쥐고) 각하! 지금이야말로 우리에게 불리한 정세를 만회하고 역전시킬 수 있는 절호의 기휩니다. 학생들과 야당은 자기들이 이겼다고 샴페인을 터뜨리고 있지만, 천만에! 두고 보십시오. 싸움은 아직 끝나지 않았습니다. 최후에 웃는 자가 진정한 승리잡니다.

　(총통, 파이프 든 손을 높이 치켜들었다고 천천히 내린다. 수락의 표시다.)

비서 : (부동자세로) 감사합니다. 각하! 신명을 걸고 임무를 완수하겠습니다.

　　　(두 사람이 퇴장하면 장면은 귀순 기자회견장으로 바뀌는데 국기가 사라지고 총통의 초상화가 걸린다. 비서, 다시 등장)

비서 : (객석을 향해)안녕하십니까? 지금부터 불로국 제1야전군 사령관 엄천석 장군의 귀순 기자회견을 시작하겠습니다. 자유를 찾아 <악의제국>을 탈출한 엄 장군을 뜨거운 성원과 힘찬 박수로 맞이해 주시기 바랍니다. (손뼉을 친다.)

　　　(천돌 등장. 훈장이 주렁주렁 달린 화려한 예복을 입고 위엄 있게 들어오지만 어딘가 어색하고 우스꽝스럽다. 천돌이 착석하자 곳곳에서 플래시가 터지고 텔레비전 카메라, 무대 아래로 몰려든다.)

비서 : (몇 번 헛기침을 하고 나서) 에, 그럼 각 언론사에서 나오신 기자 여러분께서는 뭐든지 서슴지 마시고 엄 장군께 질문해 주시기 바랍니다.

기자 1 : (객석에서 일어나) 수도신문의 박갑수 기잡니다. 먼저 장군의 성함과 연령, 계급과 직책을 말씀해 주시죠.

천돌 : 엄천돌…… 아니, 엄천석이라고 합니다. (당황해서 떤다)나이는 마흔 여덟 계급은 소장, 직책은……(고개를 뒤로 돌려 애타게 비서를 바라본다. 이하, 답변이 궁할 ㅋ때마다 뒤를 본다.)

비서 : (태연히 웃으며) 직위. (야구감독이 선수에게 사인을 보내듯 손짓·발짓으로 지시한다)

천돌 : 직위는……제1야전군 사령관입니다.

기자 1 : 엄 장군께서는 불로국의 야전군 사령관이라는 고위직에 있었는데 기로국에 귀순하게 된, 뭐 특별한 동기라도 있었나요?

천돌 : 예……여러분은 잘 모르시겠지만 불로국이란 나라는 전 국민의 4할 이상이 굶주리고 거지가 득시글대는 그야말로 생지옥입니다. 백성은 도탄에 빠져 신음하고 있으나 청색당의 간부들과 정부의 고관들은 주지육림 속에서 나날을 지새우고 있습니다. 이에 울분을 느낀 군의 소장파 장교들과 일선 지휘관 몇몇은 오직 구국의 일념으로 뭉쳐 싸울 것을 결의하고 은밀히 거사를 추진하던 중, 쿠데타를 모의한다는 정보가 새어나가 군부에 대한 일대 숙청의 회오리가 일자, 본인은 신변의 위협을 감지하고 귀순을 단행하게 되었던 것입니다.

기자 1 : 기자가 알기로는 불국로의 지엔피, 즉 국민총생산과 1인당 국민소득이 우리보다 무려 3배나 앞서 있는데 전국민의 4할이나 굶주리고 있다니 도저히 납득이 가질 않습니다. 이는 어디에 근거한 통계수친가요?

천돌 : 예 그건…… 그건 …… (뒤를 보자 비서가 사인을 보낸다)제 3세계에서 펴낸 『국제경제의 동향과 과제』란 책에서 보고 알았습니다.

기자 2 : (객석에서 일어나) 중앙방송의 성주철 기잡니다. 장군께서는 야전군 사령관으로서 국경지대의 대치상황이나 양국의 군사력을 누구보다 상세히 아시리라 믿습니다. 현재 우리 국민들은 지구상에서 가장 호전적인 전쟁광들의 집단인 불로국 괴뢰도당들의 침공 위협 때문에 밤잠을 설치고 있는데……어때요? 놈들이 확실히 쳐들어옵니까, 안 옵니까? (기자석에서 폭소)

천돌 : (확신에 찬 태도로) 분명히 말해두지만 적은 호시탐탐 침략의 기회만을 엿보고 있습니다. 특히 학생시위와 노사분규로 인한 무정부주의적 혼란은 적의 무력도발을 한발 앞당기는 도화선

이 될 것이며, 적으로 하여금 이때야말로 선제공격의 결정적 시기라고 오판케 할 가능성이 짙습니다.

기자 2 : 그렇게 구름잡는 얘기만 할 게 아니라, 불로국이 침범해 올 거라는 구체적인 사례와 증거를 제시해주세요.

천돌 : (돌아보면 비서가 사인) 불로국 야전군 총사령부는 얼마전에 5개 군단 20개 사단의 병력을 국경지대에 전진 배치했습니다. 탱크부대와 포병부대, 미사일부대가 전 전선에 집결했으며…… (차츰 웅변조로 되어간다) 명령만 떨어지면 적은 노도와 같이 밀려와 단숨에 기로국을 점령해버릴 겁니다! 아―이 나라의 운명은 백척간두에, 누란의 위기에 봉착해 있으니…… 적은 오늘 밤이라도 당장에! 굶주린 이리떼가 혼곤히 잠든 어린양을 덮치듯이 여러분의 생명과 재산을 삼켜버리고 말 것입니다.……… (침묵, 기자석은 물을 끼얹은 듯 조용하다)

비서 : (재빨리 나서서) 다른 질문이 없으시면, 이상으로 엄천석 장군의 귀순 기자회견을 모두 마치겠습니다. 감사합니다.

 (총통의 초상화가 지워지고 객석에 있던 기자1·2와 보도진 퇴장. 비서, 땀을 닦고 있는 천돌에게로 간다.)

비서 : 대단히 수고가 많았소.

천돌 : 야, 덕택에…… 혹 실수는 없었나유?

비서 : 아니오, 훌륭했소. 총통각하께서도 텔레비전 중계를 보고 아주 흡족하셨을 거요.

천돌 : 고맙구먼유.

비서 : 엄 장군, 데뷔 작품은 성공했지만 정작 중요한 대목은 이제부터요. 전국민의 시선이 장군에게 쏠려 있다오. 장군이 내뱉는 한마디가 민심의 향배를 좌우하게 될 거요. 따라서 장군은 즉

　　　　시 전국 순회강연을 떠나도록 하시오.
천돌 : (내키지 않는 어투로) ……시방 바루 가야 하나유?
비서 : 그렇소, 우리에겐 시간이 없소.
천돌 : (훈장을 가리키며) 이 옷을 그냥 입은 체로유……?
비서 : 군복을 입고 가시오. 옷은 그 사람의 신분이나 교양을 나타내거든. 엄장군이 불로국 장성이란 걸 표나게 증명할 수 있는 건 그 제복뿐이라오. 이 멋진 유니폼은 놀라운 전시효과를 거둘 거요. 어리석은 백성들은 눈 앞에 보이는 것만 맹신하는 습관이 있거든. 하하하……
천돌 : (어눌하게) 가서 뭐라구 얘기해야 되지유? 지는 사람들 앞에 서믄 자꾸 떨리는디……
비서 : 떨 것 없소. 훈련받은 대로만 하시오. 당신은 장군이란 걸 잊었소?
천돌 : 순회강연은 어디루 가게 되나유?
비서 : 전국 방방곡곡. 우선 도청소재지를 돌고 다음은 시청·군청소재지. 그 다음엔 읍·면·리까지 내려가게 될 꺼요.
천돌 : 몽땅 돌려믄 시일이 얼마큼 걸려유?
비서 : 대략 3년쯤 걸리겠지.
천돌 : (절망적인 표정으로) 아유, 이 일을 어쩐디야……!
비서 : (천돌의 어깨를 다독이며) 걱정 마시오. 끝나면 한 밑천 단단히 쥐게 될 테니까. 당신이 평생 벌어도 만져보지 못할 거금을 왕창 넣게 된단 말이오.
천돌 : 지가 아는 거라군 달달 외었던 원고 뿐인디 그게 바닥이 나믄 어떡하지유? 본전이 죄다 털리믄유.
비서 : 허허……그건 염려 마시오. 각본대로, 연습했던 시나리오만 줄

줄이 외면 되는 거요. 새로운 지역에 가면 낯선 청중이 모이니까 어디서나 같은 이야길 반복하면 되지요. 요컨대 장군은 3년 동안 사람이 아니라 앵무새가 되는 거라오……알겠소?

천돌 : (애원하듯) 비서님두……같이 가실 거지유?

비서 : 난 가지 않소. 기관원이 동행하게 될 거요. (객석을 향해) 기관원! 기관원!

기관원 : (객석에서 벌떡 일어나며) 넷! (급히 무대 위로 올라온다. 어깨에 메가폰을 멘 기골이 장대한 사내다.─)

비서 : 엄 장군을 잘 모시게.

기관원 : 네, 알겠습니다.

비서 : (천돌에게 악수를 청하며) 그럼, 수고하시오.

천돌 : (금방 울음이 터질 듯 실룩거린다)…… (비서, 겨우 손을 빼내어 퇴장)

기관원 : (메가폰을 천돌에게 넘겨주고 앉는다) 자, 타시죠.

　(천돌, 기관원의 어깨 위에 올라타면 사내는 순회연사를 무등태우고 무대를 종횡무진 누빈다. 천돌이 메가폰으로 열심히 떠들 때 호리즌트에는 봄·여름·가을·겨울이 세 번이나 바뀌고 백뮤직으로 비발디의 <사계>가 조용히 흐른다)

천돌 : (객석을 향해) 친애하는 국민 여러분! 본인은 불로국의 제1야전군 사령관이었다가 자유가 그리워서 기로국으로 귀순한 엄천석입니다. 바로 이 순간에도 전쟁준비를 모두 끝내놓고 침략의 야욕을 불태우고 있는 불로국 괴수 도루묵은 일주일 이내에 기로국 인민을 해방시키겠노라고 호언장담하고 있습니다! 바야흐로 전운이 감도는 이 일촉즉발의 위기 앞에서 외침을 막고 사회적 혼란을 수습하기 위해서는 강력한 영도자가

필요하며…… 그 분은 민족의 태양이요, 겨레의 등불인 경애하는 총통각하가 아니고 그 누구이겠습니까! 국민 여러분! 이 국가적 위난을 극복하는 길은 오로지 서양에서 들여온 핫바지 같은 헌법을 우리 몸에 맞도록 뜯어고쳐서 총통각하의 눈에 흙이 들어갈 때까지는 그분이 이 나라를 통치하게끔 해야 합니다! 본인은 헌법 개정만이 우리의 살 길이라고 간곡히, 간곡히 호소하는 바입니다-!

　(군중들의 우레와 같은 박수, 환호, (개헌! 개헌!) 하는 구호가 장내 스피커로 흘러나온다. 이때 박수를 치면서 비서 등장 기관원이 앉으면 천돌, 그의 어깨에서 내려온다.)

천돌 : (어리둥절해서) 아니, 비서님! 어떻게 여길……?
비서 : 하하핫…… 그동안 고생이 많았소 오늘이 마지막 강연 아니오? 그래서 격려도 할 겸 검사검사해서 나온 거요.
천돌 : (한숨) 휴우…… 벌써 그렇코롬 됐나유?
비서 : 아무튼 욕봤소. 우리가 예상했던 것 이상으로 대성공이오. 정보기관에서 여론을 수집해 분석한 보고서를 읽었는데 엄 장군의 순회강연이 국민 통합에 크게 기여했다는 거요. 적의 실상과 동태를 생생히 알리는 계기가 됐을 뿐 아니라, 개헌지지 쪽으로 국민 여론을 급선회시킨 기폭제가 됐다는 평가였소. 이 모든 게 장군의 빛나는 공로라고 아니할 수 없소. 총통각하께서 장군의 노고에 대해 치하와 위로의 말씀을 전하라는 엄명이 계셨다오.
천돌 : 몸둘바를 모르겄시유. 지가 벨루 한 일도 읍넌디……
비서 : 아, 아니오. 청중을 사로잡고 열광시키는 그 뛰어난 웅변술에는 솔직히 나도 감탄했소. (기관원에게) 응, 됐어. 자넨 이제

기관으로 복귀하게.

기관원 : 넷! (인사하고 퇴장)

비서 : 며칠 동안 푹 쉬시오. 당신이 거처할 집을 마련했으니까 거기 가서 목욕하고 피로를 말끔히 씻어버리시오. 아 참! 예쁜 색시도 하나 대령해뒀소. 그 일엔 아주 기막힌 기술을 가진 끝내주는 여자요. (봉투를 내민다) 그리고 이건 총통각하의 특별하사금인데 1억 원 짜리 자기앞수표요. 이 돈이면 기로국에선 기와집 열 채를 살 수 있다오.

천돌 : (눈이 휘둥그래저) 히—익! 이렇게 많은 돈을……!

비서 : 허허…… 그러게 내가 뭐랬소. 한밑천 쥐게 해준다고 하지 않았소? 자, 그럼 집으로 갑시다. 여자가 눈이 빠지게 기다리고 있을 거요. 장안에서 이름난 요정의 마담인데 웃을 땐 곱게 볼우물이 파이지. 경험에 의하면 보조갠 잘근잘근 씹어주는 미덕이 있거든 으하하하……

    (두 사람 퇴장. 무대가 핑크빛으로 물들면 갓 목욕을 끝내고 물방울이 뚝뚝 떨어지는 탐스런 나체를 타월로 가린 마담이 나와 담배를 피워물 때 천돌 등장)

천돌 : (외면한 채) 누, 누구세유?

마담 : 오우, 우리들의 영웅! 엄 장군님이시군요, 맞죠?

천돌 : 그런디유……

마담 : (싱긋 웃으며) 저에 관해서 비서님이 말씀하시지 않던가요?

천돌 : (슬쩍 보다가 고개를 홱 돌리고) 아, 야……

마담 : 아이, 뭘 그렇게 꿔다놓은 보릿자루처럼 계세요? 빨랑 목욕하고 와서 짜릿한 합환주를 나눠야죠.

천돌 : 모, 목간통이 어느 쪽이어유?

마담 : (가리킨다) 저어쪽요.

(천돌, 벌벌 떨며 욕실로 간다)

마담 : 호호호…… 아이구, 우스워라. 장군쯤 돼가지고 오입도 안 해 봤나? 근데 장군이 어째 저 모양이야? 후줄근한게 꼭 농사꾼 같애(천돌, 나온다)

천돌 : (침을 꿀꺽 삼키고) 저어……곰곰 생각해 보니께 며칠 전에 여관에서 목간을 했거든유.

마담 : 며칠 전에요? 매일 샤워를 안하세요?

천돌 : (씨익 웃는다) 에이, 고향에 있을 땐 일년에 고작 두 번밖에 안 했는디유, 뭘……추석하구 설날 하루 전에유.

마담 : (질겁해서) 뭐라구요! 그게 정말이에요?

천돌 : 그려유.

마담 : 어머 불결해라. 그런 남자하고 어떻게 살을 맞대고 잠을 자죠?

천돌 : 그래도 우리 마누란 아무 불평이 없었시유.

마담 : 나 원 참, 기가 막혀서……불로국 사람들, 째지게 가난해요? 그 나라에선 수돗물도 안 나오나 보죠?

천돌 : 전부 배급제가 돼서유……물 배급표 얻기가 하늘에 별 따기에 유.

마담 : (가상의 잔에 술을 따르는 시늉) 술이나 마셔요. 듣자하니 전 국을 도느라 발바닥이 부르텄다던데……찌든 피로를 술로 확 풀어버려요. 자, 총통각하와 공화국을 위하여 건배! (잔을 부 딪고 단숨에 마신다)

천돌 : (조금 맛보고 찡그리며) 하이구, 이거 뭔 술이유?

마담 : 최고급 양주에요. 총통각하가 애용하는 술이라고 소문이 났더

군요.

천돌 : 지는 막걸리가 좋은디……그런 건 없나유?

마담 : 촌스럽게 막걸리라뇨? 그건 농사꾼들이나 마시는 술이에요.

천돌 : (다소 불쾌해서) 농사꾼이 막걸릴 찾는 게 뭐가 나빠유?

마담 : (교태를 부리며) 엄 장군님두 차암! 지금 농담하시는 거예요?

천돌 : (성난 듯 술을 쭉 들이키고) 난 지쳐서 일찍 잘래유. (군복을 거칠게 벗고 침대 속으로 들어간다)

마담 : (코맹맹이 소리로, 갈보 기질을 유감없이 발휘하여) 아유, 장군님, 화나셨나봐. 그깟 일 갖고 영웅호걸답잖게 뭘 그러세요? 동침할 땐 말예요, 즐겁고 부드럽게 하는 거라구요. 흐응, 화내심 난 싫어…… (어쩌구 하면서 시트 안으로 들어가 타월을 벗어던진다)

  (까르르 웃는 소리. 시트 안이 이층이 되고 몇 번 깔짝거리다가 이층이 단층이 된다. 마담이 먼저 시트 밖으로 얼굴을 내민다)

마담 : 어머나! 벌써?

천돌 : ……

마담 : (노골적으로 짜증기를 발라서) 뭘 이런 남자가 다 있어! 아니, 그걸 물건이라고 차고 다녀요? (타월을 두르고 침대에서 나오며) 가위로 뭉턱 잘라서 까마귀에게나 던져줘버려요!

천돌 : (시트 밖으로 얼굴을 내밀고) 미안하네유. 하두 오랜만에 해놔서 기계가 녹슬었나비유.

마담 : (역정을 내어) 이것 보세요! 난 정책적으로 당신과 하룻밤 놀아주는 거란 말예요. 씨이, 누가 하고 싶어 이 짓을 하는 줄 알아요? 그 비선가 뭔가 하는 양반의 반의 반반이라도 해봐요.

(술을 따라 홀짝 마시고) 그이 정력하난 알아줘야 해. 백사를 고아 먹었는지 밤새 들들 볶는다니깐. (사이) 암튼 다신 날 만날 생각일랑 아예 하질 마세요. 쳇, 재수 옴 붙었네, 옴 붙었어.

천돌 : (슬그머니 시트 속으로 사라진다)

　　　(마담, 요염하고 선정적인 포즈로, 허벅지가 거의 드러나도록 다리를 꼬고 앉아 담배를 꼬나문다. 무대, 어두워졌다가 서서히 밝아오면 천돌, 일어나 기지개를 켜다 마담이 안 보이자 내의 바람으로 여기저기 찾아본다. 그러다 방에 떨어진 봉투를 발견하고 줍는다. 수표가 없어진 걸 확인하고 파랗게 질려서 가상의 전화를 들고 다이얼을 돌린다)

천돌 : 저어……거시기 저어……거그가 서기국이에유? 비서님 쪼깐 바꿔 주셔유. 야, 이쪽은 엄천돌인디유. (사이) 아 비서님이셔유? 지는 천돌이구먼유. 덕택에 자알 잤어유. 아이구, 재미는 무슨……다 그런 거지유, 헤헤……근디 말에유, 아침에 일어나 보니께 여자가 없어졌시유.……야, 사라졌다구유. 헌디 비서님께서 주신 돈 있잖유? 것도 같이 사라졌는디유. 아, 진짜라니께유! 시방 한가허게 농담헐 마음이 아녀유. 직접 눈으로 보시믄 되잖아유. (사이) 비, 비서님…… 화를 내실 일이 아니디유. 야. 그럼 기다리구 있을 거구먼유. 알겠시유…… (힘없이 전화기를 놓고) 어메 어쩐 일이디야? 참말 귀신이 곡할 노릇이구먼. 틀림없이 비서님이 1억 원이라구 허시믄서 봉툴 주셨는디……

(천돌, 봉투 구멍을 벌려 털어보기도 하고 군복 호주머니, 의자 밑, 시트 속을 샅샅이 뒤진다. 이때, 소리없이 기관원 등장. 예리한 눈초리로 천돌의 행동을 지켜본다. 침대 아래로 기어 들어 갔다가 나오던 천돌, 기관원을 보자 화들짝 놀란다)

천돌 : 어 기관원 선상! 여그는 웬일이셔?
기관원 : (싸늘하게) 비서님의 심부름으로 왔어요. 비서님 지십니다. 이 시간 이후에 장군께선 문밖 출입을 삼가시기 바랍니다. 대문에 보초가 지키고 있습니다.
천돌 : (풀이 죽어서) 그러믄……밖으로 나가지도 못한단 말인가유?
기간원 : 그렇습니다.
천돌 : 약속이 틀리잖아유? 순회강연만 끝나믄 마음놓구 자유롭게 살 수 있다구 했는디……
기간원 : 사정이 달라졌어요.
천돌 : 언제까지 이곳에 갇혀 있어야 돼유?
기관원 : 그건 몰라요. 전 상부의 지시를 전달할 뿐입니다.
천돌 : (고개를 주억거리다) 선상은 어제부터……그려, 순회강연을 시작할 때부터 줄곧 날 감시허구 있었구먼유.
기관원 : ……
천돌 : 그랬지유? 그것도 상부의 지신가유?
기관원 : ……(말없이 끄덕인다)
천돌 : 밖에도 못 나가믄 뭘 먹구 살라는 거유?
기관원 : 식사는 매끼마다 배달됩니다.
천돌 : 선상, 부탁이 하나 있는디……
기관원 : 뭡니까?

천돌 : (군복을 가리키며) 저 옷은 훈장이 너무 무거워서 걷기가 매우 불편해유. 옷 좀 바꿔줄 수 없나유?

기관원 : 옷장에 여벌 옷이 있어요. (안으로 들어가 옷을 가지고 나온다)

천돌 : (헐렁한 옷을 입으며) 크긴 허지만 저 지긋지긋헌 군복을 벗게 돼서 몸이 훨훨 날아갈 듯 개운하네유.

기관원 : 편히 쉬쉽시오. (퇴장)

　　　　(천돌, 의자에 앉아 참담한 표정을 짓다가 딱 손뼉을 마주친다. 군복 호주머니에서 라이터를 꺼내 사방에 불을 붙이고 밖을 향해 (불이야! 불이야!) 외친후. 반대편으로 후닥닥 도망친다. 무대엔 시뻘건 사이키 조명이 어수선하게 맴돌고 사이렌이 요란하게 울릴 때 암전. 잠시후, 환해지면 배경막에 기다란 철조망이 나타난다. 천돌 등장하여 갸웃거리면서 철책앞으로 가까이 간다)

천돌 : 어라? 이상허네, 이건 뭐지? 웬 쇠망태기여? 전엔 이런게 없었는디……

　　　　(이때 객석에서 초병 1·2가 총을 겨눈 채 튀어나온다)

초병 1 : 꼼짝 마! 움직이면 쏜다! 손들어! (천돌, 두 손을 번쩍 든다) 뒤로 돌아! (돌아선다)

초병 2 : 넌 누구야! 간첩이지?

천돌 : (얼이 빠져서) 가, 간첩? 간첩이 뭐여?

초병 1 : 짜아식, 개수작부리지 마라! 허튼 짓 했다간 대갈통에 구멍나! (초병 2에게) 어이, 얼른 포승줄로 묶어. (초병 2, 달려들어 천돌을 묶는다)

천돌 : (부들부들떨며) 허어, 왜들 이러는 거여. 난 아무 잘못도 없는

다……
초병 1 : (발길로 천돌의 엉덩이를 걷어찬다) 야, 이새꺄! 너 뒈지고 싶어 환장했냐? 여기가 어디라고 감히 철책을 타 넘으려고 해!
초병 2 : (초병 1에게) 지랄 염병할 놈이 통돼지 바비큐가 되고 싶었던 모양이지?
초병 1 : 밀봉교육을 받고 온 놈이 철조망에 고압전류가 흐르고 있다는 것도 몰라?
천돌 : (기가 차서) 미, 밀봉교육이라뉴? 지는 농사꾼이어유. 이 땅은 내땅이라구유. 내가 여그서 농살 지었다니께유. 우리 할아부지 적부터 여그는 우리 밭이었어유.
초병 2 : 너희 밭? 허허……이자식이 귀신 씨나락 까먹는 소리하고 자빠졌네. (초병 1에게) 이놈을 중대본부로 끌고 갈까?
초병 1 : 그래, 중대장님께 보고하고 정치보위대에게도 알려야겠어. (손으로 V자를 만들고) 월척을 낚았어. 말년에 휴가복 터지게 생겼네.
초병 2 : (개머리판으로 천돌의 등짝을 후려친다) 후딱 가, 쌍노무새꺄!
천돌 : 아악! (등이 활처럼 휘어지며 질질 끌려간다)
　　　(세 사람이 퇴장하면 호리존트에 철조망이 없어지고 얼마 후 수사관과 천돌 함께 등장)
수사관 : (의자에 앉으며) 앉으시오 (천돌, 앉는다) 중대장한테서 당신을 체포하게 된 경위를 대충 들었는데……자, 이왕지사 이리 된 바에야 숨김없이 털어놓으시오. 그래야 신상에도 이로울 테니까.
천돌 : (눈을 섬벅거리며) 무얼 털어놓으라는 건지 도무지 알 수가 없

다니께우. 아까 병정에게두 말했지만 지는 이곳에서 농사를 지어먹던……

수사관 : (말을 자르며) 연극은 그만둬! 그따위 서툰 연기에 속아 넘어갈 사람은 아무도 없어!

천돌 : 엄메? 연극이 뭐 허는 건디유? 지는 농사짓는 일 말구는 암것도 몰라유. 순회강연인가 연설인가 헌 것 빼구는 평생 농사만 지어왔다니께유. 며칠 전에 순회강연이 죄다 끝나서 고향으로 돌아왔는디…… 난데없는 쇠망태기가 우리 밭 길목에 떡억 버티고 서 있지 뭐예유?

수사관 : 홍 아주 새파랗게 물든 골수 분자로군. 당신처럼 뻔뻔스런 사상범을 여럿 다뤄봤는데 고문하기 전엔 절대로 불지 않아. 따끔한 맛을 봐야 바른말이 술술 나온다구 어때, 고문실로 직행하실까?

천돌 : (가슴을 탕 친다) 참말로 답답하구먼유. 지는 있는 그대로 말씀드리는 거예유. 저엉 못 믿겠거든 서기국의 비서님헌티 물어보믄 단박에 알 수 있다니께유.

수사관 : (비아냥거린다) 어쭈, 서기국의 비서님? 기왕이면 총통각하의 불알친구라고 하시지.

천돌 : 지난 3년 동안 전국 순회 강연을 한 엄천석 장군이 바로 나유! 나란 말예유!

수사관 : (기겁해서) 뭐, 엄천석 장군! (뚫어지게 보다가) 가만있자, 그러고보니 비슷한 것 같기도 하고……

천돌 : (약간 으스대며) 선상님은 신문이나 델레비전도 안 봐유? 나 얼굴이 사흘돌이로 나왔었는디……

수사관 : 허 참, 이거야 원…… 알쏭달쏭하구먼. 어쨌든 좋소. 우선 조

서나 꾸민 뒤에 다시 확인해봅시다. (볼펜과 수첩을 꺼내)국적은?

천돌 : 국적은 뭔디유?

수사관 : 어느 나라 사람이냐는 거요.

천돌 : 그거사 불로국 사람이지유.

수사관 : 본적과 주소는?

처돌 : 같어유. 가락도 낙랑군 수로면 380번지.

수사관 : 이름은?

천돌 : 엄천돌.

수사관 : 나이는?

천돌 : 쉰하나

수사관 : 엄 장군의 귀순 기자회견을 텔레비전에서 본 적이 있는데, 그때 장군은 자유를 찾아서 기로국에 귀순했다고 했지요?

천돌 : 에이, 그거 순 거짓말이유, 엉터리라구유.

수사관 : (불끈해서) 뭣이! 엉터리. 당신 누굴 우롱하는 거요?

천돌 : 지는 엄천석 장군이 아니라 농사꾼 엄천돌이에유.

수사관 : 그렇다면……?

천돌 : 비서님이 나보고 엄 장군 노릇을 하라구 해서 시키는 대루 했을 따름이지유.

수사관 : 그럼 귀순하게 된 동기가 뭐요?

천돌 : (절레절레) 귀순이라뉴? 지는 귀순하지 않았시유.

수사관 : 말귀를 못 알아먹는군. 당신은 불로국에서 제 발로 걸어 기로국으로 넘어오지 않았소?

천돌 : 왔지유.

수사관 : 그게 귀순이 아니고 뭐요? 누가 강제로 납치해 온 건 아니잖

소?

천돌 : 자초지종을 선상님께 말씀드려야 겠네유. ……그러니께 그때가 6월초였을 거구먼유. 송아지를 들에 놔 기르고 있었는디, 지가 꼴을 베러 간 새에 한 마리가 없어졌시유. 그놈을 찾으러 나섰다가 냇가 근처에서 무성한 풀을 봤어유. 마침 낫을 들고 있던 차라 욕심이 생겨 풀을 차근차근 베면서 아래로 내려갔지유. 한참 부지런히 베는디 별안간 등 뒤에서 누가 총부리를 들이대고 막무가내로 끌고 가데유. 기로국 병정이었지유. 아마 나도 모르게 그만 국경선을 넘어버린 모양이에유. 아뿔사, 했지만 엎질러진 물이지유. (사이, 울먹이며) 일이 그리 된 거라구유. 기로국으로 넘어올 생각은 손톱만치도 없었시유. 그놈의 송아지 때문에……꼴만 탐내지 않았었더라도……

수사관 : 흠, 그 당시엔 국경에 철조망이 없었던 때니까 충분히 있을 수 있는 일이지.

천돌 : (두 손을 비비면서) 좌우간에 지가 잘못했어유. 용서해주셔유. 고향에 있는 부모 형제·처자식들은 모두 지가 죽은 줄로만 알 거예유 (가슴이 더워온다) 3년 전에 온다 간다 기별도 없이 훌쩍 떠나온 후로 소식 한번 전하지 못했으니께유. 쇠망태기 바루 건너편에 우리 밭이 있어유. (아득한 고향을 망막속에 떠올리며) 망종이 낼 모레니께 지금쯤 우리 밭엔 누우렇게 보리가 익어가구 있을 거구먼유. 밭고랑엔 냉이와 달래·쑥·산딸기·보리콩·삼동…… 먹을게 억수루 많아유. 숭년이 들 땐 텅애쿨·게자리·하늘레기·배채기같은 풀도 뜯어다 먹구 …… 그려유, 설사엔 배채기를 삶어 먹으면 대번에 나아유. 밭이랑엔 메뚜기들도 엄청나지유. 가을이 되어 오동통통 살찐

메뚜기를 시래기 엮듯이 실로 엮어가지구 풀밭에서 구워먹으면 헤헤…… 그 맛은 둘이 먹다 하나가 죽어두 몰라유. 또 이맘때믄 밭 웅덩이엔 개구리가 바글바글허지유. 개굴개굴 울어대는 게 꼭 흥부 새끼들 밥 달라구 우는 소리 같아유.

수사관 : (손을 들어 제지한다) 알겠소. 정말 당신이 엄 장군이라면…… 그동안 국민적 영웅으로 대접받아왔는데 정부 당국에선 아무런 보상도 하지 않고 내팽개쳤단 말이오?

천돌 : 집도 줬고 어마어마한 돈두 받았시유.

수사관 : 그러면 이 나라에서 젊고 예쁜 색시한테 새장가 들고 정착을 하면 될 텐데 어째서 다시 불로국으로 돌아가려는 거요?

천돌 : 그건…… 고향이 그립기 때문이예유.

수사관 : 기로국은 불로국보다 훨씬 더 자유로운 나란데……

천돌 : 자유보다 소중한 건 핏줄이지유. 늙으신 부모님, 형제들, 마누라도 보고 싶지만 자식새끼들 얼굴이 눈에 선해유. 이 나라에 와서 단 하루도 그 녀석들을 잊어본 적이 없어유…… (눈가에 이슬이 대롱 맺힌다) 미치도록 아이들이 보고 싶다구유. 선상님도 이런 내 심정 아시겠지유?

수사관 : 기어코 가겠다면 비서님께 미리 알렸어야 했죠.

천돌 : (시무룩해서) 비서님께 부탁해두 들어주지 않았을 거예유. (주저하다가) 그리구……

수사관 : 그리고 뭐예요? 속시원히 말해봐요.

천돌 : 지가 감옥소 같은 그 집에 그냥 머물러 있다간 살아남지 못했을 거구먼유.

수사관 : (의아해서) 살아남지 못하다니?

천돌 : 총통각하께서 내게 주신 1억원을 비서하구 한 패거리인 여자

가 훔쳐 갖구 달아나버렸거든유.

수사관 : 아니, 그게 사실이오?

천돌 : 그러믄유! 눈치챘시유. 무식헌 촌놈이지만 나두 그만한 통박은 굴릴줄 알어유. 비서와 그 백여시 같은 년이 짜구서 날 없애구 돈을 가로채려 했어유.

수사관 : (연민기 어린 눈길로) 당신은 고향으로 돌아가지 않는 게 좋아요.

천돌 : 왜유?

수사관 : 순회강연을 하면서 줄창 불로국을 비방했는데 이적행위를 한 당신을 곱게 놔두겠소? 가자마자 숙청이지. (목을 긋는 손짓)

천돌 : 순회강연을 한 건 엄천석 장군이지. 엄천돌이 아니었어유. 촌구석에 묻혀 땅이나 파 먹구 살 건디 누가 날 알아보겠시유?

수사관 : 설령 우리가 보내준다 하더라도 저쪽의 수비대원에게 잡히고 말 거요. 요즘 양국간에 긴장이 고조됨에 따라 경비가 삼엄해졌단 말이오.

천돌 : (맥없이) 여그 있어두 죽구 고향에 가두 죽는다믄…… 지는 고향에 가서 죽을래유. 짐승두 죽을 때가 되믄 고향으로 돌아간다는디……

수사관 : 여기 있으면 안전해요. 도대체 누가 당신을 해친다고 합디까?

천돌 : (무릎 꿇어 수사관의 바짓가랑이를 잡고) 날 좀 고향으루 보내줘유! 동이 서가 돼두 난 가야만 한다구유, 선상님! 제발 부탁이니께 가게 해주셔유 —!

수사관 : (박차고 일어서며) 안 돼요! 넘어올 땐 당신 맘대로 왔지만

넘어갈 땐 어림도 없지! (사이) 이봐요, 당신은 운수 사납게도 덫에 걸린 한 마리 들 짐승에 지나지 않아요. 포획물을 어떻게 처리하느냐 하는 건 순전히 사냥꾼이 결정할 문제지요. 자, 또 부를 때까지 일단 들어가서 쉬고 있어요.

　　　(두 사람, 퇴장하고 곧 비서와 수사관이 나란히 들어온다)

비서 : 그래, 자넨 그 자의 진술을 액면 그대로 믿는단 말인가?

수사관 : (쩔쩔맨다) 아, 아니…… 그건 아닙니다. 전 다만 비서님께서 그간 엄천돌의 뒤를 봐줘오셨다기에 사건의 전말을 보고 드린 겁니다.

비서 : (뱉듯이) 그잔 정신병자야.

수사관 : 네엣?

비서 : 곁에서 관찰해온 기관원의 보고에 따르면 지독한 피해망상증에 걸려 있다는 거야.

수사관 : 네, 그 점에 관해선 저도 엄천돌에서 들은 바가 있습니다.

비서 : 무얼?

수사관 : 살해위협을 느끼고 있답니다. 제가 보기에도 그는 누군가가 자기를 해치려 한다는 극도의 공포에 사로잡혀 있더군요.

비서 : (득의만면하여) 후후…… 것 봐. 그 잔 애초에 넘어올 때부터 정상이 아니었어. 정상이라면 넘어올 리가 없잖아?

수사관 : 살해위협을 느끼게 된 직접적인 동기는 아마 돈 때문이었던 것 같습니다.

비서 : (안색이 갑자기 변한다) 돈? 무슨 돈……?

수사관 : 총통각하께서 하사하신……

비서 : 오오라. 그 돈 말이군. 그렇잖아도 못된 도둑년을 잡아들이라구 전국에 지명수배해놨어. 날강도 같은 년! 지 물건에 뭔 휘

황찬란한 금테를 둘렀다구 하룻밤에 화대가 1억원이야?

수사관 : 비서님…… 이 사건을 어떻게 처리했으면 좋겠습니까?

비서 : 어떻게라니? 그걸 말이라고 하나! (냉혹하게) 그 잔 이젠 이용가치가 없어졌어. 뿐만 아니라 괜히 나발 불고 다니면 우리의 입장이 난처해지지. 이번 일은 특히 보안유지에 철저를 기해서 극비로 추진하도록…… 정권의 사활이 걸린 문제란 걸 명심해.

수사관 : 그러니까 군재에 회부하란 말씀이십니까?

비서 : (버럭) 이 석두야! 장장 3년이나 전국을 누비면서 국빈으로 떠받들어 왔는데 지금 와서 무슨 명목으로 죄인을 만들어!

수사관 : (어리벙벙해서)……

비서 : 그 자는 군법에 따라 이 나라에 넘어온 게 아니야. 넘어갈 때도 법하곤 아무 상관없이 가게 해야지.

수사관 : 본인이 원하는 대로 고향으로 보내주라는 하명이시군요.

비서 : (눈알을 부라리며) 뭐야? 야 임마! 너, 그따위 썩은 골통으로 어떻게 수사관이 됐어? 이 우라질 밥통, 먹통, 똥통아!

수사관 : (점점 당혹해서)……

비서 : 그 잔 우리나라의 고급 정보를 많이 알고 있단 말이야. 더구나 불로국에 가면 놈들의 역선전에 이용될 게 뻔하잖아. 나 보기가 역겨워 가신다는데 말없이 고이 보내드려야지, 안그래? (사이, 빠른 어조로) 민간인이 허가 없이 국경을 넘으면 어떤 죄에 해당되나?

수사관 : 국가탈출죄에 해당합니다.

비서 : 국가탈출죄의 형량은?

수사관 : 그야 물론……

비서 : 알겠지? 그만 돌아가. (수사관이 미적거리자) 뭘 꾸물대고 있어! 냉큼 꺼지지 못해!

수사관 : 넷 알겠습니다! (거수경례를 붙이고 퇴장)

　　　(비서도 의미심장하게 웃으며 나가면 배경막에 철의 장막이 드리워지고 천돌과 초병 1·2의 등장)

초병 1 : 엄천돌씨, 잘 가요.

천돌 : (연신 꾸벅대며) 안녕히 계셔유.

초병 2 : 그처럼 가고 싶어 하던 고향으로 돌아가게 돼서 무척 기쁘죠?

천돌 : (누런 이빨을 드러내어 활짝 웃는다) 그럼유, 시상에 태어나서 요롷코롬 좋은 날은 처음이어유. 시방 꿈을 꾸고 있는 게 아닌지 모르겠네유.

초병 1 : 총통각하의 특별 배려라는 걸 잊지 말아요.

천돌 : (뭉클해서) 아믄요, 잊을 리가 있나유? 그 분이 내게 큰 돈두 주셨는디유. 악수꺼정 해주셨다니께유.

　　　(초병 1·2 철조망으로 가 쇠문을 여는 시늉을 한 뒤 퇴장한다. 천돌이 그 문을 돌파하면 배경막에 철조망이 사라지고 보리가 누렇게 익은 들판이 나타난다. 때마침 저녁놀이 멀리 지평선에서 붉게 타고 있다. 천돌, 객석쪽으로 돌아서서 황홀한 몸짓으로 손을 휘저으며 외친다)

천돌 : 선상님들, 자알 있어유-! 고마워유-! 참말로 고맙다니께유-!

　　　(몸을 돌려 마악 한 걸음 옮길 찰나에 따당! 한 방의 총성이 울리고 천돌이 움찔하며 어깨를 가누려는데 곧이어 연발 총소리가 장내 스피커로 쏟아진다. 천돌, 그 자리에 푹 꼬꾸라지는데 어디선가 음산한 까마귀떼 울음소리. 검은 새떼의 울부짖

음과 배를리오즈의 「환상교향곡」 제 5악장이 한데 어우러지고 핏빛 노을이 누우런 보리밭을 서서히 물들여 간다.)
 － 막

<현대문학 1990. 5>

수필

줄탁동기
내 가슴은 꽃이어라
길섶 나그네

강태국

줄탁동기

필자 소개
국제펜클럽, 한국문인협회 회원. 현대수필 이사. 제주대 명예교수(현)
수필집 『낙서의 조각들』 『추억의 조각들』 『너 그래도 돼』
논문집 『수필인가 소설인가』

줄탁동기 啐啄同機
— 깨달음의 순간

강태국

이글거리는 태양은 눈을 크게 부릅뜨고 꼼짝 말라는 듯이 째려보고 있다. 사뭇 위협적이다. 연구실 문이란 문을 모두 열어젖혔으나, 바람 한 점 없는 오후 2시다.

방학인데도 별로 갈 데도 없고, 늙은 몸을 끌고 거리를 헤맬 수도 없어 자연히 연구실에서 빈둥거리고 있다.

시간 되면 별로 배고프지 않으면서도 일을 하나 처리하는 심정으로 도시락을 푼다.

노크 소리가 있었고, "예" 하고 대답이 끝나기도 전에 한 청년이 들어왔다. 깊숙이 허리를 숙이며 절을 하고 반갑게 다가왔다. 누군가 하고 기억을 더듬노라니, 그는 자기 이름을 댔다. 이름을 듣는 순간 어렴풋이 생각이 났다.

명함을 보니 서울에 있는 버젓한 회사에 다니고 있었다. 웬일로 찾아왔느냐고 물었더니, 올가을 결혼식을 올리는데 주례를 부탁한다고 했다.

이 젊은이는 몇 년 전에 오늘처럼 노크 하나로 불쑥 나타나 상담을 했었다. 학과가 달라도 개의치 않고 그의 고민을 들었다. 누나, 형, 자기, 누이, 남동생 순으로 그는 오남매 중 셋째로 부모들 관심에 자기는 있으나 마나 한 존재라고 했다. 형과 막내에게는 큰 관심과 애정을 쏟고 있으며, 자기는 대학에 못 들어가도 되레 잘된 일로 생각했을 것이라고 했다. 선묘를 찾아 벌초할 때, 가구를 옮기는 힘든 일을 할 때 친척집에서 큰일을 치를 심부름꾼으로 자기 존재를 찾을 뿐이라서 늘 소외감을 느낀다고 했다.

요즘은 강의 듣는 것도 싫어졌고, 선배들 취직도 불투명하고 그들의 걱정하는 모습도 괴롭혀 와서, 막막한 심정으로 나를 찾아왔다는 것이었다.

나는 진지한 자세로 그의 하소연을 들었다. 잠시 침묵이 흘렀다. 나의 의식 속에서는 바쁘게 정리 작업을 하고 있었다.

사람의 역사를 거슬러 올라가서, 여러 시대에 태어나서 살다가 죽어간 사람들의 삶의 방식을 혹은 그들의 봉착한 과제였던 문제들을 생각해 보았다. 복잡하여 단시간에는 풀 수 없었다. 허나, 인간이란 왜 그렇게도 괴이하면서도 승고하고 우열하면서도 영지에 찬 존재인가고 느꼈었다.

그 욕망, 지식, 신념, 타성화(고정화) 등으로 자기 자신을 어쩔 수 없는 위기와 고뇌 같은 것을 만들어 왔을까. 아니, 그런 것들을 소화시키면서 초월하고 자신의 문명과 문화를 지키거나 탈피해 왔던가.

하지만, 오늘날 우리들만 문명의 위기와 고뇌를 짊어지고 있는 것같이 생각해서는 안 될 것 같다. 어떠한 사람에게도 인격 형성 과정에서 전환기, 변혁기, 과도기 같은 것이 있어서, 이런 때일수록 슬기롭게 당면한 과제를 타개할 수 있어야 한다.

각자의 문제를 풀어주는 참고서나 정답지는 따로 파는 데가 없고, 다만 거기에 있는 것은 확고한 원리와 현실의 리얼한 파악에 바탕을

둔 사색과 모색의 모험뿐으로 여겨진다.

젊은 층들은 육체적인 병보다 정신적인 병이 큰 문제로 본다. 이 병은 무거우면 무거울수록 자각되지 않는다. 이런 위협적인 해체 현상은 자연히 만성화되고 자각하기 어렵게 된다. 무엇이나 불안정하게 비쳐지고, 신경질에다 폭력 등을 몰고 와서 인간의 삶을 멸시하는 증세 등을 보여주고 있다.

열심히 노력하는 마음이나 미리 짐작해 보는 여유가 결핍되고 있다. 열심히 노력하는 마음이나 미리 짐작해 보는 여유가 결핍되어 가고, 고민과 회의에 찬 젊은이들이 많아졌다. 또는 경제적인 악조건에 시달리거나 가정의 풍요로움에서 오는 내면의 신경증은 내부를 외부로부터 단절시켜 성장하지 못하고 도리어 자기 자신을 파멸시키는 일도 종종 있다.

자기 파괴 현상이 심하면 통일성과 균형 감각이 상실되고, 내외적으로 대립적 충동이 생겨난다. 충돌 일부는 외계로 향해서 공격, 파괴의 행동으로 이어진다.

부모의 편애나 사랑의 인색, 무관심은 자녀들 일부의 인격 형성에 큰 지장을 주게 되고, 나아가서는 부모 형제의 살인극마저 연출하게 되는 사태로 발전된다.

생각이 여기까지 다다르자, 나의 침묵은 깨어졌다. "자네 군에 입대하게나, 자네 최전방으로 지원하게나."하고 조용히 말했다. "왜요?" 생각지도 못한 말을 느닷없이 들어 놀란 표정이었다.

"비록 학과는 다르지만 진정으로 나를 스승으로 여긴다면, 진지한 마음으로 나의 조언을 바란다면, 아무 소리 말고 군에 가게나."

그는 나의 진지한 태도에 마음을 가라앉혔는지 눈을 내려뜨리면서 조용히 입을 다물고 생각하는 눈치였다. 나는 나 나름대로 그가 군에

간 모습을 그려보았다. 최전방에서 어두운 밤, 눈을 부릅뜨고 북을 응시하면서 굳게 서있는 그림……

우리들은 그에게 나라를 맡기고 포근한 잠자리에 들어간다. 이것은 분단 조국의 현상으로 분명한 사실이다. 이 학생은 거기에 거인과 같이 서 있어야 될 것 같았다.

그는 나와 같은 생각을 했는지 "네, 알겠습니다"하고 고개를 조아리고 나갔다.

그 후 그는 입대를 했고, 최전방에서 편지가 날아왔다. 제대한 후 찾아와서 경례했다. 믿음직스러운 사나이로 다시 태어나 있었다.

줄탁동기, 계란 부화 과정에서 시간이 되어 병아리가 계란 속에 껍질을 부수어 나오려고 쪼는 것이 줄啐이다. 탁啄은 어미 닭이 그 때를 같이 하여 밖에서 쪼아줌을 말한다.

그 기회를 동시에 포착하지 않으면 병아리는 숨막혀 죽어버린다. 사전에는 동시同時로 나와 있으나, 다른 틀機로 고쳐보았다.

소아에서 대아로 초월하는 과정에서 부자지간, 사제, 선후배 사이의 묵시라고 할까.

"그래 군에 가서 무엇을 찾았는가?"

경례하는 그에게 물었다. 그는 씩씩하게 대답했다.

"옛, 자기를 찾았습니다."

사회인이 다 된 그에게 방긋이 웃었다. 그도 웃었다. 가을이 기다려진다.

김가영

내 가슴은 꽃이어라

필자 소개
제주수필문학회 회장(현). 한국문인상 대상 수상
수필집 『여자가 남자를 사랑할 때』 『남자 운이 좋은 여자』 등.

내 가슴은 꽃이어라

김가영

　이 세상에서 꽃이 없어진다면 얼마나 쓸쓸할까 하는 생각을 해 봤다. 며칠동안 접시꽃과 금잔화, 철쭉, 장미를 화분에 옮겨 심으면서 꽃의 아름다움에 마음을 빼앗기고 말았다. 그래서 아마 새삼스럽게 그런 생각을 했는지 모르겠다.
　만일 이 세상에서 꽃이 없어진다면 어린이들에게 어떻게 해서 봄이 온 것을 가르쳐 주어야 할까. 또 아이들은 봄의 풍경에 무엇을 그릴까. 여태껏 아이들은 봄 풍경을 그릴 때 꽃과 나비를 그렸다. 그런데 꽃이 없어져 버리면 하늘의 색으로 봄을 표현할 수밖에 없을 게 아닌가.
　꽃이 없어지면 '옛날에는 꽃이라는 것이 있었단다. 그것은 예쁜 것이었단다. 여러 가지 색, 여러 가지 형태의 꽃이 있어서 계절에 따라 새롭게 피고 지는 것이 있었단다.'하고 나이든 사람이 어린이에게 얘기해 줄 것이다.
　그러나 아이들은 '핀다'라는 실체를 모를 것이다. '핀다라는 건 말하자면 나타난다는 것인가요?'라고 질문을 할지도 모른다.
　그렇게되면 핀다는 말뿐만 아니라 진다는 말의 개념도 없어질게 아닌가. 예를 들어 '벚꽃이 화려하게 피었다가 한 순간에 져버리는 아름다움은 차라리 슬픔이었습니다.' 하는 표현을 아예 모를 것이다.

죽음은 소멸에 지나지 않고 어떤 죽음의 방법을 해도 아름답지도 더럽지도 않을 것이다.

꽃은 지기 때문에 아름답다. 만일 꽃이 지지 않는다면 꽃이 나타나는 정감은 모두 잃어버릴 것이다. 꽃은 시들고 지는 것에 의해 사람의 마음에 정서와 여유를 주는게 아닐까라는 생각이 든다.

꽃이 지기 때문에 인간은 꽃을 사랑했다. 그 꽃이 지는 것이 애석해서 물을 주기도 하고 바람을 통하게 하고 또 그 꽃을 손질하며 애써 왔다. 그런 따뜻한 마음이 사람의 생활에 여유를 주었다. 만일 꽃이 없어진다면 계절이 아마 꽃 대신 과일과 야채로 표현될지도 모른다. 예전에는 계절마다 야채나 과일의 구별이 뚜렷했다. 지금은 다르다. 계절에 상관없이 야채와 과일이 풍성해서 인간의 감각도 뒤바뀔 정도가 되어 버렸다.

동요도 그렇다.

'나의 살던 고향은 꽃피는 산골. 복숭아꽃 살구꽃 아기진달래.' 란 노래를 꽃이 없어진다면 어떻게 설명할까.

선흘 쪽으로 드라이브하다가 차를 세웠다. 들장미가 줄기차게 이리저리 엉켜서 아름답게 피어 있었다. 거기에 매료되어 한 가지쯤 꺾어 보려고 이 궁리 저 궁리를 하고 있었다. 야생장미는 가시가 더 날카롭고 많았다. 들장미가 엉킨 가지 사이에 빼꼼히 이름 모를 보랏빛 들꽃이 피어 있는 게 아닌가. 내가 잘 들여다보지 않았다면 거기에 피어있는 채 누구에게도 들키지 않고 지고 말았을 텐데.

이름 없이 피어서 바람에 부딪히고 태양의 포근함에 안겨서 잠시 있다가 져버리는 그 정숙함. 꽃의 아름다움은 거기에 있다.

꽃이 없어진다는 것은 인간의 불행이다. 일상생활을 풍부하게 하는 일은 꽃을 사다가 꽂아 놓은 것만이 아니다. 고요한 마음으로 찬찬히 들여다보면 누가 심었는지 모르지만 거기에 피어 있는 것, 그것은 꽃이 주는 환희다.

 행여 꽃이 죽어버리지나 않을까 하고 화분에 옮겨 심는 손놀림을 서두르며 나는 이런저런 생각을 해 봤다.

조명철

길섶 나그네

필자 소개
월간「수필문학」천료 등단. 한국수필가협회, 한국문학회 이사(현)
수필집「아내의 미소 웅녀의 미소」「신호등과 돌하르방」「가는 바람 오는 빛」등.

길섶 나그네

조명철

　머리가 무겁거나 답답할 때면 잠시 하던 일을 멈추고 '길섶 나그네'를 찾아간다. 쾌청한 날이면 더욱 좋고, 비가 내리는 날이라도 괜찮다. 해가 있고 없음이 무슨 상관인가. 소슬바람이 풍경을 울려주고, 온갖 풍상을 겪고 돌아와 앉아 미소짓는 넉넉한 여인이 있으면 그만이다.
　제주시내에서 동부산업도로를 10여 분 달리면 닿는 곳, 남조로 입구에서 동쪽으로 얼마가지 않아 길 오른편에 산굼부리 입구임을 알리는 노란 표지판이 길손을 부르는 듯 고개를 들고 서 있다. 그 곁에 허름한 듯 고즈넉한 분위기의 집 한 채 그게 바로 '길섶 나그네'다.
　마당 어귀엔 방사탑을 닮은 돌무더기가 사기邪氣의 범접을 막으려는 듯 버티고 서 있고, 맞은편 좌우엔 두 개의 오름이 비켜섰다. 어느 오름도 풍채를 갖추지 못해 시늉뿐이지만, 그래도 삭풍이 불어오면 벌떡 일어나 막아설 자세로 숨을 고르며 엎디어 있음이 미덥다.
　서남쪽 멀리에 눈을 돌리면 한라산 정상이 얼굴을 내밀고, 완만한 능선은 동남으로 뻗어 내려 꽤꼬리오름에 이어진다. 마치 길섶 나그네를 감싸 안으려는 듯한 자세다. 이만하면 누구나 찾아와 욕심을 부려 놓고 잔잔한 마음으로 쉬어 갈만한 곳이 아니랴.

집안으로 들어서면 명상음악이 조용히 흐르고, 염의를 정갈하게 입은 주인아줌마가 가벼운 미소로 맞는다. 보살이 되려고 수도라도 하고 있음인가. 그러나 번뇌를 모두 씻어내지 못했음인지 얼굴엔 때로 그늘이 진다. 몇 겁에 이어진 업의 소산이 곧 번뇌일 터이니 일거에 끊을 수는 없는 일이 아닌가.

계절에 따라 옷을 갈아입으며 고요히 선에 든 산과 마주하고, 무시로 불어오는 바람에게서 인연 소식도 들으며, 혹은 차별 없이 온 세상을 비추는 달과 얘기도 나누고, 꾀꼬리오름에서 날아오는 새들의 청아한 노랫소리와 벗하여 사노라면, 오묵은 때가 씻겨나갈지도 모를 일이다. 도가 바로 거기에 있으니 서둘 필요가 없을 것이다.

길섶 나그네! 그곳엔 언제 가보아도 마음을 녹여주는 향취가 있다. 겨울이면 난로에서 장작 타는 냄새가 옛 고향을 느끼게 하고, 봄이면 화병에 꽂아놓은 들꽃 몇 송이가 들길을 달리던 어린 시절을 일깨운다. 한쪽 구석에서 타오르는 촛불과 선향線香의 그윽한 향기는 미혹한 중생의 연화장 세계로 인도하려 함인가 제 몸을 태우며 선에 들었다.

투박한 다기에 따라 내놓은 차의 향도 그렇거니와, 점심 요기를 하려고 청한 들깨수제비의 향마저 미각을 자극한다. 어느 하나도 자연향 아닌 게 없으니 그저 취할 수밖에 없지 않은가. 자연이란 찌든 가슴을 씻어주는 마력을 가졌나 보다.

가만히 앉아 실내 여기저기를 살펴본다. 올 때마다 수가 더해지는 도자기에 눈이 머문다.

바닥에 되는 대로 놓인 크고 작은 것들, 이놈들도 어디선가 흘러온 나그네들일 것이라고 생각하며 수작을 걸어보지만 말이 없다. 고단한 몸을 풀어 쉬고 있음인가. 떠나온 고향을 그리며 한숨짓고 있는 것인가. 혹은 새 주인을 기다리며 희망의 노래라도 흥얼거리고 있는 것인

가. 일어나 가까이 서면 품에 안길 듯 다가서는 놈들이 반갑기 그지없다. 먼 옛날부터 맺어놓은 끈끈한 인연이다 싶어, 그 때마다 한 점씩 사들고 온다.

소박한 미소를 늘상, 가까이에서 접하려 함이다. 길섶에서 쉬며 나그네들의 흘리고 간 정담이라도 전해 들으려 함인지도 모른다. 비우고 버림이 열반으로 가는 길이라 했는데 이 조그만 것에도 애착을 버리지 못하니 도에 이르기는 틀렸나 보다.

이 세상에 나그네가 아닌 것은 하나도 없는 성싶다. 삼라 만상이 끊임없이 변하며 어디론가 흘러간다. 생성된 사물은 소멸하고, 태어난 생명체도 죽음을 향해 쉴새없이 길을 가고 있다. 영원한 것이라곤 어디에도 없지 않은가.

그런데도 자신이 나그네임을 잊고 산다. 영원한 존재라는 착각으로 살아가는 인생, 얼마나 어리석은가. 다람쥐 쳇바퀴 돌 듯 분주하게 돌아가는 사람들, 바쁘다 바쁘다 비명을 지르며 살아가니 번뇌를 어느 시간에 버릴 것인가.

"잠 못 이루는 사람에게 밤은 길고, 지쳐있는 나그네에겐 지척도 천리 바른 진리를 깨닫지 못한 자에겐, 윤회의 밤길이 아득하여라."

법구경의 말이다. 온갖 것에 애착을 버리지 못하고 노예처럼 살아가는 사람들에게 보내는 부처의 할喝이다.

오늘 따라 햇볕이 따사롭다. 신록이 무르익어 녹색이 산과 들을 꽉 채웠다. 황금빛 햇살과 소슬바람이 어우러져 수해樹海에 잔잔한 파도를 일으킨다. 무위無爲의 세계가 펼쳐지고 있음이다.

뜰 앞 참나무엔 빈깡통들이 가는 줄에 대롱대롱 매달려, 바람결에 흔들리며 세상을 이죽거리고 있다. 설치미술이란다. "빈 수레가 요란하다."는 말을 떠올린다.

  빈깡통들이 서로 부딪는 공허한 소리와 바람과 짝한 풍경소리를 들으며, '길섶 나그네'를 떠난다. 마음이 가벼워진다. 많은 짐을 부려놓고 떠나는 나그네의 기분이 된다.

  차창으로 흘러드는 바람이 그렇게 감미로울 수가 없다.

돌과 바람의 꿈

2005년 12월 1일 1판 1쇄 인쇄
2005년 12월 10일 1판 1쇄 발행

엮은이 • 오성찬
펴낸이 • 푸른사상사
책임편집 • 제주펜 출판소위원회

등록 제2-2876호
서울시 중구 을지로3가 296-10 장양B/D 701호
대표전화 02) 2268-8706(7) 팩시밀리 02) 2268-8708
메일 prun21c@yahoo.co.kr / prun21c@hanmail.net
홈페이지 //www.prun21c.com
ⓒ 2005, 오성찬 외

ISBN 89-5640-411-9-03810